SO MANY BRIDGES

BY PENELOPE DOUGLAS

First published in Great Britain by Woodicott Press
2000

Woodicott Press,
Week,
Dartington,
Totnes,
Devon TQ9 6JL

A catalogue record for this book is available from the British Library.

ISBN 0-9537915-0-5

Printed by Design & Print (Sussex) Limited, Rowan House, Rowan Close, Portslade, Brighton, East Sussex BN41 2QQ

CONTENTS

FOREWORD

I suppose it could be justifiably assumed that for a painter specialising in service subjects, the artist would be moving into a world dominated by men. For example, it is not easy to sketch in a V-bomber on an in-flight refuelling exercise in the dark, sitting in the 'sixth seat', wearing all the paraphernalia required in such an aircraft, but also encumbered by camera, torch and sketch pad. I have done that and that is all in the past.

I have known Penelope Douglas for many years now and I believe she blazed the trail for women artists to invade this otherwise perhaps macho world. Her paintings now hang in many military establishments and her flair for adventure and sheer guts in believing that you have to 'live' the machine that you are commissioned to paint, has earned her the respect of all the three fighting services, and she has really earned the success that she so richly deserves.

David Shepherd

O.B.E., F.R.S.A., F.R.G.S.

CHAPTER 1

DISASTER WITH A SILVER LINING

I slammed the tail gate shut on my first collection of paintings for the R.A.F., and cocooned with them in my imagination, all the fame and fortune about to alight on an aspiring artist!

Driving carefully through the February dusk towards R.A.F. Coltishall, thirty oil paintings wedged safely in the back, my heart seemed to be pumping overtime with the hope of success. It was an important celebration for the R.A.F. Station as their Lightnings had flown in the 50th anniversary fly-past, and it was a crucial one for me.

Tiers of tables and beer crates awaited me on either side of the entrance hall, cleverly concealed by white, freshly laundered damask tablecloths. As I arranged my landscapes and Lightning aircraft pictures on the pristine surfaces, I thought of the months of hard work and the relief of meeting the deadline for this exhibition. Now, setting out my one man show, I was relieved, exhilarated, and full of expectation.

Members of the Officers' Mess arrived in a steady flow. As they swept in, the chill and damp made me shiver as I stood dressed to kill, goose pimples on my bare arms and shoulders becoming a delicate blue. Nobody noticed. Worse, hardly anyone noticed my paintings. A few glanced at them as they passed, but champagne was flowing in the ante-room where it was warm, softly lit and blaring with music. Smiling, I talked to anyone who lingered long enough to view the pictures or speak to me, but there was little interest. The hope of selling several gradually receded. The procession entering the Mess fell to a mere trickle, then, along with my optimism, died away altogether. I studied one of the large pictures, a Norfolk landscape of a windmill at the edge of a dyke on the Broads, sunlight catching the creamy-white top of the structure. Why had I used burnt umber for the shadows? Cooler tones would have made them less obtrusive. Another painting had a Lightning moving off past others that were parked. What a messy background; I should have put more reflections on the undersides of the wings. In an hour of solitary confinement I found faults in every painting. Frustrated instead of exhilarated, I decided to join everybody in the ante-room.

The married couple I knew, Clive and Jenny Brimson who had arranged the invitation for me to exhibit my work, welcomed me, saying the President of the Mess Committee would purchase a painting for the Station, as a thank-you. As I would be driving home I kept to soft drinks. Soon the gulf between my sobered, sober self and the steadily drunker members of the Mess became increasingly apparent.

Eleven o'clock came, and my friends left to relieve baby sitters. I stood like a wilting wallflower at a hunt ball. The one bachelor I knew, leaning on the bar with a group of other men, almost seemed to be swapping bawdy stories about me, and the whole occasion was becoming a disaster, yet I couldn't just leave: my parents would reprimand me for not sticking it out. They knew how special the occasion was for me, the hours I had invested, the high expenses involved.

At last the P.M.C. appeared and escorted me to the entry's howling draught and my pictures. His legs appeared filled with a rubber solution, his speech slurred, his facial hues vermillion and crimson. Instead of buying a painting he commissioned a canvas for the Mess of his Labradors flushing pheasants from a cover. I clasped my hands demurely to prevent me giving him a sign that was not part of my upbringing. I longed to tell him where he and his Labradors could go, preferably stuffed, but instead put in an Oscar-winning performance of attentive listening. One thing was certain. In the morning he would not recall one word of his inane prattle.

At two in the morning I found a coherent official, saying I was going home and would return for the paintings next day. This was not on, I was informed: security was faulty, insurance would not cover my pictures; I would need to carry them to the end of the passage, turn right, along the corridor, and the second door … I interrupted,

"Don't worry, I'll load them into the car now." Outside, rain hurled itself at me. In my evening sandals I splashed through puddles. The hurt was colossal; every painting exhibited was to be taken home. I drove away, brimming with bitter disappointment, humiliation, anger and frustration. I don't cry easily when things go wrong (I weep over happy events and sentiment) and tell myself failure is character-building. As I passed the main gates the dam burst! In a gush of pent-up misery I cried all nineteen miles home! I'm sure I created as much water inside the car as there was outside on the flooded roads.

Two days later the telephone rang. It was R.A.F. Marham. They had seen my pictures at Coltishall and wished to commission a painting of a Victor on take-off for their Officers' Mess. They would make arrangments for me to be at the side of the runway and could give me all the facilities I might need. At the time I was quite unaware that because of that appalling exhibition my career, like the Victor, would be taking off. But let's go back to the beginning. How did all this start?

CHAPTER 2

THE DANCE OF THE SEVEN VEILS

Three pounds, two shillings and sixpence! I had sold my first painting! It could have been thousands, for unbelievably somebody liked my picture enough to purchase it.

This unforgettable sale which I had mentally converted into British currency, took place in Singapore where I was staying with cousins Tony and Judy Balfour, and their three small children, Peter, Ella and Harry. Tony was in the Royal Air Force, a pathologist at Changi hospital, and I joined them in their married quarter a couple of miles outside Changi village for eight months in 1964. Ah Kim, the Amah, looked after us, and with the luxury of having my bed made for me and chores taken care of, with time on my hands I decided to have a go at oil painting. A piece of bamboo from the garden, split lengthways, made a reasonable palette being non-absorbent, and I bought oil paints, white spirit and canvas board. Several brushes completed my equipment, and these included a couple of water colour brushes for detailed work. This was unorthodox, but suited me.

The first time I had handled oils was in England at a boarding and day school south of Attleborough, Norfolk, for boys up to the age of seventeen. Unqualified, I took on the kindergarten, and was persuaded to teach music and art to all age groups. I took singing lessons with my piano accordion, hoping the boys wouldn't discover that many of the songs were Girl Guide ones, learnt from my mother in a crowd of blue clad girls round a blazing camp fire! To the youngsters it was a welcome change from maths or history, and the cheerful, lusty singing could be heard miles away, the instrument being sufficiently noisy to encourage even those who were in the confused state of transition between soprano and bass! In art lessons, poster paints were used, and I had to be very enthusiastic and dream up ideas that were unusual enough to capture the imagination of boys who looked on art as either an utter bore, or the one period when they could muck about and cause chaos. Keeping one step ahead of the little blighters called for ingenuity, and it was essential that they had something worthwhile to show for their efforts, such as cutting out and painting totem poles, and silhouettes against the sunset.

Art lessons ceased at O levels, but at the request of several of the older boys I started an oil painting club. I had never used oils, so bought a book on the basics, provided the materials, and with the book in one hand, paintbrush in the other, I and a dozen budding Picassos experimented together. The club flourished, and so did the results. Inevitably there were some hilarious moments at this school. I was little older than the pupils, and being five foot two inches in height, many of them towered over me. In the kindergarten class room, the nature tables were of interest to many. I bred Privet Hawk

Moth caterpillars to moths through three generations, but was taken completely by surprise when caught and kissed by one of the older boys, on the pretext of his asking for my help to identify some furry insect in a reference book! I was shattered, amazingly naive, and furiously told him to grow up, which was precisely what he was doing! In truth, he was probably the more mature of the pair of us! Later I saw the funny side of it, but at the time I was terribly upset by the incident. I had been given the advice to start with strict discipline which could be relaxed later, but never the other way round. My only consolation was that this was a day boy, whereas the boarders knew me well enough not to attept such a thing! Perhaps it had been a 'dare'! Even so, I had a superb rapport with most of the older students, and I often produced end of term revues and skits, popular songs with words rewritten on school escapades, or at the expense of the staff, all the utmost fun.

Since small, I had been given a pony, Gypsy, by my parents, and he too was at the school, so during week-ends I could be seen tramping the lanes beside my much loved pony, teaching riding. I earned sufficient funds to buy a second animal. My oldest rider, also an art club member, was Ian Pettit. He was a 'blue baby' unable to tackle sports, but gained great pleasure from these other interests. Whilst undergoing major heart surgery the following year, he died at St. Batholomew's Hospital. It was gratifying to know that horse riding and painting had enriched his life, and I like to think that by being available to listen to him when he needed to talk, helped him come to terms with the insecurity and anxiety of his parent's separation. The art club flourished. One of the boys was a chieftain's son from Nigeria, a charming, extremely well educated mature young man of over six feet, who painted a delightful study of African dwellings, titling the painting, 'There are mud huts at the bottom of my garden'! It was a riot of enthusiasm!

The next time I used oil paints was in Singapore. My subjects were often the amazing range of colours of tropical sunsets with suitable foreground interest such as Malay huts and palm trees, and where I could include the sea, I added to those colours in reflections. I progressed through what I jokingly called my blue period, the same subjects painted in shades of blues and greys, mists and moonlight.

Early on during my time in the Far East, I met Peter Fish, an Argosy pilot who became a close friend. He insisted my paintings would sell, ignored my, "Don't be ridiculous!" protestations and bullied me into taking them to suitable shops in Changi, all wished to hang them alongside those already for sale by other artists, so we chose the smartest shop. Before I left Singapore I had sold many, and discovered they were passed off by the owner of the shop as having been done by a local artist, which presumably meant I was either Chinese or Malay! Mostly they sold to R.A.F. personnel and their friends. Aware the paintings should be signed, I had tried entwining my initials of PSD, but felt it unsatisfactory. Pete thought a scrawled P.S.Douglas was untidy, so found a solution by working the letters into one another, and I have used this ever since. To this day, Pete has my very first painting.

PENELOPE
DOUGLAS

On my return to England, I took a fourteen week shorthand and typing course in London. It was essential that I earned my living. I stayed with my mother's sister, Sylvia Makower and her husband Anthony, who owned a large, sparsely furnished, horribly tidy house in Kensington. Two other students spent the days there, and I walked home from college to join them for snack lunch. Alison Roberts made silver pendants and tea-spoons in the basement area, and Jacqueline du Pre almost at the peak of her profession, practised her cello in the drawing-room. I was in superb company! My aunt recalls that Jacqueline's upbringing had concentrated almost entirely on music and her cello, rather neglecting the more traditional school subjects. Jacqueline was thirsting for knowledge, so Sylvia arranged for Lord Clwyd's wife, Joan, who had obtained an Honours Degree at Cambridge alongside my aunt, to give tuition and fill in many of the gaps, information for which Jacqueline was craving. Her precious cello lived safely in the basement until the following day's practise, and I remember her as being refreshingly confident in playing her instrument, full of life, and happy, relaxed company. (The last time Jacqueline and I met was at the Albert Hall for a concert. Both of us had booked to hear a particular piece of Haydn, she had chosen to miss the first part of the concert, and was in her wheel chair waiting for the interval. I had got there late, so we spent the time together happily talking about mutual friends and the past).

Having achieved the necessary secretarial speeds, I returned to my parents' home in Barnham Broom, near Norwich. The house they had bought was one of Bullard's pubs, de-licensed. In view of the fact that my father, by then a retired parson, considered one drink made one a raging alcholic, this was rather amusing!

Norwich had its Assembly House, a charming period building with a restaurant, meeting rooms, and two galleries with high ceilings in which local artists could exhibit paintings, sculptures, embroidery or whatever they chose, for one or two weeks at a time. My family used the facilities regularly, and we enjoyed the current exhibitions. It was during one of these, studying the paintings, that I felt I could do almost as well. Daunted by having to produce thirty or forty paintings to do it justice, and having met the daughter and son-in-law of the auto-gyro builder, Ken Wallis, as both were painters and were delighted to exhibit their work alongside mine, I booked the gallery six months in advance for the following June. The worst that could happen was the loss of my meagre savings. I was prepared to take that risk.

Unease and doubt crept in as I talked to friends of my plans.

"If they are established artists, why are they exhibiting with a total amateur?"

"They won't produce the pictures, because they are so artistic they only paint when the mood is right." I painted like mad in case anything should go wrong. I cannot hurry the work, but I packed in more hours than ever, painting landscapes of Norfolk. Coastal scenes of the marshes became known as my mudscapes! Wishing to present the exhibition properly by having catalogues printed that people could pick up and keep, paintings numbered clearly and boldly so that even those squinting through their glasses couldn't fail to see which they were about to buy - I was prepared to give them every assistance possible - I asked my fellow exhibitors for their list of titles and prices for the printers. I was given a straight answer. They had no paintings whatsoever, and more important, could they have their booking fee back! I was on my own!

I had seen paintings of colourful characters from the Middle East painted on black velvet. They were very striking. Having been in Singapore I had appropriate photographs to work from, bought some velvet, and produced some portraits. They were a nightmare for the framer, but my first exhibition consisted of twenty-eight landscapes, four of these being of the Far East, all on canvas board; six portraits of Thai Classical dancers, Chinese and Malay people, and three dog portraits all on black velvet. The dogs belonged to the local doctor, Tony Hamerton, who had seen my paintings, and suggested I tried animals. Finally I had a head and shoulder portrait of my father on velvet.

My parents and their attitude to life was best summed up by my brother David, at the age of seven, when, riding our ponies we met the local farmer's wife, who asked,

"How are you getting on with your riding David?"

"Mummy says I'm doing very nicely, but Daddy says I'm absolutly hopeless." Nothing had changed! The exhibition had the full backing of my mother, but as regards my father, the fact that he was worried sick over my finances, was a minor point. More ghastly, was that his daughter was choosing to exhibit herself! He was utterly horrified! If I had been doing the dance of the seven veils on the altar during mattins it would have been nothing by comparison. With the exhibition hung, he refused to appear anywhere near it. However as the days went by and he heard excited words about numbers seven and eighteen selling within minutes of it opening, his natural male inquisitiveness began to crawl to the surface. The room I had booked happened to have two entrance doors, and with great courage, he shot in one door, and equally quickly straight out of the other! Next day he lingered a moment, during which a couple studying the portrait of him, made obvious signs that the sitter was 'over there! Look!' Pride at last came to the fore, and feeling a total celebrity, my father never left the exhibition for a second after that, and before leaving home could be heard muttering firmly to my mother,

"Hurry up my dear, or we'll be late!"

Oil paintings on velvet were new, so deciding to handle publicity myself, I had asked the Press if they could come and write up the exhibition for the local newspapers. They took me up on the idea, and Hamilton Wood from Eastern Counties Newspapers wrote the following about the paintings on black velvet.

"... what is curious about the pictures is the employment of straight realist painting techniques upon a material which is plainly decorative. This juxtaposition causes an initial shock, which would not have arisen if the motifs and the painting method had been purely decorative themselves. It is not the shock caused by the juxtaposition of images, such as the surrealists employed. It is a technical shock, more likely to be felt by practising painters. Sacking, charred paper, deliberately blistered paint, we have had the lot from the avant-garde. Here is a conventional painter who takes painting off prepared canvases and puts it on furnishing fabric and thus poses aesthetic questions over again. There is no doubt about the immediate effect - it is like discovering a new flavour which many will enjoy ... she is a forceful painter, often tackling a job like a young worker fresh to something which the old hands tend to labour at." Having had no formal tuition of any sort, I wondered if this gave me a fresh and original approach to my work? As a result of the newspaper article, I was interviewed on television for the B.B.C. Look East programme. I was extremely nervous as the seconds were counted down before this started, painfully aware of my appalling, stuttering sentences. Thankfully one of the cameras went wrong, and we started again. Judging from the comments of some of the visitors to the exhibition,

"Oh! It's the girl we saw on the telly!" the exposure had done me good!

With the exhibition over and a large number of commissions from it, I made the decision to try and make painting a full time career. My parents were enormously supportive, my mother realistically suggesting that instead of my paying rent, I could do all the domestic chores instead! Financially this would help me, and she could enjoy the outdoor interests that gave her so much pleasure, breeding pigs, Guiding, and rallying the village to the W.I. with her usual organisational flair! While working for this first exhibition, I had also been doing a variety of short term secretarial jobs through a Norwich agency, and the thought of quitting on these was wonderful! With an enormous amount of enthusiasm, I launched myself officially as an artist.

To achieve the animal portrait commissions, I drove to meet my four footed client, took a large number of slide photographs of the head and shoulders of the animal, and at home, was able to project these onto a wall and have my subject life size, motionless! I tried taking my paints into somebody's house, working from life. The conditions were hopeless. On one occasion the owner became fearfully agitated at the threat to her carpet from spilt paint and white spirit, and every precaution taken on my part did nothing to ease the situation. On another, help from a two year old proved a major hazard, I had nothing to show for my hours of labour except a velvet background covered in chocolate and orange juice, neither of which mixed satisfactorily with my client's expectations! Apart from that, an extremely mobile dog rushing out of the room just as I thought I had him poised, was no help whatsoever.

Originally I had stretched the velvet on to a board, pinning it into place, but on having it framed, the material got pulled slightly out of line, giving the dog portrait a lop sided leer that meant it had to be jettisoned into the dustbin, with hours of work wasted. The answer was to frame first. I painted most dogs looking alert, just as if their owner had whistled for them. The majority of breeds were obedient models, though some were surprisingly difficult. I recall asking the owner of a pair of gun-dogs to fetch a gun, in the hopes that this might check the sloppy behaviour of the dogs, and make them alert; she came out of the farmhouse with a twelve bore pointed at my chest, murmuring feebly,

"I don't know whether this is loaded!" I also had a problem with a Border Collie which insisted on looking utterly miserable, and although I made mewing noises and did all I could, she continued to look very dejected, so finally we tied her to something suitable, and I persuaded her owner to give the appearance of leaving without her, to get into her car and start the engine! It worked beautifully!

On only one occasion did I have a dissatisfied client. The subject was two rather charming Pekingese dogs, to be painted together in one frame. Although the downward turn to the mouth gave an air of disdain, their eyes were alluring, huge liquid pools reflecting such gorgeous highlights that when the portraits were finished, they gave the impression that if the eyes were touched they would water. These Pekingese were owned by an eminent surgeon and his wife. She knew my family, having done Guiding with my mother. They lived in a wealthy area, and in teenage days, my brother and I were invited to parties given for their three sons, events we loathed because of the heart-sinking games we were compelled to join, and my mother loathed because living twenty-eight miles away, she was forced to spend the evening there with other parents, and had nothing suitable to wear for the fashion one-upmanship torture she had to suffer. They knew the costs of the commission, but when I appeared with the portraits, the wife was adamant that she was only prepared to pay half. She sat behind her antique, leather topped desk like a headmistress doing her utmost to intimidate me! I had driven nearly thirty miles, but there was no offer of a cup of coffee or warmth from her. Inexperienced at dealing with this situation, desperately trying to avoid feeling threatened, I reached out for the painting, saying as firmly as I could,

"Please don't worry. You don't have to buy it. I can always do with extra portraits for exhibitions," whereupon she snatched the picture towards her, clasping it tightly, saying,

"No, I want it!"

"In that case you will have to pay me the price I quoted please." She kept the portraits. I got my money, and my mother exploded with fury when I told her what had happened!

January 1967, and I was commissioned through Wing Commander Tabor for seven Norfolk landscapes for the Officers' Mess at R.A.F. Watton. The largest was to be twenty-four inches by thirty-six, most of the others twenty by thirty. It needed great thought and planning, but with all painting, a third of it is done before I ever pick up a brush. I chose a wide variety of subjects, season of the year, time of day, and mood of nature. When the paintings were hung, the Ladies Room was renamed the Norfolk Room as a result. R.A.F. Swanton Morley also commissioned two landscapes.

CHAPTER 3

A LITTLE SHEPHERDING AND A BRUSH WITH A TIGER

Cruft's Dog Show, held at Olympia, was bound to have my dog portraits circulating the globe, so I booked a space, eight foot by six, wall backed, on a main avenue. It had to be fire proof. Various estimated for building the stand whistled through the letter box mentioning, 'a bituminous felt base linoleum laid direct on to the permanent floor ...', and, 'erect standard size lockable flush door,' and, 'partitioning and fascia unit to be decorated with two coats of emulsion paint to the colour of your choice'. They even dared to add that electrical installations were not included! I was left dazed yet amused. I might as well have a complete bungalow built! The quoted costs were colossal, acceptance out of the question. Instead I created the stand myself. I bought yards of white flame-proof flannelette nightie material - I wouldn't have been seen dead in it, but as for my great-grandmother - then I covered an old, six foot high Japanese screen with this as a background on which to hang several portraits, also sewing a cover for a folding card table which would be in the front of the stand to take an unframed portrait that people could handle, and my first business cards, about to be printed. Along the front I had white curtain cord draped from a series of posts, these made from half broom handles nailed into a one foot square block of wood. This would control the crowds that would be queuing up to commission my work, assisted by my taking a full page advertisement in Cruft's catalogue. Finally I fixed my floodlights so that the portraits would look their best.

The stand looked good. I enjoyed the exhibition. The hoards did not flock to me. Dog owners were far too busy guarding, grooming and fussing neurotically over their pampered pedigree pets, the public wandered the aisles aimlessly, some taking a mild interest in my pictures, but most presumably didn't own anything larger than a goldfish! I received two commissions, one of which was from a Gianfranco Boero in Genoa for his spaniel Broomleaf Bright An' Gay. Try calling that! I sent the painting to Italy, and it took me months to get payment. He answered my requests with cheerful letters telling me repeatedly,

"I am young and single and you know how it is". I felt like replying,

"I am young and single, and if you send me my money, I too, can discover how it is!"

Undaunted by the failure of Cruft's, and fervently still full of ideas to spread my vast talents to the nation, I wrote to the Director-General of the World Wildlife Fund, suggesting that from their vast library of photographs, I could produce an exhibition of wildlife paintings for them, all profits going to their fund. I work on the theory that I approach the head of an organisation, and work downwards if I have to, rather than have ambitions and ideas blocked by a tea-boy! Ian MacPhail must have sighed deeply after reading my letter! However, sensibly he felt such enterprise needed guidance, spoke to David Shepherd - the artist not the bishop - then wrote to me suggesting that I go to see him, take some paintings, and that he would, 'make some helpful noises, I trust'. It was indeed a charming and helpful way of turning down my misguidedly ambitious ideas, yet giving me the positive approach.

In David's studio, surrounded by several wonderful oil paintings including an unfinished canvas of his much loved elephants, we went through my pathetic efforts. David does not give tuition. He is far too busy. That afternoon must have been an exception. I came away overflowing with enthusiasm, one of the most vital points being that he sorted out my palette. The selection of paints I was using had been chosen at random with no experience or guidance other than from books I had read. From David I learnt which colours to buy, how to use them for tone to get more depth, and received a great deal of expert help for which I have been extremely grateful ever since. He was immensely encouraging, not least because I couldn't fail to be influenced and infected by his enormous warmth and passion for his profession, and for the subject matter. He has the largest heart of any man I know! We have kept in touch ever since.

Now my paintings started to improve, I exhibited pictures locally in Norfolk whenever possible, joining other artists prepared to sell work with a percentage going to charity. I also had a landscape bought by the print firm, Solomon and Whitehead, though to my knowledge they never used it. I had a one man show in Woodbridge Gallery, Suffolk, and my second at the Assembly House, Norwich.

As a full time artist my work load was unbelievable! I seemed to be at it all day, every day. Painting in artificial light I found ineffective, though I could continue if paint was already mixed. By artificial light I once created what I thought was a lovely, orange glow on the side of a combine harvester in a wheat field in evening sunlight, only to discover by daylight that it was a hideous puce!

It was by chance that I met Clive and Jenny Brimson. He was a pilot at R.A.F. Coltishall. Knowing that I painted landscapes, Clive asked me to reproduce a photograph of him taking off in a Lightning aircraft for the flypast at Winston Churchill's funeral. I had no hesitation in attempting a subject that was new, but only on the understanding that if he didn't like it, he needn't buy it. However, it was the first of two paintings he purchased, and I presumed they would be the only aircraft I would ever attempt, but Clive suggested I put on an exhibition in the Officers' Mess at R.A.F. Coltishall, the following February.

Prior to this, the R.A.F. Jubilee display was to take place at R.A.F. Abingdon, so I decided to ask the Ministry of Defence whether, as aviation artist, they would grant me a Press Pass. Adopting my usual attitude that it is always worth trying hard for something, however impossible because I never knew what might come of it, I was delighted when they agreed. I booked into a hotel nearby, watched several rehearsals for the air display, and found the experience tremendously exciting and rewarding. I had no painting equipment with me, merely my camera, an ancient Leica. My mother had owned one since before her marriage, my brother and I taking it in turns to have it at boarding school, so I had bought a second hand model. David had worked in the Public Relations department of the Army after his degree at Trinity College, Dublin, also using a Leica, and from there went into television advertising in Madison Avenue, New York. My mother's hobby and encouragement had indirectly influenced both our careers!

At Abingdon I discovered what it was like to be with the Press. As Her Majesty the Queen and Prince Philip toured the vast number of aircraft and their crews from the back of a Landrover, I was jostled and pushed, struggling to hold my ground to get good material. I had never been so close to the Royal Family - except when officially Presented at Buckingham Palace, footmen in the side isles making me laugh with their demonstrations on how we should curtsey - and couldn't believe my luck at having such a superb position. Being battered by the Press became irrelevant!

The air show was impressive, so was the noise and the smell of the aircraft and fuel. The Falcons did a spectacular display of free-fall parachuting from an Argosy aircraft flown by Peter Fish, a link with my past. I met the display team afterwards, and later painted Fred, their live falcon mascot, on black velvet. Another link with my past was the Vickers Gunbus, which was to feature in the first of two paintings I worked on, the initial one being of The Queen inspecting the Royal Guard of Honour formed by the Queen's Colour Squadron, with a Vickers Gunbus one end and the Harrier the other, and the painting included the Royal Dais and visitors. The firm of Vickers had a family connection, and worth researching.

In 1927 Vickers Limited and W.G.Armstrong Whitworth formed a joint company, Vickers Armstrong, for mutual defence interests. My great aunt Katie (Katharine) married Douglas Vickers, Chairman of this armaments firm. My aunt, now nearly ninety-six, remembers him from her childhood as a dour man. She never heard him say more than 'yes' or 'no', but his silent romp with the children every Sunday evening was one of the highlights of her week; his technique went far beyond anyone else's, including holding her up by her ankles above her bed. They all loved him, but respectfully. On mentioning to my aunt that the family must have been delighted at Katie making such a good marriage, she replied with a twinkle,

"Good heavens no! She had married beneath her, she married trade!"

(From my cousin, Philippa Luard (nee Chetwynd), I learnt that Katie had written an account in 1941, of much of their life from shortly before their marriage on 8th November 1893, until the end of the First World War, and has very kindly lent me these papers.) Staying in Scotland with her sister Ida, Katie and Douglas corresponded, and Katie writes,

"He always had a certain difficulty in expressing his deepest feelings, but not in his beautiful love letters. I learnt more about what he felt for me in those letters than in all our forty-four years together."

Before she married, Katie learnt the violin at the Guildhall School of Music, and deciding she should earn her living, studied painting at Wasse's studio in St. John's Wood. After she married Douglas, much of their life together was spent in travelling, partly because of his work, and it was quite usual to travel abroad for better health, or socially. On one occasion in 1894, Douglas returned from the office and said,

"I am going to St. Petersburg on Monday. Will you come?" Due to their travels, Katie became fluent in French, German and Italian. They had three children, Oliver born 1898, Sholto born 1902, and Angus born 1904. Douglas built Katie a studio and their great love of music and painting was shared in visits to galleries all over Europe. The works, were in Sheffield, and Katie writes,

"King Edward and Queen Alexandra visited the works ... .glass screens had been erected behind which they saw the molten metal poured into moulds." On another occasion a Russian visitor remarked how wonderfully they had concealed all the police and detectives; he couldn't believe there was not one policeman or one detective in the works atall.

Oliver broke his leg in a fall when skating. "Dr Selby brought him home saying he was sure it was not broken, but after two days I was not satisfied and took him up to London on an ironing board. Mr Bowlby, the surgeon, said it was a green fracture, had a leather splint moulded on to his leg, which hardened and was quite comfortable, and he was able to go out driving but looked very white. I poured a wonderful prescription I had of belladonna, menthol and chloroform on the poor leg with very good effect!"

She mentions their first car, 1902. "We seem to have started having a motor this year! Amusing to look back on now (written in 1941) as to its comfort and shape - it was a small wagonette, open! The second chauffeur we had rejoiced in the name of Ezra Carr! The children thought it so appropriate."

Although Douglas only drank wine occasionally, he suffered from gout, but "managed to hobble to his installation as Master Cutler" - 1908. As Master and Mistress Cutlers they gave an afternoon concert for six hundred guests. Ninety guests visited the works for the Cutlers Feast, and Katie tells of their drive home from Sheffield, "The suffragettes, Sylvia Pankhurst, were trying to make trouble. We drove through a tremendous crowd and the front car had a window broken! Sylvia Pankhurst tried very hard to get into the Cutler's Hall first as a guest, and even as a charwoman in the kitchen but did not succeed and finally had to be rescued from the crowd, got into a train and taken away!"

Douglas Vickers visited both Russia and Japan for his work, and he and Katie took Oliver with them. This was a second visit to St. Petersburg. "It was unfortunately near the Russian Christmas so the Kremlin, which I wanted so much to show Oliver was shut, but we called on the Governor who received us very kindly indeed, he and his wife quite charming, and next day the Kremlin was opened for us! We saw all its marvellous treasures again we did some sightseeing including a most interesting, very old, Russian peasant's house - belonged to the great grandfather of Peter the Great - about two hundred years old, and untouched. We have invested in some high felt boots, come right up well over your knees, and I can't think what we should have done without them later, as crossing Siberia, the train only burning wood, it had to stop three or four times a day to load up. We all pulled on our boots and walked up and down the platform for air and exercise. We had a private sleeping car put on to the train at Pekin, most comfortable in every way but we had to jump on to the restaurant car for meals. Luckily the train was not going fast at all, but it was quite sad to leave it and get out at a very icy snowy station at 5.0 a.m. as we had to change trains for Moscow. The rest of that journey to Harbin was rather a nightmare and most uncomfortable. We were so glad to get into the luxury of the Siberian Express. The journey crossing the Urals was quite indescribably lovely, the silver birches shining up against the snow. We stopped ... where they had an interesting little booth of precious stones found in the Urals. I was very pleased with some green stones which afterwards made a brooch, which always reminds me of that lovely scenery."

In 1910, the Vickers household clearly very musical, often had well known musicians staying in the house. The boys had learnt the piano and could write the notes down as their tutor played, and Katie says all went well until they went to school at Eaton. "I always remember one of the Governors of Eaton saying, 'No BOY should be musical.'" Eaton was not a success, the housemaster proved very unpleasant, and the poor lighting in the school affected Angus's eyesight for the rest of his life. Cantley was the Vickers home in Sheffield, and they rented a house in Tulloch, Scotland, for three months of the year. The lifestyle seemed to be one of shooting parties and skating, balls and concerts, visits to both opera and ballet. Both Douglas and Katie took on endless public engagements, and Douglas always spoke beautifully. Katie, not satisfied with her first public speaking effort, had tuition.

1914 saw the outbreak of war, Douglas extremely busy at the works, Katie packing parcels for prisoners of war. For a while, much of life continued as before. She writes,

"I was very anxious that Sargent should paint Douglas so I wrote to him (he did not want to paint any more portraits) but I was able to say that IF he would paint him it would be the eleventh Vickers he had painted! He wrote me a charming letter saying these were eleven good reasons why he should, and would Douglas come and sit the next Sunday morning and would I care to come and watch! It was a most marvellous privilege to watch that magic hand paint - at the first sitting he turned to me and said, 'I shall enjoy doing THIS.' I said I had felt sure he would! It is a most beautiful picture. The story of Sargent's painting so many Vickers is interesting; in early days my three sisters in law were in Paris with an old friend of their mother's Mademoiselle Hautier. They saw some very good photographs in a window and said they would like to have their portraits painted. Mademoiselle Hautier who painted very well herself ... wrote that she knew of a clever student in Paris who would come over to Sheffield and paint the girls there. She sent Sargent! He first painted the famous picture of the three Miss Vickers, Mabel, Mildred and Evelyn, which is now in the Mappin Art Gallery. It was left to me with all the other pictures but we arranged if I could not hang it, it should go to the Sheffield Art Gallery - they had no Sargent there - it was very well received."

At Tulloch, Katie had several convalescent officers to stay, having ninety in all through the house that year, which she found interesting but quite hard work. (Her manuscript is difficult to follow regarding where they lived, and when, but) they owned a house in London, Chapel House, which she also filled with convalescent soldiers. She was involved with a society called the 'United Workers' with weekly meetings and "a brilliant list of speakers." Katie thought that much economising was in the hands of domestic staff, so got groups of these together, eventually with a large gathering at Drury Lane. She organised an economy exhibition in the unfinished building of London County Council, a series of speakers on coal, education, welfare work amongst boys and girls in factories, and Trade Unions, and had a visit from Queen Mary. She continues, "It was not possible to go on having semi convalescents at Chapel House any longer. Douglas desperately over worked and tired, had to have a quiet house. As a consolation he said if I liked he would furnish and equip a hospital for the Flying Corps. I found a very good house 82 Eaton Square and went to see Lady Henderson who was interested in a small hospital in Bryanstone Square. We arranged to join our forces and she remained chairman of the house committee until I took it over ... I set to work and furnished the hospital making the very good airy rooms as nice as possible and making a very comfortable mess room of the big dining-room with a polished table at one end for meals, and endless comfortable chairs and stools for tired limbs. The Scottish Red Cross gave me and fully equipped the sterilising, operating wards etc: as our patients came straight from the Front. We were a good band of workers. I admired one splendid woman who sorted uniforms and clothes and saw to cleaning such as were possible, to be used again ... some of our V.A.D. helpers bore distinguished names, three Baldwin daughters amongst them! We had seventy beds."

1917 Katie says, "I started the first communal kitchen! Then three big kitchens in Westminster and fed a thousand a day! The first big one in Smith Street was opened for me by Princess Beatrice! We had a splendid French woman as head cook, many voluntary helpers. The difficulties were very many, but there was always a dinner of a meaty dish two vegetables and a pudding. Some girls came one day to me and said could they eat their dinner at the kitchens, so I got a carpenter, put in a partition, for a table, crockery etc: and it was easily organised! I set up a very good committee, which was most helpful. A representative of the School for Cookery, a representative of the Gas Company, etc. and a truly invaluable Brigadier from the Salvation Army did all our accounts for us!" Most of the equipment was given by Douglas.

1918, Katie heard that a military hospital in Hampstead were, "badly in need of comforts," and in order to raise money, "Lady Drogheda was splendid - she got up an exhibition of drawings etc: of early Air Force, balloons etc. a great success and she made quite a lot of money for arm chairs, stools, bath chairs etc:." By this time Douglas and Katie's son Oliver was in the Flying Corps in 20 Squadron - or was it 24 Squadron - and soon got his wings. "We saw him off to France, a perfectly tragic and miserable parting ... he had had a good training as when he joined they found he was a good pilot and he went from one training camp to another rapidly. Finally to Gosport the best." August 1917, "Had a thrilling letter from Oliver with an account of his wonderful fight with a German Circus found to be Richthofens. Jack Hone was his observer, between them they shot down four machines and a fifth out of control twelve miles over the German lines. Managed to get back over our lines before pancake landing - under carriage shot away - in the middle of the fight the propeller stopped. Oliver said, 'I knew the top tank had been shot through but there might be some left below the shot.' There was. He was recommended for the M.C. but his General refused it! July 25th. Heard he was coming home. Apparently his nerves had suffered (he was not yet nineteen) and he applied to see Air Marshal Trenchard who asking his age said, 'What are you doing here, go home.' It showed by his being sick in the air, the first time in his life." Some time later, a friend called on Katie. He had been in hospital, and in the next bed was a badly wounded man just back. Katie continues, "He asked him if the German planes had worried them much, and he said, 'No not since a young pilot named Vickers smashed Richthofen's Squadron up.'"

October 7th - "I went up to Sheffield for the annual Vickers meeting, Douglas's first as chairman. What a splendid reception he got. I felt so proud of him." The following June, "Douglas came out into the garden really excited and said, 'They have done it!' Captain John Alcock and Lieutenant Arthur Whitton-Brown had made the first non-stop crossing of the Atlantic, from Newfoundland to Clifden, County Galway, in a Vickers Vimy. It won them a Knighthood, the Air Force Cross, and a cheque for ten thousand pounds from the Daily Mail who had offered this as a prize to the first person to fly the Atlantic.

"They landed on what looked like a nice smooth green field - it was a bog! Oliver got his car out and drove across Ireland to fetch them."

Great Aunt Katie's notes end soon after 1920, much of it family news. They are difficult to decipher in places, and I have tried to pick out the most relevant parts, and give a glimpse into the past.

Now back to painting ... To return to my own career, after being at the 50th anniversary of the R.A.F. at Abingdon, I was commissioned by the Red Arrows for a painting of their nine aircraft in flight, with below, on the Royal Dais, The Queen and Prince Philip, The Duchess of Gloucester and Princess Marina, plus the crowd of guests either side. It was presented to their team leader, Ray Hanna.

My brother persuaded me it was time to have my own notepaper printed and become more businesslike, saying that my small Basildon Bond would get lost among official letters! My artist's signature was at the top on the left, the address on the right, printed in red.

Having painted domestic animals on black velvet, I moved on to the big cat family. A cougar was shot by my brother ... on film, in a commercial for the Cougar car in the United States of America. It featured slow dissolves - when one image slowly takes over from another. The television commercial showed the car being driven up a hill, then slow dissolve to the animal romping down the other side, and so on. Tame, this beautiful creature was invited on to the back seat in order that the interior could be filmed. She sniffed, whiskers twitching with curiosity, then like a back-yard moggie on a log, sharpened her claws on the upholstery which disintegrated satisfactorily beneath her paws, ripped to shreds by extended claws! The commercial never showed the interior! David had given me photographs of the cougar, so she was the first wild animal I painted, followed by lions, then newly born giraffe with unsteady legs braced.

I was surprised to receive a commission for a tiger's portrait from a lady in Sussex. How she knew of me, I never discovered. Her instructions were clear. It must be snarling! With great eagerness I headed for London Zoo, tracking down both the tiger enclosure and their keeper.

"Snarling?" He laughed out loud. "Come with me Miss." I followed. He ducked under the outer safety barrier, called the tigers over to him, and put his hand through the bars while they rolled on their backs, purring as his hand fondled them. So much for that! Where was I to go to get the material?

Robert Brothers' Circus was to visit Norwich, so perhaps they had a tiger? I went to see them. What a fascinating world opened up to me. Marie Roberts was a marvellous, warm, friendly person. She was apologetic, they had no tigers. But, they commissioned a portrait on velvet of one of their Appaloosan horses, a North American breed with dark spots on a light background, and a pretty animal to paint with its neck arched in true Circus style. It was not easy on the black background, for like a Dalmation, I had to make sure the spots looked solid, and not that the animal was riddled with bullet holes! The subject gave me great pleasure. They also bought several small landscapes to hang in their trailer, a large and comfortable mobile home, full of an astonishing collection of china animal ornaments. Marie was an enchanting person, full of fascinating anecdotes of life in the Big Top, which I revelled in as we sat in the trailer drinking coffee.

They had been so good to me, I thought I should go to a performance - I prefer animals in the natural state than as a circus act - taking with me my God-daughter Brigid Menin and two of her school friends. Performers in travelling circuses have many jobs outside the ring, and when I handed over my ticket money, it was taken by Marie, and mysteriously I discovered my bank notes returned neatly folded under the tickets, my requested seats upgraded to the best ringside view! The various acts got under way, then they brought in a large, single horse, asking for volunteers to ride it bareback in the ring and to try to stand up on it. I was wearing trousers, and with great persuasion and shovings from the children, I volunteered, was collected and escorted by one of the circus folk to the side of the ring, where they fastened a belt round my waist, the safety harness. The rope from this went up to the centre of the Big Top, through a ring, and down into the hands of several clowns. Thrilled at riding a horse in a circus, beyond my wildest dreams, I ran towards the spring-board which was arranged in a helpful position for mounting, scrambling astride the live rocking-horse as it cantered round the ring. I felt the steady movement beneath me, the warmth from being bareback, the discipline and power of this magnificent horse, the neck arching in front of me, and I felt a million dollars ... until I was asked to stand up. I got into a crouching position, straightened my knees, and I was there! Standing, I lasted about three seconds before I lost my balance! Now the act really took hold, for I became a pendulum, my height controlled by the clowns. When they pulled on the rope, I was dangling twenty feet up, when they let it out, I swept past at the height of their heads, causing them all to flatten themselves on the sawdust. They would start to get to their feet, when with frantic warning shouts to each other, I would hurtle past again while they sprawled beneath me or leapt out of the way. The audience loved it! The slapstick appealed to all, and I seemed to swing for ever!

Finally, standing at the side while they unbuckled the harness, I was laughing so much and was so dizzy, I was reeling! Perhaps it is the dream of every little girl to ride a horse in the circus ring! If so, I'd fulfilled my dream!

Eventually I completed my tiger commission through material from a zoo. But, I was to fall in more ways than one shortly afterwards.

CHAPTER 4

NIMROD, THE MIGHTY HUNTER

Now came my disastrous exhibition in the Officers' Mess at R.A.F. Coltishall, but in spite of this, I had been asked to paint a Victor taking off from its base at R.A.F. Marham. Having worked from borrowed photographs for the exhibition of Lightnings, at Marham I was taking my own, my escort in a Landrover in contact with the control tower. I could therefore ask the pilot to lift off sooner, or delay this to suit my position at the side of the runway. My immediate impression was just how fast this shark-like aircraft was tearing past me. I was lucky if I had time for one photograph with the aircraft in the position I'd planned; two were the most I could take, and those would have the aircraft too far from me or too close. It was a nightmare as there were limits to how long the aircraft could remain in the circuit, and it left no room for any error regarding shutter speed or exposure. Yet absorbing the atmosphere, the noise and the sight of this monster of metal quite so close, heightened my professional attitude. The colossal change from working from somebody else's photographs to seeing the aircraft, made a profound impression on me. Uncertain whether to paint the aircraft lifting off from the runway or airborne, I painted two pictures, giving a choice. The Mess bought both.

Farnborough Air Show followed, and the ground vibrated beneath me as I stood beside the runway watching the aircraft thundering past. A few were familiar to me, many were not, especially those from foreign countries. With my Press pass, I was in a privileged position which was ideal for photography. One of the aircraft displayed in flight was a reconnaisance aircraft, the Breguet Atlantique - the French equivalent of our Shackleton - and having demonstrated the 'feathering' of one engine, banked low over the buildings at the end of the runway, starting up the second engine as it turned to come in to land. Whether the pilot appeared to be flying too slowly, and too low, only an inquiry would tell, for the tip of the port wing caught the roof of the tallest hanger, and the Atlantique cartwheeled, bringing the fuselage nose down on to the side of the R.A.E's garage, exploding, flinging the tail section on to the roof of the staff canteen. Thick, dark smoke billowed skywards. The crowd of ten thousand, stunned, stood silent and still. The Press tent became a hive of activity. Five of the French crew were killed instantly, and in the burnt out canteen rest room the body of a lorry driver was found. Had the aircraft crashed a few minutes earlier, the canteen would have been packed with people, but thankfully it had emptied. Rumours that the Atlantique crew had their wives with them for the display kept the Press seeking urgent information, but fortunately this was not so.

I was to have a maritime connection with my next painting. In Plymouth at five in the morning, I left the friends with whom I had been staying in their Navy married quarter, Elizabeth and Robin Violet, and drove across country along a labyrinth of lanes, and reached R.A.F. St. Mawgan on the west coast of Cornwall in time for a crew briefing at eight. I was to have a Shackleton flight to get material for a painting of the Nimrod. This was not yet in service, but I had taken some paintings to the Headquarters of Coastal Command at Northwood, with the subsequent commission. Discussion made it clear that the aircraft should be depicted in the murky conditions under which she would be operational, flying over the Atlantic ocean. I murmured firmly that I had never seen it, the upshot being my flight in the Shackleton. I was enormously elated at the prospect of my first ever flight, kitted out in flying suit, life jacket and headset, I curled up in the nose of the aircraft in the gun turret, from where it was felt I would get the best opportunity of studying sea and sky. The day was grey, overcast, with the sky breaking to the west giving me wonderful glimpses of light, shades of ivory to dark cream, and the waves below, white crested and a million shades of greys and greens, quite perfect. If the conditions and colours suited me, the flight did not! We were flying in a figure of eight, working with an R.A.F. launch towing a target, on a simulated bombing exercise, swooping down low over the boat, then rising round the loops of the pattern. All was fine, photography going well, quick sketches achieved, but was it just me, or was it becoming warm? Two hours into the five hour flight, I began to feel horribly hot outside my body, and extremely uncomfortable inside, and knew I was about to be airsick. Thank God for the man who'd shoved a sick bag at me, 'just in case'! I filled it! I felt awful. Until I learnt to drive, I had been car sick. Stupid pride, just not wanting to miss a second of this flight in my excitement, and the fear of becoming drowsy, I had not taken a tablet. More fool me! Every time the aircraft headed for the distant Cornish coast, I prayed silently we were going back to base. We weren't! Again and again we turned out to sea, while I vomited uncontrollably until, I imagine, I was empty! Cheerfully, the quartermaster offered to refill me by bringing plates swimming with sausages, baked beans and other food, the sight of which was quite beyond me, and the rest of the flight, still in my turret, was simply, endured! On boarding the aircraft I had felt extremely privileged to be flying in an aircraft of such age and distinction, linked with the names of its Avro forbears, Lancaster and Lincoln. Now I wondered what the hell I was doing in this incredibly noisy, rattling smelly old crate! When at long last we landed, I was interviewed immediately for an article for the R.A.F. News, printed under the caption, 'Putting Penelope in the Picture', I was thankful the photographs had been taken before the flight, though in black and white, my pea-green skin tone would not have shown, but forget publicity, all I wanted was a cup of tea!

I had been given excellent material of the Nimrod, and the canvas size chosen by Northwood was three foot by four, the painting seemed to take up the entire room at home, and was Christened, Big Nim. It was the largest I had painted, and my first stretched canvas, quite different to work on. The surface had none of the hardbacked resistance that I was used to, and from the start, I felt more professional. Framed, I could just get it into the car. Fortunately I had an estate, and due to my chosen profession, only this or a hatchback model was suitable. The Big Nim painting appeared on television when I had a second interview for Look East. Soon I received a letter from Air Marshal Sir John Lapsley at Northwood, informing me the painting was to be presented to Coastal Command Headquarters by Hawker Siddeley Aviation, and Sir Harry Broadhurst would be formally handing it over at 'a luncheon', to which I was invited. It was a memorable and very special occasion. Even the menus were printed, 'Presentation of Nimrod Painting', and Big Nim was officially unveiled. I made myself a cream, mini shirt-dress, very fashionable, worn with a dark green cowboy hat, and felt highly honoured to be the cause of such an occasion. Had I known Hawker Siddeley were paying for the picture, I might have added a few noughts to the sum, perhaps they wouldn't have noticed! When working, I wore jeans and casual clothes, but because artists seem to have a reputation for looking thoroughly dirty and scruffy, when it came to the presentation of Big Nim, I made a point of dressing smartly for the occasion.

The Kronfeld Club was a meeting place for all interested in light aviation and gliding, with the Kronfeld Society, formed in 1966, as part of this, encouraging aviation art. Robert Kronfeld was the Austrian gliding champion who came to Britain in the early days of gliding, was involved in the birth of British military gliding, and was killed testing a new tail-less glider at the end of the war. Having seen one of their exhibitions, I achieved having three paintings accepted for their Annual show. One of these was a Nimrod over Malta. My brother, when in Public Relations with the Army, was based on the island, so had material for the background, though when I visited Malta a couple of years later, from the position I had portrayed the aircraft, it would probably have taken off from a side street in Valetta! Nobody appeared to question this, and I was elected a member of the society. At the exhibition, a Full Member, who had been commissioned for the same subject, stood in front of my painting, saying,

"Break that girl's arm!" Little did he realize I was close by!

As a result of painting Big Nim, Hawker Siddeley published a two page spread about, 'The remarkable girl who puts aeroplanes on canvas', which was read by John Hellings, a fellow artist I had met through the Kronfeld Society, who also worked at Hatfield for Hawker Siddeley. With his marvellous sense of humour, he sent me his own version of the article, words deleted here and there with thick felt pen, so that it read in a totally different way, suggestive and highly entertaining!

The Queen had visited Norwich to open the new County Hall, and with a selection of photographs from which I could get the material, I presented Norfolk County Council with a painting. A sherry party marked the unveiling of the picture, and somebody whispered to me that it was the same cloth that Her Majesty had used! As a thank you, members of the Council gave me a gift of artist's materials, which was probably more generous than originally intended as the acknowledgement of the painting's arrival had got lost among a sea of papers, and never sent to me! Studio 69, the firm that provided me with my paints and framed my work, were a great help over this gift, for a few of the tubes of paint given to me were not colours I used, so they changed them.

Through David Shepherd's suggestion, my palette held the following paints, titanium white, ivory black, burnt umber, burnt sienna, light red, cadmium yellow, yellow ochre, winsor red, ultramarine blue, cobalt blue, olive green, and alizarin crimson. These were my basic colours. In addition, I had raw umber, flesh tint, cerulean blue, Prussian blue, and cadmium orange. By constant use, I had got to know these colour intimately, and did not wish to have any other particular shade introduced, as the learning process of the qualities of a new colour would have to start all over again. Some were strong in pigment, just the smallest squeeze of the tube needed, others were the opposite. Oils could take over two weeks to dry, much depending on the weather and the time of year.

Tone was vitally important, helped mainly by the use of cool colours for the distance, warm colours for the foreground. When painting the sky, I usually started at the top of the canvas and worked downwards, so if it was a landscape with brilliant blue sky, I would use the warm colours at the top, which out of doors would be in the sky up above my head. So, titanium white, with ultramarine blue, plus a small amount of alizarin red. This would give me the warmth of the sky overhead. As I worked downwards, no more alizarin would be added, but by grading the strength of the paint, the ultramarine would take over and the alizarin phased out. Mid way down the sky, I would gradually bring in the coolness of the cobalt hue, letting it take over from ultramarine as I worked towards the horizon, and close to this a tiny amount of light red would produce the softness of distance and dust particles. In the same way, distant trees would be the combination of the cool colours of cobalt blue, yellow ochre, a touch of burnt umber, with titanium white. Foreground trees would use the hot colours of ultramarine blue, cadmium yellow and burnt umber. I did not possess a tube of green paint, always creating the colours I wanted from mixing, but olive green was an exception, a wonderful dark, muddy green, ideal for immediate foreground.

So, by keeping cool colours for the distance, hot colours for foreground, the tone of the painting gave the feeling of distance and that the viewer would take a long time to walk to the horizon! The same rules applied for any object within a painting. Working on aircraft wings, it was possible, indeed essential, to push the far wing away, and the end of that wing further than where it joined the fuselage, and with the nearer wing, the point closest to the viewer needed to come out of the painting towards them. (An obvious exercise for a child, is to draw a row of posts as if they are looking along a fence, therefore the posts fairly close to one another, yet each drawn smaller in size. Paint the nearest, dark, making the colours paler on each post, and distance is achieved. How confused the mind becomes when the paint is applied in the opposite order!) Another way of achieving distance was to use thicker paint in the foreground, even quite large blobs or streaks of paint that are in relief. The two most obvious faults of an amateur artist - indeed I made them myself - are failing to achieve distance, and bright emerald grass which has little reality with nature's softer, muddier shades. With clouds, being condensed watery vapour, I felt it important to keep the paint thin. I added a small amount of linseed oil when I mixed my colours, and I used white spirit or substitute turpentine, as I couldn't stand the strong smell of real turpentine!

With the animal portraits on velvet, I used the same oil paints, but slackened the mix with more white spirit than I do when painting on canvas. Painting on velvet was not a novel idea, for the Victorians used it, perhaps as a background for flowers, some of it still seen to-day.

CHAPTER 5

THE ROYAL NAVY HEAVES TO

The Battle of Britain film was being made, starring Kenneth More and Susanna York, when I unwisely had one of my bright ideas of working with the film company to produce a selection of paintings from the film. These could be exhibited around the foyer where the Premiere was to be shown. With my usual fertile, or should it be futile, imagination, I almost pictured myself in the line-up for presentation to The Queen! Fame at last! Trying to appear as businesslike as possible, I approached the film company who liked the idea very much, took me up on it immediately, responded by producing a variety of photographs, and arranged that I could watch the filming taking place at Duxford. I was brimming with enthusiasm and secretly congratulating myself on my brilliant idea!

As I arrived on the film set, I stepped back into the past! The noise of the Merlin engine is unforgettable, and seeing even a tiny part of the Second World War brought to life so vividly, really infused the soul with nostalgia. To my left, several pilots relaxed outside the wooden shack of a crew room, talking, reading the paper, playing cards, their clothes so different from the modern flying suit. Beyond them was a row of Spitfire aircraft. To see one is a privilege that brings back thoughts of liberty, freedom, but a row of them, then ... scramble! A sudden shout from the depths of the crew room, instant movement from all the pilots grabbing their gear and running to the row of Spitfires. The sound of the engines and the aircraft taxiing for take off was a sight I drank in with great reverence. I wasn't even aware of the cameras rolling beside me. I watched several takes, towards the last the sun was dropping out of sight and the sky was tinged with softest tawny-pinks and golds, the Spitfires silhouetted, a sight indelibly printed on my mind. I was well into my painting production programme, when suddenly, everything went wrong. The film company became ominously silent. They were unable to tell me what had happened, no amount of questioning got me anywhere, but finally I was informed that my whole idea was cancelled for good! It was so unexpected and very peculiar. I was asked to return the information they had given me. I didn't! I was angry about the whole thing, and felt it was all so odd, and the least they could have done was give me an explanation, especially after showing such eagerness in the first place. Some months later, I went to see the film, and in the foyer the mystery was partly solved, for there around the walls were paintings from the Kronfeld Society members. Was it they, or one particular Full Member who was to blame, for his strange behaviour led me to believe the truth of what had happened - he was clearly embarrassed to see me at the next Kronfeld meeting, watching me yet looking away the moment our eyes met, unable to speak to me, and his strange manner aroused my suspicions - I could only conclude that I had been ousted from the project in favour of others, perhaps by one particular artist. I fell neatly between two stools, for I was not invited to hang paintings through the Kronfeld Club, so my ideas had been taken up by other people without my having the opportunity even of being included. I had stopped work on the project immediately, and was left with five pictures, eventually exhibiting them in the Foyer in Norwich when the film was shown there, and much later at the International Air Fair at Biggin Hill. It was a hard knock which left me hurt and indignant, and brought home that I was 'a girl in a man's world', competition was fierce, and I had been pushed aside without consideration. I would not argue that those exhibiting were more experienced artists than me, but still felt I had been treated badly.

So far, my paintings for the Armed Forces had been limited to the R.A.F., but the presentation of a New Colour to the Royal Navy gave me an introduction to painting ships. On 29th July, 1969, armed with an official MOD Pass, I headed for Torbay. Weather conditions over the past twenty-four hours had been exceptionally appalling, and gale force winds and torrential rain had forced hundreds of ratings from various ships anchored in Torbay, to spend the night ashore. Clutching the directions I had been given, I searched for the Press assembly point, and presuming I had found the right place, innocently opened a door into what appeared to be a civic building, and the one I needed. I shut it extremely quickly! It was filled wall to wall with sailors lying like sardines, and the sight of a female standing lost in the doorway got instant cat-calls, whistles and invitations for I dare not think what! I fled, blushing!

The Queen was to present the new Colour to the Fleet on board H.M.S. Eagle, accompanied by the Duke of Edinburgh, Prince Charles and Princess Anne. The Western Fleet was comprised of well over a hundred ships ranging from small coastal craft and minesweepers up to the most modern and powerful frigates and submarines; both conventional and nuclear powered; guided missile destroyers, amphibious ships carrying Royal Marine Commandos, and aircraft carriers. Weather eased sufficiently for everybody to return to their ships. The Press were taken out to H.M.S. Eagle by boat, and the aircraft carrier seemed colossal, especially when approached from well below her bows, and climbing out and onto the fixed ladder up into the ship in the rough seas needed careful judgement. I was lucky to have one camera bag, but many of the Press were laden with thousands of pounds worth of valuable photographic equipment, nobody found it easy, particularly as sea water and cameras don't suit each other, so this little adventure was orchestrated by a fair amount of colourful language!

I had experienced one previous encounter with an aircraft carrier when I was in Singapore. I had water skied about thirty feet from the Ark Royal coming through the channel to the Navy Base on the island. With Peter Fish handling the ski boat, I had been on a mono ski waving to those on board who were lining the decks and presumably wishing that the 'bird in the two piece' would somersault off her water-skis and come a cropper, for I was showing off for my captive audience abominably and loving every second of it! Now, on board H.M.S. Eagle, due to the poor weather, arrangements for the event had been altered at the last moment and it was to take place in the upper hangar, instead of up on the flight deck; Russell Flint junior, his canvas on his easel, was frantically painting over the blue sky achieved while watching rehearsals, changing it to a muddy brown interior. Perhaps because I was the only girl amongst the Press, I was adopted by Westward Television who invited me up on to their stand, instead of my being with the Press. Normally for mountaineering scaffolding, I would have been dressed suitably in trousers, but very aware of the occasion, I was wearing a mini-dress! So what! Up I went, seeing the funny side of the fact that I was doing so in front of rows of ratings standing at ease facing me! When I reached the television crew at the top I had a superb vantage point. The Armed Forces, with their immaculate uniforms, Massed Bands, and talent for displays on ceremonial occasions, are always tremendously impressive. I felt enormously proud to be British, and witnessing the event.

The Old Colour had been presented to what was then the Home Fleet in 1937, superseded by the Western Fleet in 1967. The Western Fleet's area of operations included the North and South Atlantic and the Mediterranean as well as home waters. The Old Colour was paraded on this occasion, the drum party piled the drums in front of the dais for the presentation of the new Colour which was consecrated by the Chaplain of the Fleet, The Ven. Archdeacon A.W.M.Weekes, assisted during the short service by other clergy, and the new Colour was presented by The Queen. It was the first time a new Colour had been presented to the Navy at sea and the first to be received by the Western Fleet. The Queen inspected the white gaitered guard who were standing rigidly with fixed bayonets, and the entire ceremony was full of grandeur, colour and precision. A fly-past of more than ninety aircraft from the Fleet Air Arm followed the service, Wessex, Wasp, Gannet, Buccaneer, Sea Vixen and Phantom. To watch this, the Press were transferred to the flight deck on the aircraft hoist! Then the Royal Family went on board the Royal Yacht, The Queen led her Fleet to sea, from where the members of the Royal Family could watch four miles of ships steaming past, led by H.M.S. Eagle. The sight of this penetrated right to the heart, I found it all very moving, seeing HMY Britannia so close and such a gleaming, beautiful ship to look at, the elements - the waves, a somewhat angry sky, the reflections, and yet, at the end of the day my most lasting memory was the brilliant scarlet of the coat worn by Princess Anne!

I had been given a Press Pack with fascinating information on all these ships. From it for instance, I learnt that H.M.S. Eagle R.05, had a tonnage of 50,000 tons, a length of 811ft, beam 112ft (167ft overall), and draught 36ft. Her captain was J.D.Treacher, and she was flying the Flag of Admiral Sir John Bush, KCB,DSC, the Commander-in-Chief of the Western Fleet. Her laying down was October 1942, she was launched in March 1946, accepted into service in March 1951, and had been modernised in 1959 - 1963 at Devonport with Angled deck, ADA - large digital computer, SeaCat etc: She had been built by Harland and Wolff Ltd, Belfast, had 250 Officers, 2,300

Ratings, had four shafts and a speed of 30 knots, had been launched by H.R.H. Princess Elizabeth, and she had just returned from the United States. On board were Buccaneers, Sea Vixens, Gannets and Wessex aircraft. The Royal Fleet Auxiliary Service, the Merchant Fleet that supports the Royal Navy were very well represented. I looked forward to recounting the day to my parents, particularly my father, for it had been enormously special, and visually, wonderful. Back home I worked on a large painting, an overall scene of the upper deck with the Queen presenting the New Colour in the foreground. It was bought by the Life Assurance Company of Hobbs, Savill & Bradford, who presented it to H.M.S. Eagle.

Soon after this sea-going event, the Kronfeld Society chose seven Battle of Britain paintings for an exhibition in New York. One of them was mine, of St. Paul's cathedral choked by smoke during the blitz, a Spitfire banking overhead. While in America, in an unprecedented situation, all seven were stolen! Thankfully the Kronfeld had them insured so my expenses were covered.

I too, had my paintings insured, usually taking out a special insurance during a personal exhibition. It was very unnerving to have perhaps fifty paintings in the car, representing a great deal of time, trouble, and investment, with the thought of, 'what happens if I have an accident?'

It was no accident however that I could not go out to the British Virgin Islands to join the Royal Engineers 53 Field Squadron, who were building a new runway on Beef Island, off Tortola. This would allow the Avro 748, the civil version of the Andover, to land there and promote tourism. Having been commissioned to paint this for the Royal Engineers, for one glimmering second I thought I might get out there but only the Hercules as a troop carrier was going, and strict rules at the Ministry of Defence would not allow any woman to fly in a Hercules. This was partly because the loo is a flimsy bucket affair dangling half way up the side of the fuselage. It was no good saying I wouldn't drink, so wouldn't need it! There was no question of my having a flight, therefore no way whatsoever of my obtaining information at first hand. The Commanding Officer's name was Richard Bird, and the fact that he was known as Dickie Bird amused me sufficiently to cheer me up while I made determined efforts to sort out the material I was offered.

I was shown a series of aerial photographs and a magnificent model of Beef Island, at Waterbeach near Cambridge. The canvas was to be five foot six inches by three foot nine inches, and I grappled to put the jigsaw of material together, placing the LIAT aircraft in the correct livery, over the sea so as not to hide any of the landscape and new runway, pictured down below. The painting was to be unveiled at a guest night, at which I would be guest of honour. I was the only woman present. I had chosen a scarlet, full length skirt and white evening blouse, and with Dickie Bird and Officers in full dress uniform which included scarlet jackets, I was thankful, by pure chance I had chosen a matching red! Tony Balfour, my R.A.F. cousin, briefed me on the traditions of a formal Regimental dinner including the toast to the Sovereign, so that I would know what to expect, but although I did well most of the way through the dinner, I blew it completely at the end by stirring my Irish coffee! What a peasant I am! My sixty mile drive home after the dinner, was filled with both delight and horror, delight from having been presented with a stunning bouquet of flowers the scent of which filled the car, and utter horror when, on a wide deserted piece of straight road, I had spotted a cat hunting in the darkness on the verge, and in order to leave it undisturbed, I had steered well away from it by crossing over to the wrong side of the road, and it suddenly shot across right under my wheels. I felt the car hit it. I was shaken and very upset. I just couldn't go back, as I felt unable to cope if it wasn't dead, there was nobody around nor any dwellings anywhere near me where I might have got help. I just hope death was instantaneous.

Having had problems producing the Virgin Islands painting, the next commission of two Lightnings refuelling from a Victor tanker over the Niagara Falls was another headache! In this case I was to work from somebody else's photographs. Being the first of two paintings for Strike Command at High Wycombe, I was ecstatic at being commissioned by them, that was, until I was handed the small transparency from which I was to work.

"Is this the original?" I asked, aghast at the overall faded green colouring and lack of contrast. I was told it was. I felt desperate as my knowledge of flight refuelling was nil. After quiet but firm insistence that I must know more about the subject, I was told to report the following week to an RAF Station, where I sat in on two refuelling lectures and films. The photograph I'd been given showed the Victor and Lightnings in flight, the former with the background of a wood down below. This caused a dilemma. A camouflaged aircraft, seen from above with landscape below, is not meant to be very obvious! It is the whole point of the camouflage! Trying to achieve this in paint, and yet show the aircraft clearly, was not going to be easy. For the sky, I painted the tones of colour from the warmth of the sky at the top of the canvas to the coolness of horizon shades. This was how I worked on the aircraft too, using the ultramarine blue and burnt sienna with other warm tones in the part of the aeroplane that was closest to me, and keeping the cobalt blue and light red (a rusty brown) for further away, achieving the contrast in tone as much as I could. I wanted to create as three dimensional a painting as possible. Yellow ochre used in distant landscape with other cool colours contrasted well with chrome yellow and warm colours in the aircraft camouflage. I could manipulate the shape of an aircraft by the use of tones of colour, I could push the far wing away, and bring the nearer one closer, using this method. Although it seemed complex, by painting almost non-stop, it had become fairly straight forward for me to mix the right tone I wanted, from the right tubes. I couldn't add to the thickness of the paint in the foreground, but used every technique I could think of to make the viewer aware of the space between the closeness of the aircraft and the far-off landscape. Since I had received advice from David Shepherd on the choice of paints to buy, my palette had not changed since. He had guided me against using flake white, which by comparison with titanium white, looked dirty. I had the same group of about ten tubes that I worked from, and a further eight or so, used less often. Having become familiar with these colours, I stuck to them.

Back in my studio, I studied the one photograph that Strike Command had given me. The colours seemed incredibly uniform from the Niagara Falls to the aircraft, and it seemed extremely unlikely that it was an original, but they confirmed this again on the telephone. It was months later I learnt it was a reproduction, hence the distorted colouring. Put off by the poor material, my brother came to the rescue. From Madison Avenue, he had produced several French speaking television commercials in Toronto, had not only flown over the Niagara Falls, but had taken a mass of photographs. It was a great help on the colours. The frothy, pale spray from the water made the Lightnings, painted against it, really stand out. I toned down a rather ugly breakwater in the distance so it would not distract the eye from the aircraft. I worked long and hard at getting the correct balance between camouflage and background, and two weeks after I had completed it, the paint was dry. I got it framed and drove down to High Wycombe from Norfolk with the picture.

There was no reception for it, and having delivered it safely, I sent the account shortly afterwards. I heard nothing. In the meantime I had acccepted an invitation from the Officers' Mess at Strike Command to put on an exhibition of landscapes at R.A.F. High Wycombe for two weeks in November, which I duly achieved, and I also gave them a painting on velvet for their Christmas draw. High Wycombe had asked that their first commission be completed by the end of October, and I had delivered it well inside the deadline. On December 18th, the Officer dealing with the painting wrote to me saying there were problems with the background, he suggested cutting down the height of the picture, and perhaps painting out the breakwater. 'Alternatively,' the letter continued, 'it might perhaps be better to change the background completely to a cloud effect or something of that nature.' They had made arrangements to return the painting to me, so that I could consider the problem. I was very down and dejected. As always, I had painted the picture to the very best of my ability, and felt unconfident how to deal with the situation.

On 29th December, with my torn up efforts of composing a suitable reply littering the floor, I settled for the following letter;

' ... It seems you are not altogether happy with the picture, and suggest that perhaps the height of it should be cut down, and the breakwater painted out. You will remember that we discussed the actual size of the canvas before I started work on it, and I would like to point out that to cut the size down now, would upset the balance of the subjects depicted. Also, from the material you gave me, and from other material collected, the background is now pictorially correct, as you had commissioned the aircraft over Niagara Falls. I did in fact, tone down the breakwater so that it would be less obvious. You also suggest it might be better to change the background completely, possibly to clouds. Technically this is an impossibility. It would mean a completely new picture from the start. I am quite prepared to do this on the understanding that it would be a second commission, and that you would be paying me for both paintings.'

The picture arrived home, and as requested I worked on lifting the aircraft from the background slightly, then when it was dry I returned it to the Mess. Months seemed to pass and I could have done with the money. Again, I heard nothing. During this period, the P.M.C's changed, and the new one at long last wrote to me. By then it was 16th April! To say I was feeling indignant at their lack of business acumen was an understatement! Again the P.M.C. was a Group Captain, and told me that the Mess Committee were not satisfied with the picture, but he saw little hope of achieving any improvement by making radical changes in the background or size. He added, 'no good purpose would be served by taking any other action at this moment'. At the same time I received a letter from the previous Group Captain saying he had given instructions for the Mess to pay me! They seemed in one hell of a muddle! All this, and from one of the more important R.A.F. Stations in the country? Again nothing happened. What about paying me? Clearly things were meant to drift ... No cheque arrived. Mentally I gave them a deadline to get their act together. They didn't! So, I wrote, telling them I would be collecting the painting on 29th April, as I saw 'no purpose in your keeping it in the circumstances'. I asked for five pounds towards the expenses of producing it. It was all I got, and was nothing compared to the actual costs of petrol, let alone the rest! I was extremely naive to have asked for such a ridiculous sum! (There is a sequel to this story which will come later!) In spite of feeling miserably uncomfortable about all that had happened, I still felt it was important to try things even if they failed. I honestly believe the failing is less important than to 'have a go'. Telling myself I'll never make the same mistake again however, is a waste of time! In life, the identical circumstances never do present themselves a second time, so ... I go on making mistakes! And trying!

During dealing with the High Wycombe commission, I continued to paint landscapes and animal portraits. My next Assembly House exhibition in Norwich did not go well. To be honest, I was feeling a total failure all round! Perhaps it was a bad time of year or poor choice of subjects. As a family we had great fun before an exhibition, each choosing four paintings we thought would sell. My father amused me by being unsure if this was betting, perhaps to be disapproved of, or not! My mother's choice often went first. Mine seldom sold! Perhaps this showed I was no judge of my own work or at picking a subject. On this occasion I received plenty of commissions but the exhibition paintings remained mainly unsold. I had heavy bills to pay, materials, the majority of the framing and the hire of the room. In desperation on the last day I reduced the prices drastically, advertising it as, 'A Sale'. I felt cheap and unsuccessful but it seemed unavoidable. I sold two pictures which would probably have sold anyway. At home after the exhibition was over, I felt I might be forced to quit my art and get a secretarial job for a while, depressing but realistic. I had no extra funds behind me and from the moment I had achieved a qualification on leaving school, had never asked my parents for a penny. For one thing they didn't have it, but it was mostly my own pride. That day the doorbell rang and I found two complete strangers looking hopefully at me.

"Are you Penelope Douglas?" I nodded, wondering what on earth they wanted. "We couldn't get to your exhibition and we so wanted to buy a painting. Do you have any left?" They bought two! I could have hugged them!

This painting career has taught me a great deal. It has shown me that when things go wrong, I get nowhere by sitting and moping. It's up to me and me only, to pull myself together. Nobody else is going to do this for me. I've learnt resilience and thankfully I'm an optimist by nature! Telling myself failure is character building does not mean I'm a blue-eyed goodie-goodie! It is my way of forcing myself to be positive and move forward. No amount of dwelling on a disaster will alter a thing, sitting back is useless, and I feel better if I take charge of a situation and DO something! Although this lesson was a hard one to accept, it has stood me in good stead, time and time again.

CHAPTER 6

WINCHED UP OVER CYPRUS

My mother, Enid Chetwynd (before her marriage), had been a rally driver, taking part in the very first three R.A.C. Rallys, usually with her first cousin Joan Chetwynd, on one occasion driving for Fords. Their best result I believe, was to come first of the ladies teams and third overall. Sir Henry 'Tim' Birkin, Bart., another of my mother's first cousins, was racing Bentleys - one of 'the Bentley boys' - Archie his brother shared his love of racing. This was the golden age of motoring. My mother's aunt had married Sir Thomas Stanley Birkin, head of a rich lace making family in Nottingham, and Tim was born on 26th July, 1896. By 1921, he was married and living in Norfolk as were many of the family, and devoted to the county. Tim started competing at Brooklands and seldom took part in a road race without putting up a remarkable performance. 1927 was a sad year however, for Archie was killed in a motorcycle TT race in the Isle of Man, and Tim and his wife divorced. At that point Tim threw himself into the motor racing, and my mother was soon old enough to be driving and competing in the R.A.C. Rallys. Inevitably and happily, there was much family interest and support between them all. One of the delights they enjoyed was visiting the North Norfolk coast and the marshes, all of them good shots, and they got on very happily with the locals. There is an enchanting story, (to quote Peter Dunn), of Tim hiring a charabanc for three days to take the local fishermen and the entire lifeboat crew to London and Brooklands to see him win the 1928 Six Hour race. Few of the fishermen had ever worn anything other than their traditional smocks, and having to don neckties provided complications. On returning to Blakeney the first words of old 'Bob' Bishop to his wife, were,

"Sarah, get this bloody thing off me. I've had it on for three days," and so he had, because he and the others knew that once off, they would never get their ties back on!

There is no doubt that Tim was one of the greatest racing motorists the world ever produced. It was also the time of the socialite, brave and daring good looking young men and pretty 1920's 'flappers', and the age of the hero, and I look back on this time for my mother as being exhilarating and exciting. Tim was brilliant, but tragically he died after coming third in the 1933 Tripoli Grand Prix, leaning across the engine to top up with oil, he burnt his arm on the exhaust pipe. Although these were only superficial burns, septicaemia set in, and he died three weeks later. He was only thirty-six. Years later, through Rosemary Scott, who's father (Clive Russell Vick) owned a Bentley, I was one of the few people allowed to drive it. In order to see over the bonnet I sat perched as high as possible on a pile of folded rugs! Changing gear was astonishing with the double declutching, it seemed to take hours for the engine to respond! What would it have been like to race these? It would certainly have needed much physical strength and stamina. To travel as a passenger in such a car would have been a treat of a lifetime, to drive one was even more so!

In those days of R.A.C. Rallies, the contrast between the cars, conditions and communications compared with the current Rallies, couldn't have been greater. I had listened to the stories my mother had told me, seen photographs of the Chetwynd cousins grouped around the bonnet of their car, studying the route maps, so it was with special interest that I worked on a picture of the London to Sydney Marathon, with David Carrington and his team in a Hillman Hunter driving through the Khyber Pass, representing the R.A.F. Sports Association. It was bought and presented to him by Rootes. I also did an oil of Chris Amon in a Ferrari, which hung and sold in the Steering Wheel Club in London. Although I enjoyed the new subject, particularly the Khyber Pass background, I hadn't a great deal of enthusiasm in painting the modern racing car in the circuit, as I found the background of endless advertisements a real pain to paint. Depending on where these were situated in relation to the car, to indicate the latter's speed, wording often had to be blurred. Michael Turner is a brilliant artist and captures all this with apparent ease, but I did not. If I was going to paint hard cold metal subjects, then to me there seemed much more scope with aeroplanes and ships.

But I certainly had no cold views about Concorde, for she was flying by 1969 though not as yet in service. British Aircraft Corporation allowed me to see round the first ever Concorde that was built. The interior had no seats, but instead, equipment monitoring and recording information, equal in weight to a full passenger load I gathered. I found it immensely exciting, her design wonderfully graceful especially in flight, and quite exquisite.

The painting I had completed as a result of the fiftieth anniversary of the R.A.F. was unframed - it showed the Queen inspecting the Guard of Honour with Gunbus and Harrier - and I had taken it to Group Captain Norman Hoad who was Station Commander at Abingdon where the event had taken place. As he was a talented artist, clearly the painting could not go there. I still remember his words when he saw it, that I had painted two separate pictures on one canvas and got away with it! Unsure of what outlets there were for the painting, I made an appointment to see the Director of Public Relations of the R.A.F., Air Commodore Peter Brothers,CBE,DSO, DFC,RAF, taking the painting with me. Due to the unusual shape the subject demanded, I had painted on hardboard, it was several feet long and about two foot six inches in height, and a nightmare to handle. I longed to fold it up and pocket it, and as I struggled through the throngs of people to the Ministry of Defence, it was one of the times when I felt making thimbles would have proved easier to transport! Thankfully, it was undoubtedly to my benefit that I couldn't afford to frame such a large size unless I knew I could sell it, or it would have weighed even more! At the suggestion of Air Commodore Brothers, I took it to the R.A.F. Regiment, at Uxbridge, whom I had painted lined up as the Guard of Honour, and they were delighted to purchase it, many members crowding round and recognising themselves much to their satisfaction.

Pete Brother's daughter had married a Harrier pilot of No.1. Squadron based at R.A.F. Wittering. I had already got a commission from the Officers' Mess for a Harrier painting, was enjoying the social life involved with the Squadron, and at a cocktail party, met Pete Brothers again.

"How's the painting going Penelope?"

"Not very successfully at the moment. Every time I try to get material of the Harrier, it rains!"

"Well the Squadron's going out to Akrotiri shortly, so I don't see why we shouldn't put you on an aircraft and you can join them out there." Once again, I found it unbelievable! On 5th March 1970, I duly reported at R.A.F. Brize Norton, and was soon on route to Cyprus!

I stayed with the C.O. of the Lightning Squadron, Wing Commander Bill Kelly, his wife and family, who were immensely kind. It was the first time the Harriers had been to Akrotiri as a Squadron on detachment. They were there for two weeks, plus R.A.F. photographers. The aircraft caused quite a stir! Nine or ten Harriers hovering above the runway, moving in unison, was an unforgettable sight. If it is possible to have a ballet of heavy metal, this was it! Wonderfully spectacular, they had an audience every time they flew.

Wing Commander Ken Hayr was Commanding Officer of No.1. Squadron, and it was clear from the start he was enormously respected. The first time I joined them, encouraged by some of the Squadron that if climbed the ladder up to one of the Harriers I would get better photographs, I did so, taking great care as I straddled the side of the aircraft, one foot on the seat. Ken Hayr was waiting for me as I came down and ticked me off soundly! It was after all, an ejector seat. He spoke with firmness but charm, and instantly I fell head over heels in love with him! He enabled me to get all the material I needed, and couldn't have been more helpful. Being with the Squadron, I joined in all the evening fun, going to night clubs or kababs out in the town, and had a fantastic time. Lynn - I believe she worked with air traffic control - had also flown out with the Squadron, and she and I were the only females with them. I have many gloriously happy memories that make me chuckle to this day! One evening, well after midnight in a nightclub, somebody suggested they should all drink champagne from my shoe, and did! As I had been dancing non-stop for several hours, it must have been absolutly revolting, but nobody cared! A sweepstake was run on guessing my weight which meant they all picked me up one by one, we drank the rough red wine, Kokkinelli, renowned for having a headache in every glass (usually diluted with water by most women), devoured fish mezzes at The Pelican in Paphos with the tame pelican sitting on the pillion seat of the motor-bike parked nearby, consumed delicious food everywhere we went, and with the wonderfully balmy air of the Mediterranean, it was superb. Seldom have I had such an amazing week, enjoyed myself or laughed so much, and understandably, with only two girls as company for all those men, it was a sure way of being extremely popular! One evening, the only transport back to Akrotiri was a Station mini. Eight of us got into it! I was closest to the roof, horizontal, and couldn't believe I had so many hands holding me in place! We even circled a roundabout twice, 'just to prove the mini could hack it'! The Squadron photographed me for their diary, in a flying suit and wearing the largest bone-dome they could find, and the caption with it was unrepeatable! They were superb company, incredibly generous towards me, and as I often think the tone of a Squadron is taken from the boss, then Ken Hayr was worth his weight in gold, and entered into all the evening fun as much as the rest of us. My time with them was magical. During the daytime however, it was a working programme, as much packed into it as possible. The Harrier, with its vertical take off and landing ability, was an entirely new concept, taking it away from airfields and concrete runways, and giving it the ability to be operated in a way that helicopters had, but fighter aircraft had not, so the Squadron was, in a way, Boy Scouts in a field with a high performance jet aeroplane which was also great fun to fly. To the pilots it must have been one of the most exhilarating experiences in the world.

During our visit in Akrotiri, one of the British national newspapers was running a series, 'Man plus bird plus flying machine,' and permission was sought by 1 Squadron, to send a photograph for this, the MOD publicity department agreed, and I was photographed in front of a Harrier with one of the pilots, Mike Shaw (later, author of, 'Twice Vertical' the history of No. 1 Squadron, from hot air balloons to Harriers,) For this I wore a mini-dress that I had made from material Sally my sister-in-law had given me. She felt my dress sense was appalling, the material was dark brown with tiny white flowers - I was not bowled over - she insisted I made a long sleeved shirt dress with white collar and cuffs, and it not only became my favourite but proved very popular with everybody who saw it, probably because being the period of the mini skirt, it barely covered my bottom!

Before No.1 Squadron left, I had an Argosy flight accompanying the R.A.F. photographers watching an echelon of five Harriers beside us. The photographers bagged the best positions for photography through the open door, and I used one of the windows. Later I did a painting of this group of Harriers over Aphrodite's rock and the Cypriot coastline, calling it, 'Aphrodite's Nightmare.'

I felt full of emotion as I watched the Squadron leave Akrotiri for their return to the U.K. I stood close by as they taxied past, knowing who was flying each aircraft. Just before their departure, the P.M.C. at Akrotiri commissioned paintings from me of the four aircraft that were operational out there, for the Officers' Mess. To this day I wonder why? It wasn't as if my paintings were around very much, for I hadn't been painting aircraft long. Those that had been commissioned in the past were hanging in the R.A.F. Stations concerned, so did they take a gamble on an almost unknown artist? I shall never know, but the commission was totally unexpected and I was thrilled. I stayed on in Akrotiri. I was given a further Pass allowing me free access to wander round the aeroplanes concerned, walk from Squadron to

Squadron along the airfield, and the attitude of all those I met was warm, friendly and helpful. I was often picked up on route somewhere and dropped where I needed to be, and all the time I was planning how to paint the aircraft in their role, get the best background, and important, talk with those who were flying the aircraft and get all the ideas I could.

The first was the Lightning. This I painted landing on the runway, as I had been given little instruction as to how each aircraft was to be shown, so wished to produce as diverse a collection as possible, so one on the runway seemed appropriate. To portray the speed of the aircraft I painted it in sharp detail with both background and foreground a blur.

Next came the Vulcan and as I collected all the details I needed, when watching it in flight the design was so graceful that I felt it had to be shown airborne. For this, a flight in a Canberra was arranged for me, the canopy polished and left uncovered in the blazing sun so that it would be spotless for my photography! This was my first jet flight with the R.A.F., and I made sure I took an air sickness tablet. They kitted me out in suitable flying suit, life jacket, 'bone dome' and oxygen mask, though I must have looked faintly amusing as all were far too large for me, and instead of flying boots I wore my totally unsuitable court shoes! Before the flight I was briefed and given full instruction on how to deal with an ejector seat in the case of emergency, and the different drill needed if I found myself floating down on the end of a parachute for a land or water descent. I sat in on briefings and debriefings, and got to know and appreciate all those I worked with. Finally we climbed into the aircraft which was by then very hot inside, and after listening to all the pre flight checks, we taxied out onto the end of the runway. This was the first time I had ever been in the cockpit for take off, and I found the thrust and speed very exciting. Once we were at a reasonable height, we were joined alongside by the Vulcan! I really had to pinch myself that all this was happening for my benefit! What's that song ... 'If they could see me now ... ' I got my camera ready and photographed furiously, for this would be my one and only chance to capture this magnificent aircraft in flight. If I wished, they would fly higher or lower, more ahead or behind, bank away or appear on the other side of the Canberra altogether. Wow! It was quite something! Was this really me? At this point I was concentrating solely on the aircraft, not the background. Finally, after a flight of about half an hour we headed back to the base. Usually I had only been aware of landing on a runway by watching from a side window, but this was all absorbing, listening to the crew at the controls, seeing the runway ahead as we came in to land, I was engrossed in our descent and far more conscious of the sense of speed and all that was happening. It was a revelation. Later I was taken to look at Paphos from the air and put the Vulcan, viewed from the underside, banking slightly over the background view of Cyprus and the harbour.

The third subject was an Argosy. It was suggested by both Mess and Squadron, that this be depicted in flight with the base of Akrotiri down below. My instructions were delightful! I was not permitted to photograph this for security reasons, but while I was having the Canberra flight, would I make quite sure I had my camera with me! I got the message! We made several passes over Akrotiri for my benefit!

A Whirlwind helicopter was the fourth aircraft I was to portray. Again, wishing to show the aircraft in its role and with much discussion with the crew, we decided the painting should be of an injured person on a stretcher, being winched up into the helicopter for transference to hospital. I was therefore to fly with the Search and Rescue Squadron in the Whirlwind. We went via the loo! We hadn't been in flight long; I was seated in the doorway on the end of a 'monkey' strap, with my feet hanging out. I loved it! With plenty of fresh air - feeling sick just didn't seem to occur - we were out over the sea, the cliffs of Akrotiri not far away, when the helicopter slowed and hovered, manoeuvring slightly, and there below me was a tall pinnacle of rock with a perfectly normal porcelain household lavatory perched at the very top of it, in fact, I was gazing down into the bowl! It was hilarious, and the delighted faces of the crew at my complete surprise at coming on such a sight, said it all! We had indeed gone via the loo! On one occasion another Squadron had sabotaged and removed it, so it was now cemented into place!

The cliffs along the coast were sheer in places, steep and dangerous. Accidents had happened, some fatal. We found the best place for a background, and some low rock stretching out to sea, from which I could watch them working on the rescue of a stretcher patient. The helicopter flew lower, hovering on these rocks and I scrambled out, then photographed them while they dealt with an imaginary casualty. Once again I was relying on photographic material, transferring all I was watching to memory and film, the superb lens of my Leica an essential. The crew had decided to winch me up into the aircraft, so when I had all the material I needed, I signalled a 'thumbs up' to them, and with helicopter hovering above, the winchman came down for me and we were winched back on board - a novelty again, and great! The winch brought us up level with the doorway, and one of the crew who was kneeling inside, leant out and took hold of the webbing strap or handle that is part of the winch harness and lies on the small of the back, pulling us inside the helicopter. The stretcher work had taken place over a relatively safe area, I had obtained plenty of coastline material, so could paint a background of a steep cliff from which a person might well have fallen. The Squadron were a super bunch! I had several flights with them and adored every moment. These also gave me a spectacular view of the Cypriot countryside: I felt extremely fortunate to have such marvellous experiences, and all because I just happened to have become an artist!

I was also commissioned for paintings by individuals, one of these was for Group Captain Mike Beavis, of the flight deck of a VC10. Having been shown inside the aircraft, I worked from photographs, the co-pilot having his head-set round his neck. On completing the painting, Mike requested the head-set was repainted so that his co-pilot was wearing it properly, and as, with oils, I could paint on top of the existing picture, it was easy to alter.

Before leaving Cyprus I was interviewed on radio for the British Forces Broadcasting Service which I thoroughly enjoyed. Another novelty! It was newsworthy that during my stay in Cyprus there was an attempted assassination of President Makarios.

Back home in the studio in Norfolk I worked on the paintings, the first being of the Harrier and No.1 Squadron, for the Officer's Mess at R.A.F. Wittering. It showed the aircraft under camouflage nets at the side of a wood, and one taking off vertically from a clearing in front, and was full of activity. Painting a puddle in front of the main Harrier emphasised that it was taking off vertically and would not be taxiing through such wet, boggy ground, and also gave me the opportunity of adding reflections that were distorted and dancing from the thrust of the nozzles. Without fail, I listened to music while working, invariably from the classics, sometimes from the ballet or musicals.

By now I had developed more techniques for creating my pictures, for throughout my work, continuously I was attempting to extend my knowledge, intensify my portrayal of the subjects I painted, rectify any bad habits that had crept in, and upgrade my standard where I could. I was extremely critical of my own work. For the Akrotiri collection I did far more underpainting before working on the top layer. It was particularly effective in the case of a pale coloured aircraft that had to stand out from its background in as much of a three dimensional way as I could manage. The Whirlwind was a supreme example being bright yellow against rocks, some of which had pale yellow and sand coloured hues to them. A silhouette of the chopper was painted with the warmest tones and darkest pigments that I could mix. When it was completely dry, I could build up the colours of the aircraft on top. Frustrating as it often was, I could not hurry this, for if I worked on the final details with underpainting slightly sticky, the top coat would pick up this colour and create a horrible, muddy mess! As a result of endless patience and this improved technique, there was much discussion and laughter when the painting was hanging in the Mess, as to whether the chopper was a cut out image that I had pasted onto the canvas! It seemed I had achieved the three dimensional effect for which I was striving.

CHAPTER 7

SPOTLIGHTS ON BLACK VELVET

Carthorses were still being used on a farm near Ely, and it was nostalgic to see them, and totally irresistible. They were walking along the A10, but the advantage for me as a painter - I could leave out television aerials and telegraph poles and change the A10 to heathland! The completed painting sold to Felix Rosenstiel's Widow and Son, fine art publishers, for reproduction as a print. David Shepherd had elephants in Boots, I hoped to have horses in Boots! To my knowledge it never happened, but I loved the subject matter so much I painted a similar picture many years later.

I produced many paintings of these carthorses, muck spreading, harrowing and harvesting, and had another of my annual exhibitions at the Assembly House, Norwich. If I had been asked to organise the Olympic Games, probably I would have accepted and achieved it! (Thankfully nobody is likely to challenge me to that!) The hanging of these exhibitions was highly organised. There are right hand pictures, and left hand ones. Some colours and subjects look correct hanging next to each other, sometimes they kill one another. If a panel took perhaps five pictures they would be strung together, and loaded into the car as a unit of five. My chart of which group was for each panel accompanied me. The hanging was fairly slick as a result, and I was always enormously grateful for the support of Michael Brett who was totally reliable and would come and help me at every exhibition. My mother, also extremely practical, never missed a hanging session. Somebody steadied the dangling pictures, Michael climbed to the top of the step ladder and slipped the cords over the hook. I had my own spotlights for highlighting the animal portraits on black velvet, and these I hung as a group. Catalogues were always printed and available to be taken away and were free, flowers on the table, the most alluring subjects hung on the wall on view to anybody entering the building down the long passage. I hoped to seduce the public into the exhibition by any means I could! To achieve these paintings, usually around forty to fifty, I drove all over the county and worked incredibly hard, long hours. Each picture was individually framed to suit. Pricing was always difficult. At first I had priced them according to which I felt had come off best. Then I had one indignant customer saying crossly,

"Why is number five cheaper than number two? They're the same size, so what's wrong with it?" Clearly my pricing needed a more professional approach, so I changed things, pricing on size. It's not a good policy for a customer to feel they are buying an artistic work at so much a foot! But it is professional. If somebody has room to hang a twenty inches by thirty canvas, all pictures of that size are priced the same. If somebody wants to commission a landscape, I quote them the price for each size. Labour does not come into it. Various people have told me it should, but that would make things just too complicated! Like chocolates, I had a soft centre, occasionally lowering my price to a customer who genuinely couldn't afford the money. This was especially true of the commissioned dog portraits. It wouldn't make me rich, but it gave me pleasure and satisfaction to see the delighted expression on the face of the dog's owner. It didn't follow that pensioners were on the bread line, but it was often the case, their much loved dog probably being their only companion and meaning a tremendous amount to them, and I seldom turned down a commission if the full asking price was not available, and hope my judgement of a situation was correct.

With the portraits on velvet, my craftsmanship was improving. I had sketched the details of the dog on to the material with blackboard chalk, not a very fine line, but one that could be removed. Then I changed my methods, tightening up the whole process by producing a template in paper, and transferring that to the material in oil paint. It was vital I didn't go over the outline of the head, as if I removed the paint with white spirit, the velvet would remain marked, I would have no option but ditch that attempt and start again. The best silk velvet is very expensive! Within the outline, I could remove the paint and work on it again while the paint was wet. Once it started to dry it was too late. I had to assemble a portrait without making any mistake whatsoever.

Life was full of interest. I was asked to judge paintings for prizes at the Young Farmers' County Rally at the Norfolk Showground. Commissioned, I painted Buccaneers and Basset Hounds, Canberras and canaries, Dakotas and Dalmations! I was learning all the time, frequently questioning my methods.

With my next commission I made a major blunder. While I was at Akrotiri, IX Squadron had flown the Vulcans, but during the war it was a Lancaster Squadron, and I received a letter from Ron Goebel saying there was going to be a Squadron reunion in Cyprus for the wartime V.C. crew, and they wished to present the current IX Squadron with a painting of a Lancaster over the Dortmund-Ems canal, and would I do the painting? The story recounted that Flight Sergeant George Thompson was posthumously awarded the Victoria Cross after saving two fellow crew members in a burning Lancaster bomber towards the end of the last war. One man, mid upper gunner Ernie Potts died immediately afterwards from his burns. Now, five members of the crew, Harry Denton DFC (pilot), Ron Goebel (bomb aimer), Ted Kneebone (navigator), Wilf Hartshorn (flight engineer), and Haydn 'Taffy' Price (rear gunner), were returning to Cyprus.

On a historical note, Lancaster 'U for Uncle' had just released her bombs over the Dortmund-Ems canal on New Year's Day in 1945, when two anti-aircraft shells scored direct hits, one in the middle of the fuselage and one on the nose of the aircraft. Fires broke out, one engine was wrecked, the nose was blown off letting in a 200 mph gale and the hydraulics were shattered, leaving only Denton's strength to control the heavy, crippled aeroplane. Despite the damage, 'Uncle' could, incredibly, still be flown, and Harry Denton set course homewards with his feet braced against the control column to keep the aircraft level. Wireless operator George Thompson meanwhile was standing astride the hole in the upper gun turret where he was being burned alive. Thompson then went aft to the damaged rear turret, where he fought through more flames to rescue 'Taffy' Price who was about to jump not knowing his parachute had been burned and would not have functioned. Harry Denton successfully crash-landed the aircraft in a Dutch field and all the crew escaped. Ernie Potts died the following day and George Thompson three weeks later despite tremendous efforts and use of the new wonder drug, penicillin.

The painting became a nightmare for me, because although I had got material on the Lancaster, and a photograph produced by Ron of the canal from the air, I made the fatal error of painting the canal far too large, thus reducing the height of my aircraft to far too low a level for bombing anything! There was a deadline for the picture as the crew were to be flown out to Akrotiri and would be taking it with them. Panic set in! Total panic. I had to scrap my first effort completely and start the whole painting again. The hours I put in were unbelievable! This time I painted the canal glimpsed through broken cloud which obscured the ground beyond the limits of the photograph. Had I invented the land outside this, it would have been from imagination and therefore inaccurate. However at long last I had the Lancaster flying at the correct height. Adding cloud was a neat answer which I should have thought of in the first place. With the help of George Baillie - retired from the R.A.F. - who lived locally, and who was driving south and offered to deliver the painting to the crew, I got it to them just in time for their departure to Cyprus. They were delighted with the picture and had no idea of the hideous mess I had made at the start, and I quote, 'Climax of their one week stay as guests of the Royal Air Force came … when the captain, Harry Denton, awarded the DFC for his skill and determination in bringing back the blazing, crippled aircraft, presented a painting by Miss Penelope Douglas of the Lancaster 'U for Uncle' to the CO of No. IX Squadron, Wing Commander R. Dick, at a farewell dinner in their honour.' On the second day of their visit to Cyprus, Air Chief Marshal David Lee at the NATO Headquarters in Brussels, close to where George Thompson was buried, sent the following signal, 'On behalf of surviving members of crew, I have placed a wreath on his grave to commemorate reunion of his colleagues'. This was in July 1970.

By November the four paintings for Akrotiri were completed and framed, and the Ministry of Defence felt I should fly out with these for a formal presentation. Packing them for the flight was laborious and made them unwieldy and heavy to handle, and I arrived at R.A.F. Brize Norton, checking them in with my luggage at the terminal. But having done so, standing at the desk where I'd reported for the flight - I had no ticket or documentation - I noticed an unusual label, pale yellow with a diagonal black cross upon it being fixed on to my luggage, looking as if I was suffering from the plague, and one of the R.A.F. officials stepped forward and asked me to,

"Come this way Miss." I followed him through behind the check in, uncertain why I had been singled out, anxiously going over details such as my passport being in order, and was about to ask what was wrong when he opened the door into the V.I.P. suite! How fantastic! I knew I'd got to make the most of every second of such star treatment, it was unlikely to be repeated. I waited for my flight in luxury and when everybody else was seated on the aircraft, was escorted out, even my camera bag carried for me! On arrival at Akrotiri, Tony Balfour and Judy, by then stationed in Cyprus and with whom I was to stay, were unable to find me amongst the usual scrum of passsengers, and when finally they discovered me in the V.I.P. suite, the stifled giggles of delight from Judy said everything!

We travelled to their quarter, the four paintings safely with me, and I was really looking forward to the pleasure of the official presentation, when suddenly there was a very large hiccup! Somebody important in the Mess refused to acknowledge the existence of any pictures having been commissioned! I stayed quietly in the quarter with Tony and Judy, utterly perplexed by what was going on. I would hardly have been given the run of the base to get all the material for nothing, nor would I have been flown out to deliver the pictures. It was embarrassing. Various 'top brass' came to see me, apologising profusely, asking me to wait patiently while the situation was sorted out. I gathered the Mess budget had been exceeded, and when faced with the prospect of having to find funds for four paintings, somebody just opted out! Whether this was true I don't know, but soon the problems appeared solved, and a reception was held in the Mess with the Station Commander Air Commodore Stacey, Group Captain Mike Beavis, and Wing Commander Keith Hepburn accepting the paintings officially. Drinks were provided, photographs taken. The R.A.F. newspaper article said I was well known throughout the Royal Air Force for my aircraft paintings, and the authenticity of my work was the result of thorough research and the lengths at which I was prepared to go to be as accurate as possible. It is easy to make mistakes but I do everything in my power to get things pictorially correct. As I laughingly say,

"The paintings usually sell to those who either fly them or work on them, and who know them backwards. You can't put two tails on a VC10 and get away with it!" Again I had the delight of being interviewed by BFBS.

Whilst in Cyprus I was commissioned by No.3 Wing R.A.F. Regiment for an action painting of a Bofors L 40/70 gun being fired. In order to give me suitable material, I was taken to see the site for the gun, which was to be the background. It was an attractive area with the parched and dusty Mediterranean landscape, the sea behind and across the bay, Limasol and the distant Troodos mountains. While I was being bounced along the rough perimeter track in a Landrover for this, the driver suddenly exclaimed with horror that he had forgotten to ask me to sign a blood chit! In the case of an accident, my signature would mean I could not hold the R.A.F. responsible if I was injured. He drove a little more slowly after that! The gun itself and guncrew handling the shells was set up for me back at the depot, and was transferred to the correct background when I worked on the canvas. I'm told that now this painting has joined the others in the Officers' Mess, sometimes they are hung with the gun pointing directly at the Lightning painting, and sometimes they are swopped round so the barrel is pointing away from the Lightning, depending on who is in the Mess!

I am often asked which subject I enjoy painting most? It is the variety that is stimulating; I am content to switch from aeroplane to Afghan hound portrait, from a landscape of White Boats on the Broads to galloping racehorses on Newmarket heath. Often, with an animal portrait, it is commissioned by one member of the family for another as a birthday or Christmas surprise. Then all is stealth! I am whisked into somebody's house to see the dog, while the owner for whom it is to be a present is out. When I telephone to say the portrait is completed, I'm left lying like a trooper if the wrong person picks up the 'phone! Roger and Diana Harrison had commissioned a picture of Sophie, a white Standard Poodle, a lovely natured dog who posed most beautifully. They were so enchanted with the portrait that Roger, who farmed, kept giving me sacks of barley for the handful of sheep we had at home, with the balance becoming so uneven that I decided to paint his Yellow Labrador's portrait unknown to them, and just prop it up on the mantelpiece in their sitting-room for them to discover! They were friends of mine, I had met the person who cleaned the house, and she entered into my idea with great amusement, and the portrait was painted. It became almost impossible for me to deliver it without being caught, Diana had retired from her job and, it seemed, was always at home. The one occasion that presented itself was the day of the Royal Norfolk Agricultural Show, to which they would both be going. I telephoned to see if they had left the house. Diana answered so I put the receiver down, saying nothing. I could get away with this once. In half an hour I tried again. Diana answered. They were still there. Knowing their telephone number was three one four, disguising my voice as best I could, I said,

"Is that three one five?"

"No, it isn't. You've got the wrong number." Yet another half hour passed, and I tried once more. Diana picked up the receiver, and this time I became a three year old.

"Hallo Gwandma, can I speak to Gwandad?" Roger and Diana had no family, she was not a grandmother, and furious at yet another wretched 'phone call when she was trying to leave the house! I got a few fairly sharp staccato words in reply! I then drove to their area, parked in a gateway within sight of their drive, ducked down as they passed, and got the picture on to the mantlepiece as planned, to the great satisfaction of the 'daily' who looked on this as being the best adventure to have happened in the village for some time! The earlier 'phone calls were admitted later!

Another Assembly House exhibition was the climax to several months of intensive work. On Saturday evening, with pictures hung, I used to drive home exhausted but satisfied. It usually lasted over the Sunday! I was always present at every exhibition, all the time. Half way through the first hour, I was already dissatisfied with my efforts, criticising this painting here, that painting there! It was inevitable. Although I have met artists who genuinely say they produced a marvellous painting and were really pleased with it, I am seldom one of those. I am relieved to get the whole lot up and an exhibition ready, but I am not often satisfied with the individual paintings though perhaps more so with the animal portraits, but they are different. Of the landscapes and aircraft paintings, I am my own worst enemy. Sometimes perhaps I have nearly achieved what I have been striving for, and there are times when I have felt proud to see a painting in the Mess several years later. It is much like greeting an old friend. I am comfortable with it! Without exception I produce my best possible standard. I am a perfectionist without, I hope, being too nauseating! But I feel strongly, if I can sit back and say it is marvellous then something must be missing, some intangible freshness, I might as well throw my brushes in the dustbin, and give up!

At the Assembly House exhibition I had several paintings of the stalls in Norwich. This is a permanent market, and pure delight to explore. Covered with striped, coloured awning faded from the elements, their fruit, flowers and vegetables overflow into the narrow aisles, goods are for sale from fish to buttons, the sweet yet pungent smell of the fresh produce is wonderful. Stall owners heard of the paintings and arrived to view them, a group of noisy, cheerful people. I think the Assembly House staff, who prided themselves on the high standard of clientele, were slightly appalled! I thought it was lovely, and we all had such a laugh over the pictures! They were very touched to discover themselves! One time, apparently my pictures inspired Guy, a seven year old to rush home and produce drawings and doodles which were sent to me by proud father. A particular admirer, a very charming man, made several visits to see me, telling me,

"I know what you want, and I can give it to you!" He was married, so my reply was,

"Ah, but you're one of those things called 'somebody else's husband!'"

Sometimes at these exhibitions, visitors discussed a painting as if I was merely somebody on duty, not the artist. My sense of humour had to remain well controlled, for I was tempted to say,

"Yes, poor thing, tragic accident, six feet down now," to see whether, if I was apparently dead, my paintings would sell better! It was tempting to tell some story about 'the artist' and have some fun! On one occasion a man studied the pictures, said he had been ill and having psychiatric treatment, had progressed sufficiently to have a job at the local hospital, and inspired by my pictures, wished to paint again; if I chose to visit him, he informed me, he could be found at the hospital between the mortuary and the laundry! Another artist exhibited animal pictures on velvet, whole dogs with a brightly coloured toy at their feet, so tongue in cheek I asked the artist why she had chosen velvet? I got a whispered reply,

"Well, I saw them here, done by somebody else, so I thought I'd copy them!"

Flight International magazine published a two page spread about the Kronfeld Aviation Art Society's annual exhibition, and printed a photograph of a painting of mine illustrating a Royal Navy Phantom in flight over the Atlantic. Exhibited with this was my canvas of a Victor aircraft, landing. I had watched this during my visit to R.A.F. Marham, totally captivated by the stunning contrast of the shark-like, hard metal aeroplane, and the gentle, floating billowing form of the break parachute out behind. The latter was white, so a dark sky would emphasize this contrast. How I loved working on that painting, indulging myself in portraying a soaked runway and plenty of reflections. In the magazine they described my painting, 'Wet, is Penelope Douglas's Victor in 'Victor Far East'. Landing across a shadowy waterlogged airfield with pools glinting light against the dark ground, the aircraft comes in fast with drag 'chute ballooning out like a full moon against a threatening orange monsoon sky.'

The International Encyclopaedia of Stamps published a magazine, on the back cover of which was a full page spread on the different ways mail was carried. They approached me to do a painting of the Short-Mayo composite, (the "Piggy back aircraft"). A war always accelerates technology and with the arrival of peace after the first war, regular mail flights increased. The limited flight duration of commercial aircraft made this difficult, especially across the sea, needing endless refuelling stops. By 1939 great strides had been made with the design and construction of trans-oceanic aircraft, but the North Atlantic still presented a problem. The Short-Mayo composite was a unique design and idea. The Short Empire flying boat, known as Maia, had a smaller aircraft Mercury on its back, the latter heavily laden with mail. Mercury, unable to take off due to the heavy pay load and fuel, would be carried into the air by Maia, the two aircraft separating at the desired height. This was to take place in the skies over Rochester where my parents were living, and my mother remembered the enormous publicity covering such an event. Whether Shorts got cold feet or not, is not revealed, but she told me that instead of Mercury's first launch from Maia taking place on the planned day with full publicity coverage, the aircraft slipped into the sky unannounced the day before, Mercury separating successfully from the 'mother' aircraft, and carrying the mail to Canada in its floats. It was an exceptional feat. Shorts gave me all the material and my painting was reproduced for the back cover of the International Encyclopaedia of Stamps magazine. A second painting followed showing the early American airmails. Of all coincidences, it happened to have the name 'Douglas' on the tail fin! It was an open-cockpit biplane, rather more sophisticated than the British built De Havilland 4, and the Curtiss Jenny - one of the first all-American aircraft to be built in numbers. This painting was also published on the back cover of the magazine.

I too had unusual post delivered, which read as follows, 'Air Commodore P.M.Brothers, CBE, DSO, DFCk, RAF, Director of Public Relations (Royal Air Force) requests the pleasure of Miss P.Douglas at a reception in the Senior Officers Mess, Ministry of Defence ... to mark the occasion of his retirement and to introduce his successor ...' I went! Eighty men, and me!

A request from R.A.F. Honington, Suffolk, for a landscape for the ante-room meant an unusual size, for they wanted it for a particular panel and the picture was 3′ high, 7′ long. I thoroughly enjoyed working on this, and chose West Mersea as my subject, boats on the mud, and in the foreground a pile of lobster pots gave the landscape a greater impression of distance.

At Christmas I reached the real summit of fame! A large local poster advertised a Christmas Fare, and billed together in equally large writing, firstly, 'Display of Paintings by Penelope Douglas' and below, 'Father Christmas in his Grotto!' I could hardly have been in more elite company!

CHAPTER 8

LONG SKIRT FOR MASIRAH

March 1973, with the luxury of being considered a V.I.P again, I flew out to Cyprus in style, having been commissioned for a fifth painting for the Mess, this time a Hercules. It was while I was down on the airfield sketching her that I was arrested! It amused me so much that the R.A.F. Policeman came up to me, questioned me, then told me to stay exactly where I was and disappeared to return with two more Police! Was I such a handful that it required three of them? I went quietly! Apparently neither the Officers' Mess nor 70 Squadron had informed the R.A.F. Police of my visit, and in order to get across how important this was - the group known as Black September were fairly active at the time, with security on the base tighter than ever - the Police apprehended me. I was taken to the their Headquarters. I remember reading a fascinating framed article hanging on the wall with instructions for Police many years ago on, 'How to look after your camel'! My arrest was logged in the record book officially for, 'doing an unlawful act upon the airfield'! After several telephone calls and strong words, an hour later I was released, and the P.M.C. who happened to be a Medic had a few hilarious words to say about it all when he poured drinks all round to celebrate my return! "Who was he Penelope?" and, "Couldn't you have waited until you got to the crew room?"

Although a Hercules flight to the Virgin Islands had been forbidden, due to working with 70 Squadron, I was allowed to join the crew for a short local flight, during an exercise to find a man in a dinghy at sea with a 'homing' device. On the flight deck, I was amazed how difficult it was to sight the stranded airman. Waves, reflection, movement, the combination showed me what a surprisingly tricky operation it could be. Having found him, even as we circled away he was lost to sight far more quickly than I expected, merging into the background in spite of the bright orange colour of the life jacket.

The Hercules was able to take off and land from a desert strip. Consultation with Wing Commander Alan Curry, the C.O. of 70 Squadron, and several of the Officers, confirmed this was a very dramatic sight on a sand runway and a good idea for the painting. However it would mean, unbelievably, I was destined for R.A.F. Masirah, a small island off the coast of Oman, a staging post for the R.A.F. and it was from there I could watch an aircraft land on a desert strip. I could not see this at Akrotiri.

My flight was in a Britannia, and having been told there were no women at Masirah whatsoever, I kept expecting some 'red tape' would make us turn back! The co-pilot was inexperienced and on doing his first landing, hit the runway so hard, we bounced sixty feet into the air! Every pilot has to start somewhere! It would be drinks all round on him that evening! After that the Captain took over! When we finally taxied to a stop, the Commanding Officer Group Captain Swalwell and two Officers met me at the bottom of the aircraft steps with the C.O's Landrover complete with fluttering pennant! I felt a million dollars and very humbled - a glorious mixture!

I was to sleep in the Medical Centre, a sign saying, 'The Masirah Hilton' had been fixed up over the door! That evening I joined everybody in the Mess for drinks, then dinner, then more drinks. I was left in the care of Ken, one of the Officers, as the 'top brass' had a meeting, others gathered telling Ken, 'not to hog the goodies,'! Stories were told, the conversation was riveting and my cheeks ached with laughing! One serious story was that a cattle boat had sunk three days earlier, forty-five miles out to sea, and a ship, the Osprey happened to find the crew in a dinghy. They were extremely fortunate, as with the currents they would never have made it to land, sharks had been circling their dinghy for seventeen hours! The crew of the Britannia arrived, the co-pilot still having his leg pulled about bouncing the Brit. I'd been given instructions to lock my ward door at night and have breakfast in my room, being easier than chaperoning me from various areas of the Mess where men would be 'starkers'! I had so many compliments that evening, the boost to my morale should last me for years!

"Something special around to-night!" It is very easy to be popular as the only 'piece of skirt' around!

Next day, the C.O. offered me the use of his patio when I wished to relax, mainly as a sanctuary from staring eyes! I was advised against going to the swimming pool for obvious reasons. Various Officers were planning that the aircraft I was to depart on, was definitely to 'go u/s' (unservicable)! It was all wonderfully complimentary and great fun. The C.O. took me in his Landrover, off the base to see a rubbish dump, an extraordinary sight because it was such an incredible contrast of Shell's huge cylindrical storage tanks in the distance, and in the foreground, wild camels, gulls and donkeys all rummaging through old tins and anything they could find of interest. Work on the Hercules followed and before lunch, a walk on the beach and my introduction to Shelagh's fawn, a gazelle. There are about four hundred wild gazelle on the island of Masirah, and Shelagh was found injured, and with nursing became tame. She spent much of the day curled up asleep under the C.O's table, and was always accused as being the culprit if any papers were mislaid! The fawn was extremely friendly and so beautiful, amazingly dainty, an exquisite little head with exceptionally large and beautiful eyes. Jack, the Senior Medical Officer, in charge of the Medical Centre, sometimes took me to the beach and if we met Arab women and children, these would rush to the Landrover and crowd round staring at me, for many of them had never seen a white woman nor one with her head uncovered. I wore a borrowed long sleeved shirt so that sleeves could be rolled down and cover my arms, to dress politely and appropriately for the Arabs. The beaches and rock pools were full of sea life, hermit crabs, iridescent anemones, prickly sea urchins and brightly coloured fish. In that heat, inviting as the sea looked, it was unsafe for swimming, sharks cruising up and down. Like an uncle, Jack told me there wasn't a man on the island who didn't want to rape me!

"They will all do so given half a chance, and as long as you know this you'll be all right!" What a lovely statement!

In the Mess, some men couldn't face me and avoided me. I had seen more pin-ups of women in various stages of undress to complete nudity in Masirah than I'd ever seen in my life! I was probably considered as a trivial piece of sexual fluff by a few, but all those I came across respected me as an artist and the reason for my presence out there. I wore trousers for work, when off duty I changed into a long skirt and enjoyed being female amongst all the men. Evenings were immensely enjoyable, the atmosphere of a group of only men working together, totally unique. There is a comradeship which is very apparent, enormously special, and it was fascinating to be the 'only girl on the island' and a real privilege to become part of this and to be welcomed so warmly. Invitations poured in to show me anything from Police dogs to the sunset! The following day a Hercules was scheduled to land on the desert strip. I stood at the side and watched, getting all the material I could, and they 'rolled' for me - landing, rolling along the runway, then taking off again to repeat the process. It was an amazing sight, for the props acted rather like a fan amongst shredded paper, stirring and blowing up the sand all round the aircraft, creating a dust storm that obscured parts of the fuselage. What a painting to work on! I felt enormously excited! How was I going to capture the atmosphere of heat and dust?

While with my cousins I had enjoyed a coffee table book on the popular twentieth century American artist, Norman Rockwell.

Born in 1894, he had created over three hundred covers for Saturday Evening Post (1916 - 1963), painting sentimental images of America's dream of itself, idyllic scenes of small town and rural life in the United States. His 'Four Freedoms' series were reproduced as posters by Office Of War Information during World War II, and he had illustrated the official Boy Scout calendar (1926 - 1976). A photograph of one painting in particular had specially impressed me: it was the head and shoulders of a Boy Scout, the wide brimmed hat shading his eyes from the glare of the sun, and underneath was written information that the artist had underpainted in red. This lingered in the back of my mind and now, as I watched the Hercules landing, the prospect of experimenting with scarlet underpainting to enhance the atmosphere of intense heat I wanted to capture, was tremendously stimulating. I found it frustrating that I couldn't grab my brushes and start painting immediately! It would of course have been impossible, for each time the Hercules rotated we had to turn our backs and duck our heads as the sandstorm swirled around us. After the aircraft left finally, Arabs, in pairs, wandered out onto the runway, and with wooden rakes smoothed the sand for the arrival of the next flight. They were dressed in an entertaining concoction of Arab and British clothing, and as this was their official job, I felt they would make an ideal foreground subject to the painting, giving it a three dimensional appearance. It would also be obvious where in the world the subject was placed, for one of the disadvantages of working on pictures of runways and airfields is that they are wide open places seemingly very much alike.

Masirah had beaches where green turtles come ashore to lay their eggs. Sadly it was not that time of year, but walks along the beach showed the scrapes that had been left by the adults, and scuffing my way through the sand I found one or two bones and pieces of turtleshell lying bleached by the sunlight. Several turtles about six months old were kept in an open aquarium by the R.A.F., so it was interesting to see them before they were released. When the young hatch, the lights surrounding the parked aircraft at night were switched off so they couldn't confuse the baby turtles who make for the reflection of the moonlight on the surf. The green turtles grow to an enormous size, their bite strong enough to snap an oar in half. One evening I was taken to the top of a Jabal, from where I had an excellent view of the island. Down below was a Bedouin home plus accommodation for the three wives. I heard a story about piracy in the late 1800's: although asked not to cause trouble to the British, the Arabs massacred the crew of a British ship. The Sultan's punishment was that no proper house could be built for many years, none above head height or permanent. Consequently we could see a complete settlement made out of old oil drums, wooden boxes, and every building material imaginable. I believe the period that this was to last has ended.

Amidst all the light hearted banter about the Brit taking me back to Cyprus going u/s, news had come in that it had! That meant I could go on working, and Jack took me down to the R.A.F. Police Dog Section, where the snarles, growls and barks from the dogs were quite intimidating, but Corporal Evans introduced me to a beautiful Alsatian, Judy, and once she and I had met I could stroke her, talk to her.

On return to the Medical Centre, Ramis, who worked there, said he wished me to meet his wife, so I went with him to the entrance of the building, and found a huge crowd of Arab women and children, the adults clad from head to foot in black, their faces covered except for their eyes. Many shook hands with me, children touched my clothes wanting to feel Western cloth, a new experience to them. It was hard to tell what people were thinking with only their eyes visible. How much the mouth tells, the suspicion of a smile or anger. Ramis said if I went with them to their huts, once inside I would notice the colourful garments worn beneath this sombre, black covering, but somehow black seemed right for the heat and the country.

As I was in Masirah longer than planned, it was arranged that I could join David Old and Mike Cross in one of the Landrovers, a second following behind, on a desert rescue exercise, an essential part of training in case an aircraft ever crash landed on the island, and a thoughtful suggestion made by the C.O. to give me a chance to see more of the terrain. It was a wonderful opportunity for me, through the village made of the oil drums, boxes and corrugated iron, into other villages, my sleeves rolled down as we approached them so as not to insult the inhabitants, the vehicles each time surrounded by excited Arabs, the children swarming all over them. We drove to a beach, checked on a particular fishing boat for security reasons, and then drove inland, the rough road becoming much narrower, a vast area of volcanic rock, yet with it a far wider range of colours to the sandy, rocky surface than imaginable. It was an eye-opener for me to see what harsh and rugged conditions could be tackled successfully by these Landrovers. We had vast water containers strapped to each vehicle. We drove into a sudden lush patch of date palms, with a well full of frogs! Then along a dried up river bed and out onto a dusty, rocky track again, a moonscape! After several hours we returned to the base. That evening I watched the sun set from the top of the Jabal. I was not alone. The colours of the desert and the skies were wonderful, drifting like a series of gossamer veils through shades of orange to deepest purple, beautiful to witness, and wonderfully romantic. Should ideas of, 'their bodies lay together on the sand, the need was there for both of them', crop up, then no, it wasn't actually quite like that, though there were just two of us and certainly gloriously romantic! When it was dark we went down to the beach in the moonlight, and the curve of each wave glowed with a kind of phosphorescent light, pin heads of which could be found at the water's edge, apparently organic matter. Deliciously ridiculous, I felt like a top model ready for the cover of Vogue or a romantic novel, paddling through the shallows in a full length skirt, handsome escort by my side! Well, a girl can dream! We sat on a rock and talked for ages then wandered along the water's edge again, sploshing through the sea, silver reflections dancing, the tang of salt and seaweed, sand and shells. Thousands of girls would probably have given their eye teeth to be where I was, and being an aviation artist certainly had its rewards! I had to be the luckiest person ever! We punctured on the way back! It had to happen and brought us down to earth! We felt like kids who had been caught doing something they shouldn't, like being discovered out of bounds after 'lights out'! On returning to the Medical Centre, Jack was dealing with the bloody results of a drunken brawl. He must have noticed our soggy, wet feet, covered in sand, but said not a word!

The following day it came to light that I had had no 'jabs' that would cover me from various illnesses for that area, and they decided this should be rectified immediately. The only vehicle available to take me to the Medical Centre happened to be the ambulance, so off I went in it, to be given a cholora jab in one arm, smallpox in the other. I was not working that morning for once, for the Brit had arrived, my visit to Masirah over. The C.O. in Landrover with pennant fluttering, saw me to the aircraft. As we took off, after such a wonderful time, tears poured down my face. It must have been a bit shattering for the men seated either side of me, but word had got around, and it seemed they knew about me and we were soon talking. I joined the crew on the flight deck very soon. I was the only woman on the aircraft and spoilt with it, staying with them for the landing at Sharjah, where a large lorry was to take us to the transit lounge during the refuelling stop.

It's much easier for the men to get up and down into a four tonner, a wallet tucked in a back pocket, but quite difficult for me with camera equipment and handbag. The airport lounge was unbearably stifling. After an hour, when we were queueing for the truck to take us out to the Brit, somebody came to me and said,

"Would you and your husband like to come this way, we have a Landrover available to take you out to the aircraft." I looked at the men around me, wondering if any would like to take up the challenge and an easier form of transport, and addressed a young, newly recruited airman behind me.

"Are you my husband?" I inquired, twinkling up at his six foot four frame. Poor man, he didn't know where to put himself, and was far too embarrassed to take me up on it!

Again I was on the flight deck of the Brit for take off. We had a heavy payload, had just refuelled, and by then were in the real heat of the day, these three together not a good combination. I was standing behind the Captain's seat. We rolled along the runway, on and on ... It seemed as if we were never going to get airborne. 'Just my inexperience, this is probably quite normal', I told myself, until as we continued bumping along the ground, I saw the knuckles of the crew going white, the quartermaster was sweating profusely, and the coils of barbed wire and the sea at the end of the runway seemed to be rushing ominously towards us! We still hurtled along the ground, four green lights had now lit up on the instrument panel showing it was too late to abort, and then ... after what seemed forever ... we began to lift slowly and laboriously, j..u..s..t clearing the wire! The relief felt all round was tangible to say the least!

During the flight I realized that stupidly, the crayfish which I had been asked to bring back by the P.M.C. at Akrotiri, and my cousins, had been left in the fridge. The crew said not only would we send a signal to get it put onto the next available aircraft, but that I should send it. It read as follows, 'FOR SMO PLEASE PUT CRAYFISH BELONGING TO FEMALE PASSENGER ON HERCULES BOUND AKROTIRI'. With laughs all round, word came back that the message was not received properly and must be repeated! This was done correctly with each pair of words being repeated twice. I was told that all this had been enjoyed by everybody, making the routine flight more fun. The sunset was glorious as we touched down at Akrotiri after the ten hour flight. It had been an exhilarating few days, I had worked hard and played hard, and now I was arriving back I realized I was desperately tired, so thoroughly appreciated the staff car that whisked me away to the V.I.P. lounge.

On starting work back in England, the first thing I did was to underpaint the canvas I intended using, scarlet. It would have been difficult to find a stronger, brighter red. There is something in the make up of the red pigment that requires far longer to dry than any other colour, and the wait nearly killed me! Only when it was totally dry, could I put the pale colours of the sky on top, and discover what effect I was going to create. Clearly I was taking a massive risk, but the worst that could happen was to scrap the painting altogether, and begin in a more conventional way. Whatever the result, time would not be wasted. I planned a cloudless sky, and usually start with the background of a picture, working from the top downwards. The canvas on the easel was vertical. When the sky and far side of the runway was completed, I underpainted scarlet again, for the shape of the Hercules, (this was the third layer of paint) and so it went on. In the shadows, I ran the brush loosely on the canvas, leaving minute glimpses of the scarlet paint visible. Arabs were underpainted scarlet, (the fifth layer) and put in the foreground as planned, the painting was completed, with no doubt about the results whatsoever, for it was very obvious that this was a scene set in the blazing, unrelentless heat of the Middle East. It had worked! I found it wonderfully rewarding. A second painting showed a Hercules on the airfield in Masirah, with Corporal Evans and Judy in the foreground on duty. When getting the material for this, he had changed into his uniform specially for me, and later I wrote to him, sending a photograph of the completed painting, and a close up of he and Judy, receiving a delighted letter in return. The painting was the second bought by the R.A.F. Museum at Hendon, the first having been of a Whirlwind at Akrotiri, from my previous flight to Cyprus. Wing Commander Alan Curry arranged for a photograph of the painting to be the No.70 Squadron Christmas card that year. (Later, I was to see him on television as Yeoman Usher of the Black Rod at the opening of Parliament.)

By now I had a very good relationship with the local Press in Norwich, and they wrote an article about the paintings under the caption, 'Herculean task for artist'.

The Kronfeld Club had grown in size and needed to stand on its own, so it became a separate entity with the new name of, 'The Guild of Aviation Artists'. This was formed in 1971 as a body of professional and non-professional artists. I was a Founder member and exhibited with them annually, and they put on other displays of paintings at a selection of venues, such as The Shuttleworth Trust, Yeovilton Museum, and at major flying days such as The Biggin Hill Air Fair.

The subjects I painted still ranged over as wide a variety as before, with the animal portraits, landscapes, private aircraft, and my own annual exhibition in Norwich which always brought in many commissions.

My next painting was requested by Squadron Leader Keith Batt for the R.A.F. Regiment, based at Catterick. It was suggested that I go up to the depot to see them, and for once, instead of driving, I was offered a lift by one of the Regiment. Whether the car was faulty or the driver faulty, I don't know, but his foot on the accelerator had no gentle touch whatsoever, we leapt into space to go faster, or braked to lose speed, travelling the entire route from London to Yorkshire like a kangaroo with hiccups!

My painting was to portray a piece of history from 28th November 1944. The Regiment achieved the distinction of being the first unit to shoot down a jet-propelled aircraft in an action which took place on the Dutch/Belgian border. The aircraft which was shot down by No. 2875 Squadron, was a Messerschmitt 262, probably re-designated 262A-2A because the original aircraft were converted to bombers in the summer of 1944. All the relevant information would be found for me, along with photographs of the terrain at Helmond and the wartime L40/60 gun with the detachment wearing the battledress of the 1944 period. The extract from the operations book read as follows:-

'Weather was very cold indeed and rather overcast. Another Me 262 very unwisely visited the airfield with fatal results. Squadron guns opened up, and the crew of B11 gun were successful in shooting it down. The guns opened up on the machine, but Tempests appeared. The guns ceased fire. The Tempests moved off, and the guns re-opened, shooting down the machine. The Tempests then followed it down. Later in the day, the Squadron was informed that it had been credited with destroying the machine. During the evening, a personal message of congratulations was received by the Squadron Commander from the AOC 83 Group.'

A 20 × 30 inch sized canvas was requested and I was given all the information and photographs from this event. The R.A.F. Regiment had formed a museum of their history, and after being shown round, as we were leaving I was informed that a lift to the Mess for lunch had been arranged for me. I thought this very odd as the buildings were not only next to each other, but I had already walked between them without suffering any major disaster, so ... were they completely off their rocker ... then, as I stepped outside, I discovered an enormous fire tender awaiting me! I mountaineered up into the cab, three of us in front, Keith Batt smugly said he would see me later, and off we went! They had arranged to drive me on the vehicle assault course as a surprise, telling me proudly that they had taken Princess Anne through the same course the previous week. Had they hung on to her, to steady her as we rolled and pitched through the mud and water, down into troughs of unbelievable filth and squelch, grinding steadily up the other side as water poured off the fire tender? They hung on to me! I think I'd have been tossed through the windscreen if they hadn't! On route we passed several burnt out hulks of old aircraft, some broken apart yet still recognisable from their shape, used by the R.A.F. fire service for practice. Our vehicle must have been a six wheel drive, possibly eight, and was the greatest of fun to be in as well as educating me to the appalling conditions it could tackle without a fault.

The painting was completed back in Norfolk, and only then did we all realize that no one had thought there would have been empty shell cases lying on the ground, so these were added.

It was some years later I received a telephone call from the Public Relations of the Ministry of Defence, to say that a photograph of this painting had been seen by somebody in Belgium, who was questioning whether the Regiment had indeed been the first unit to shoot down a jet aircraft, as he felt they were not. Could I help? Thankfully I had a copy of the official report on the action, and had the answers available.

CHAPTER 9

BRITANNIA

Paintings in the Mess at Akrotiri were seen by many people, and led to more commissions. One of these was from the P.M.C. of the Officers' Mess at R.A.F. Brize Norton, commissioning a 'Big Nim' sized painting of a Britannia. I drove to Brize Norton to discuss it with the Squadron, and discovered they wanted the background of R.A.F. Gan, in the Maldive Islands. Set in the Indian Ocean, this is a staging post for aircraft. I received a letter of confirmation that I was to report to the Passenger Terminal at Brize Norton for a flight on 20th November. The signals that went to and fro during these arrangements were certainly unusual and amusing. The first said,

'... IS ANXIOUS TO SPONSOR ARTIST MISS PENELOPE DOUGLAS TO GAN FOR PURPOSE OF DOING PAINTING OF A BRITANNIA A/C WHICH IS SCHEDULED TO BE HUNG IN THE RAF MUSEUM PD APPARENTLY MISS DOUGLAS WANTS THREE DAYS ON GAN AND IS AVAILABLE TO TRAVEL ... GRATEFUL YOU ADVISE IF CANST ACCEPT AND ACCOMMODATION AVAILABILITY'

The reply was as follows,

' ... SUBJECT VISIT OF ARTIST MISS PENELOPE DOUGLAS TO GAN PD WE ACCEPT VISIT AND ACCOMMODATION WILL BE AVAILABLE ... AND PRESUME MOD UK WILL PROVIDE NICE SHINY BRITANNIA FOR DURATION OF VISIT.' Then followed a signal giving change of dates, and a final one saying,

' ... ACCOMMODATION RESERVED PD HAVE LARGE STOCK OF PUCE PAINT AND MANY WILLING HELPERS TO PAINT BRITANNIA A/C'! Lovely!

I left the UK on 20th November, to return on 25th. Once again, miraculously I flew as a V.I.P. on board a VC10, in my view a stunningly beautiful aircraft. On arrival at Gan at about 3.20a.m. local time, 10.20p.m. in the U.K. I was met by Flight Lieutenant Mike Sugg, and we watched the VC10 take off. Alongside us were the crash vehicles and fire tender, engines going, R.A.F. firefighters dressed in their protective silver coloured clothing, not an emergency but normal standard procedure. I was given a room in the V.I.P. 'suite', which was a single story, low wooden building which had its own bathroom attached, and as I drifted off to sleep, listened to the clicking noise of the cicada lizards, and the weird sounds from the fruit bats which resembled the squeals of a piglet being squashed by a very large sow!

Next day Mike Sugg showed me round Gan, about four and a half miles. Once it was purely date palms but many of these had been replaced by tropical trees and shrubs: the beautiful, feathery casuarina trees that I remembered so well from Singapore, cascades of purple bougainvillaea, scarlet hibiscus trumpets, and the waxen cream coloured frangipani with the intoxicating scent. The Department of the Environment had a nursery there, a small botanical centre where trees, shrubs and orchids were raised. We passed a water catchment area. Unsurfaced roads were creamy white in colour from the coral. Bird life abounded, a hawk, herons, little birds like the Dunlins of the Norfolk coast, others with turquoise wings and not unlike our British jay, and a breed a little larger than a blackbird, with white wings on a creamy, chocolate covered body. Lizards scuttled away amongst the fallen leaves and bark. Bordering our route, fruit bats hung upside down from the low trees and bushes like dark socks hanging on the line to dry. I got within ten feet of one that had been swinging through the branches. It stopped and gazed at me, light chestnut body soft and furry, and then flew away, a two foot wingspan. They go to the loo in flight, so you need to be alert to this when they get airborne! I learnt one had been caught, and R.A.F. roundels painted on its wings! Certainly at dusk, from a distance, they didn't look unlike a Canberra!

Gan is one of many islands in the horse-shoe shaped Addu Atoll, and many of the Maldivians, tough, thin, darkskinned people, arrived by Dhonie, a local boat, from neighbouring islands at dawn, to work on Gan with the British. Many of them suffered from malnutrition, rickets, TB and other diseases, and those at the R.A.F. Medical Centre were able to help with the prevention and cure of these. As a staging post, there is the Blue Lagoon hotel. No aircraft were permanently there, work centred round the arrival and departure of the many flights in transit.

This first day on Gan I met Norman Hoad again, whom I had last seen as C.O. at Abingdon. I found him depressing, as he said the painting commissioned was almost impossible, as either I could do the Britannia justice and forget Gan, or the other way round, but to show both would be extremely difficult. Clearly I had a challenge ahead of me! He wished to know how I planned to do the painting, but I had arrived with an open mind, as I prefer to form ideas when I see the background and gather material. If I have pre-conceived thoughts, I usually have to change them.

There were seldom any women on Gan, though occasionally they passed through on route. Consequently the Maldivians greeted me with, "Morning Sir"! The road sign Bat Alley hung upside down, and a many fingered signpost read, 'Cocos 1806, Perth 3524, S.Pole 5358, London 5750, Hong Kong 4055, Tokyo 5100, Karachi 1850, Moscow 4125,' and included Cape Town and Paris.

There had been discussion in the U.K. that the painting might show the Britannia in flight with the Atoll down below, but it became apparent that this would be impossible, the only aircraft coming through from which I might have got the material was the Canberra, but it was the two seater version without the facilities for extra crew. Thankfully they had made no special demands on how the Britannia was to be shown, it was left to me. I can't have enough praise for the attitude of the Services when commissioning paintings, for they seldom tied my hands. This made an enormous difference to my attitude towards the commission, giving me every advantage of looking freshly at the subject and background, and the freedom to make my own decisions, and give my artistic scope full range. I have always been immensely grateful for this. On the rare occasion when I have been given a detailed brief that had to be fullfilled, it has often proved very frustrating and notoriously hard to get the material I need, the atmosphere and original pictorial arrangement that I am longing to produce, stifled. Now, the Canberra crew took my camera with them on a flight, while Mike and I lay on a raft floating on an azure sea, my sense of humour coming to the fore as the aircraft circled high overhead, with me doubled up with laughter saying,

"Left hand down a little," giggling instructions to the distant pilot! What a life! A coral island, wonderful beaches, the amazing colours of the sea, and all these men! What more could any girl want! That night I was invited to dinner at the civilian Mess, eight of us in all, sitting outside with the soft, balmy air of the tropics, palm trees stretching their fronds to the darkened sky overhead, gentle sounds of the sea lazily swoshing its way up onto the sand, excellent company, and a delicious meal. The visit to Gan was proving a wonderful and complete contrast from the endless hours spent in the studio alone, and certainly made it all worthwhile! The following day was Sunday, and I had been invited by Keith to work on the local Family Favourite's radio programme, reading out messages from loved ones back in the U.K. After I'd dealt with the second request which sent special devoted greetings from the family pets, I thought I'd end up weeping with emotion, but hastily pulled myself together! I had forms in front of me which gave the details of the message, and as the programme progressed, I soon got the knack of changing the order, reading the words from loved ones and the chosen music in a more professional way, all very stimulating. The afternoon was spent snorkelling, the underwater life teeming with interested, nosy tropical fish! I have to adapt to my own methods for this, as having nearly drowned twice in my life, I have a natural fear of water, but with my feet firmly on the sea bed, I could watch them through my mask, able to stand up within my depth if needed. I can swim, but putting my head under brings instant fear and panic. It was windy, the palm trees swinging to and fro along the edge of the beach like metronomes, care needed with the coral to avoid shredded legs! However, it was time to work for a Britannia arrived at last.

People had said,

"Well if you're here to paint the Brit on Gan Penelope, we expect both to be axed!" They were correct. Now, thankfully my subject was there for me to see for the rest of the day, and I worked hard until dusk. That evening, Charlton Heston in, 'The Ten Commandments' was shown. Watching any film with a bunch of men in the Forces was an experience not to be missed, for at the most dramatic or serious moments, some wag called out a comment that made everybody explode with laughter. It was unforgettable! I'd had a schoolgirl crush on Charlton Heston, a real photograph of him had lived amongst my underclothes, hidden from my father who has insisted all my collection of pictures of film stars - many of them precious 'swaps' at school - must be burnt. I was considered cheap at enjoying such trivia! He didn't understand it was a passing phase and I would move on to something else equally dreadful! My collection became bonfire material, charred beyond redemption, but guiltily I had smuggled Charlton Heston into my pants!

On Gan the Station Photographer had developed some of the films I had taken, and it was a great relief to know ahead that my gathered material was all right, for I could hardly go back to the U.K. to request another flight because I had used the wrong exposure! Watching the aircraft, and trying to come up with some ideas for the painting that would show the background as Gan, as well as the Britannia to advantage, I decided to put in the foreground two Maldivians with the 'honey wagon'. They pushed this wheeled, yellow container affair out to the aircraft to empty the loos, hence the name! It would be a perfect way to incorporate local Maldivians and add to that three-dimensional visual impact. Finally I had all the material I needed. Before leaving, Mike Thomas took me off to show me the meteorological balloon, hydrogen filled, being sent up to record data which is sent to Britain, building up information on the weather world wide. He too, like Mike Sugg, had looked after me at intervals, and both were superb company. And so my flight home was due, I clocked in to Air Movements with its comical notice outside of the Pink Panther and the message, 'Breakfast in England, dinner in Gan, luggage in Hong Kong', and returned to the U.K. via a two hour refuelling stop at Akrotiri, and as on my way out, Judy Balfour managed to join me in the V.I.P. lounge. It was not long before the Britannias were phased out, and Gan closed as an R.A.F. base. My painting would become history.

I started work on the canvas for Brize Norton, and once again I used the scarlet underpainting. To discover that this technique had worked so well had given a real spark to my passion for painting, firing me with new enthusiasm. While working on the canvas, Anglia Television decided to do a film on me for their programme, 'About Women.' They spent the whole day at the house, the producer insisting her minions be sent off to the local pubs to find the exact make of wine that she wished for, and we produced food for the production team of seven. The programme was edited later to just under ten minutes. They had asked me questions but cut these, creating a documentary film with commentary by me, inserting footage of Gan, producing a very pleasing programme. The painting of the Britannia was under way at the time, I was filmed working on it but surprisingly they never asked why the canvas was scarlet. To me it had been the most obvious question! I did a second large painting 4′ × 3′ 'Portrait of Gan' which had twelve small aspects of Gan painted round the edge, the Adu Atoll from the air in the centre, all linked with lizards and fruit bats. It was bought by the R.A.F. Museum at Hendon.

The P.M.C., Wing Commander Ian Semple at R.A.F. Brize Norton wrote to me immediately after the delivery of the Britannia painting, commissioning two more large pictures, the first of a Belfast at Brize Norton, the second of a VC10 at a staging post 'as yet to be decided.' Once again, I was over the moon! However, before this I was to be sent to the Tower!

The Ceremony of the Keys takes place late at night at the Tower of London, completed as Big Ben strikes the hour of ten. It is a tradition that takes place every night including Christmas Day, and Regiments take turns to be on duty, escorting the Keys of the Sovereign to their place of safety for the night. The custom started when the Chief Yeoman Warder locked the gates of the Tower in the evenings in the reign of Queen Elizabeth I when unruly mobs tried to mug him, so he required an escort. The military came to his aid, and ever since then the guard of the day (now part of the Buckingham Palace Guard,) escorts the Yeoman Warder as he locks the doors. This is the oldest, longest surviving ceremony in the country, has taken place for several centuries, even through both wars. Apart from Christmas Day, the public may request tickets to allow them to watch, and the Tower is closed to the public several hours before the start of the ceremony. The Queen's Colour Squadron were on duty in November 1974, and the R.A.F. Regiment wishing to purchase a painting of the event, arranged for me to see it. I was therefore expected at the Tower after it was officially closed, let in at the outer gate, and given directions to find the Squadron.

November, the chill of the evening heightened by the darkness, and I walked over the drawbridge and along Water Lane, the Thames smacking at Traitor's Gate as I reached it. Nobody about, not a soul, just the heavy atmosphere of history, the raw coldness of late autumn, the damp environment, all contributed to an unforgettably eerie experience, and so strange without the public present. The very emptiness of the grounds made the buildings seem even more impressive, and I was aware of the huge, stone walls that seemed to tower over me in such an oppressive manner. I wandered alone, slightly scared, the Black Tower on my left, and as I passed under the portcullis felt compelled to linger, shadows cast by the old lamps, my own shadow startling me, even the smell of dankness and dampness from the Thames, the events of the past several centuries causing me to shiver a little. Somebody stepped towards me from a doorway unexpectedly, my imagination was working overtime, and it was a slight shock that they were there atall, and surprisingly, in modern clothing! I made my way up the steps where the Ceremony of the Keys ends as Big Ben strikes ten o'clock, and walked on to Wellington Barracks and the glare of electric lighting in the Guardroom. I was to join Air Commodore Bumstead and party, and watched the ceremony, gathering material frantically for the painting, the Queen's Colour Squadron immaculate, their sombre blue-grey greatcoats a total contrast to the brilliant scarlet uniform of the Yeoman Warders. Photography was the nightmare I dreaded because of the dimly lit passage, even with suitable film. I took photographs as best I could, for the ceremony was neither going to pause for me, nor be set up afterwards. It was an unusual subject, and back in the studio, a demanding and difficult task to paint the figures captured in the lamplight, and I made sure I included the heavy shadows cast by night lighting. The completed painting went to the R.A.F. Regimental museum.

I was extremely hesitant to take on the next commission by Air Commodore Geoffrey Bumstead. Although I do many portraits of animals, I don't do portraits of people. As with photographs the results are usually controversial, some considered flattering, others that they don't do the person justice, so it was with some reluctance and trepidation that I took on a portrait of the Commandant General of the R.A.F. Regiment, Air Vice Marshal D.A. Pocock O.B.E. I had done a study, the head of Peter Nicholls from three different angles - he had such Nordic features that I felt compelled to paint him - but I tried to avoid portraits. The picture was to be presented to the Air Vice Marshal on his retirement. Although it was to be done in secret creating even more of a problem, arrangements were made for me to meet him, with reasons given that I was working on oil paintings for the Regimental Museum. As we were introduced at the Ministry of Defence, he must have thought me a strange woman, unable to take my eyes off him, studying his facial features as if my life depended on it! There was a similarity in appearance with the actor Jack Hawkins. I was given photographs, and set to work. With the painting completed and framed, Geoff Bumstead came to the flat in London to collect the portrait. With him came his driver, and I made coffee for us all. The driver paced the room, then to my amusement explained that he had been driving Air Vice Marshal Pocock for some time, and thought the painting so like him that he didn't feel able to relax. I turned the portrait's face to the wall, the problem solved!

Now a Royal Review is notoriously difficult to portray, either you get the back view of The Queen and the faces of the Regiment, or the reverse. Painted from the side, it looks as if there is nobody else on the parade ground, or figures are too distant, but I was to show just two figures, one of which was The Queen, to be done from Regimental photographs from 1967. Although I had impressed on the 'powers that be' of the R.A.F. Regiment that I need to see an event if I am to do it justice, they were building up a series of pictures of historical, past occasions, so it was impossible. For this, permission from Her Majesty was requested through Sir Martin Charteris, the Queen's Private Secretary. I gathered that Her Majesty was 'interested to learn of the project that Miss Penelope Douglas should paint a picture, and certainly had no objection to the painting.' In spite of permission from Her Majesty, I didn't enjoy working on the picture! It was thoroughly unsatisfactory not to have seen the event and selected my own angle from which to work.

Elected a Full Member of the Guild of Aviation Artists with a letter of congratulations from Roy Nockolds, continuing to exhibit with them, I did my stint as committee member and enjoyed the various social functions. One of my tasks was to organise the Annual Dinner which coincided with the Annual Exhibition. I did this over several years, a fair amount of work involved. Yvonne Bonham, who was so efficient at organising the Guild, worked with me on the seating of members and their guests, and I made a plan of this, put flowers on tables, and where possible, decor in the theme of flying and painting. I hung model aircraft below lights, or used kites with long tails draped across the wall. It added to the atmosphere, caused amusement and interest. Guests numbered over a hundred, and included a variety of interesting speakers.

Held at different venues, Terence Cuneo was a guest speaker at a dinner held in the R.A.F. Club, Piccadilly. Well known for a mouse in his painting, I made one that would parachute across the ballroom to him. I stood on a window seat the other side of the room with my old fashioned cobweb brush held up above my head, and from the top of that, had a thread strung right across the ballroom to a window catch behind the speakers on the 'top table.' Through gravity, when I let the mouse go, it would descend over the heads of the diners towards Cuneo, a match tied in the thread stopping it two feet short of him, and Michael Turner seated nearby would break the thread with his lighter flame and present the mouse to Cuneo. With a run through beforehand it worked perfectly, the cobweb brush giving me the necessary height. Dudley Burnside was the Chairman that year, had been briefed on everything, but completely forgot that the mouse was to arrive first, and instead, launched off on his speech. My arms began to get desperately tired held above my head, and I was just losing all feeling when he spotted me, signalled a gentlemanly, 'Ah yes,' and hastily announced the arrival of the mouse, which on release, floated down beautifully, much to the enjoyment of all those present, especially any who were used to the pranks of R.A.F. dining-in nights! In his speech Cuneo said he was often presented with a mouse, but never one arriving by parachute, and planned to take it home to hang in his studio! As years went by the dinner proved too expensive, many people having to arrange overnight accommodation, and they came to an end.

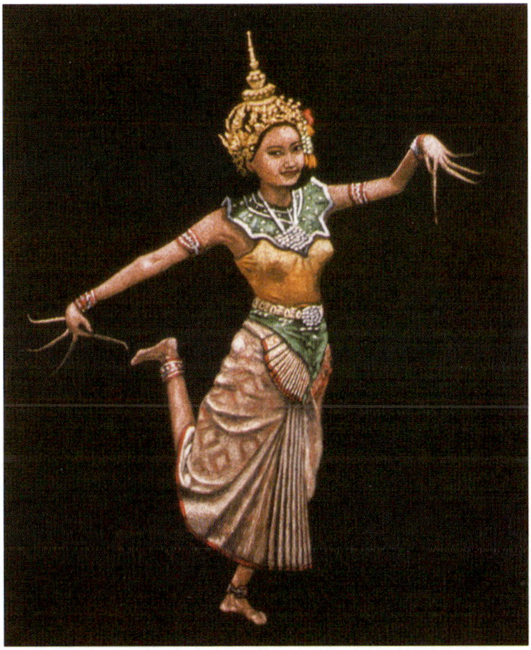

Thai dancer

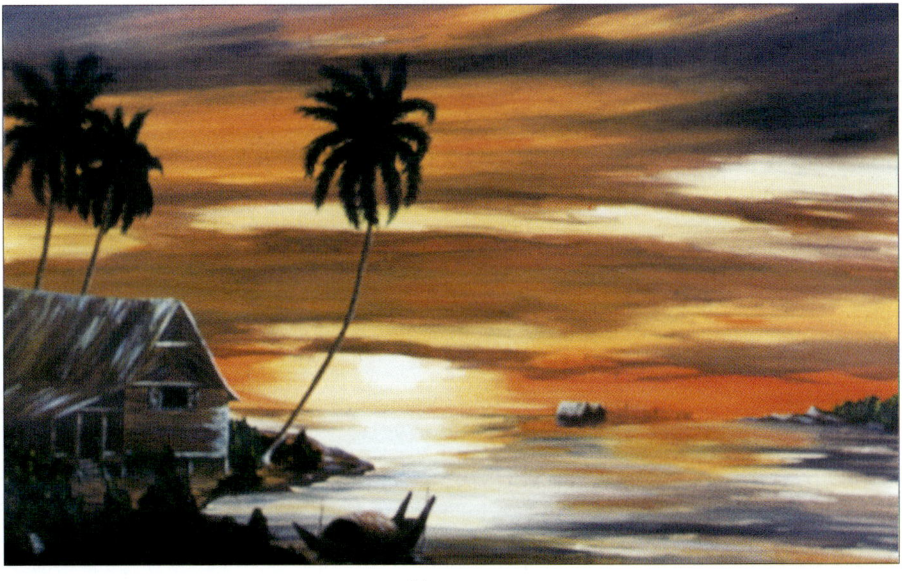

Singapore

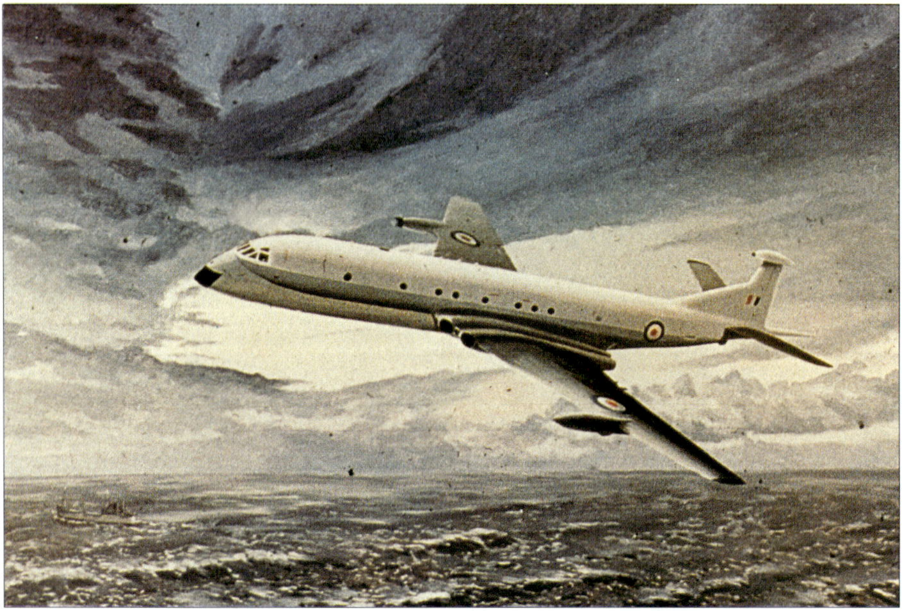

Nimrod

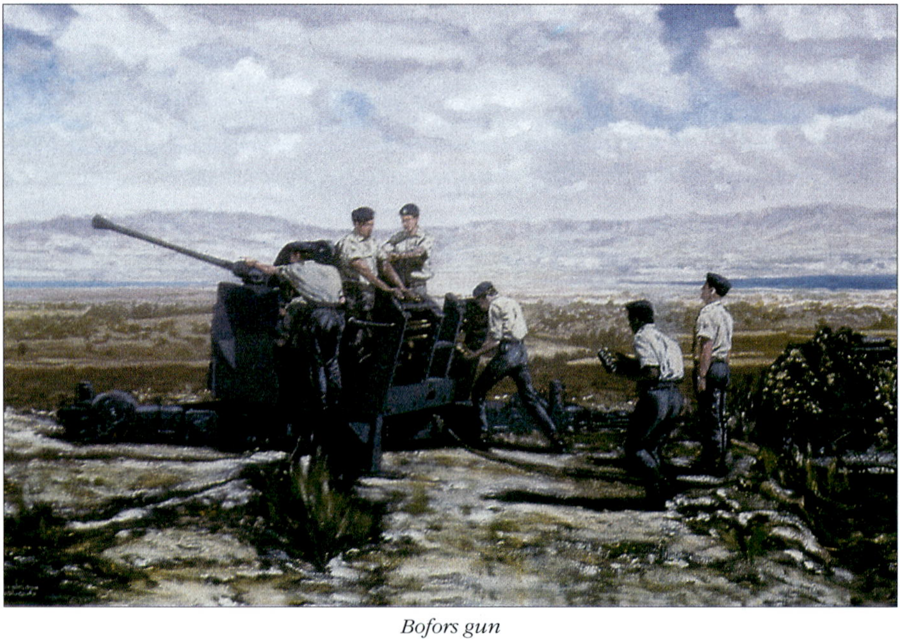

Bofors gun

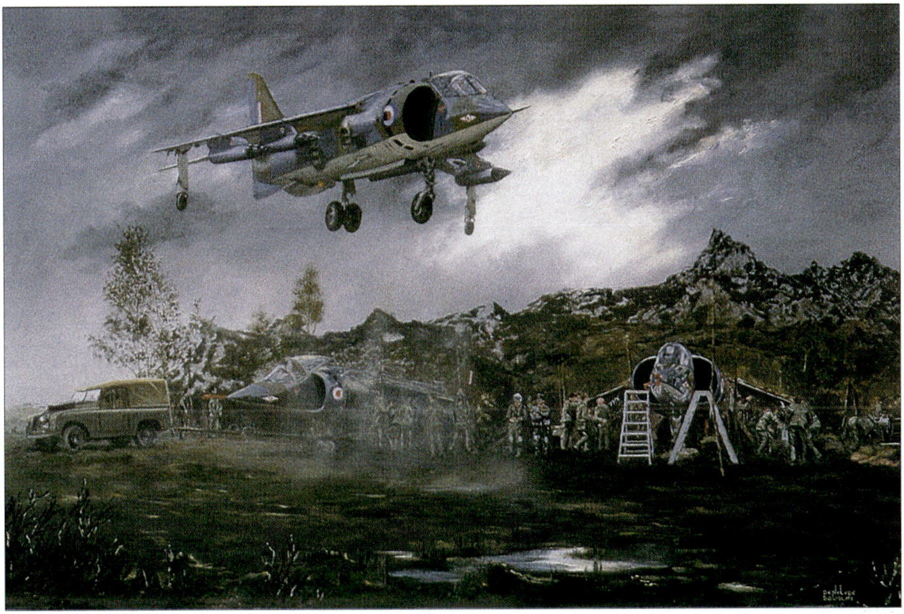

Harrier

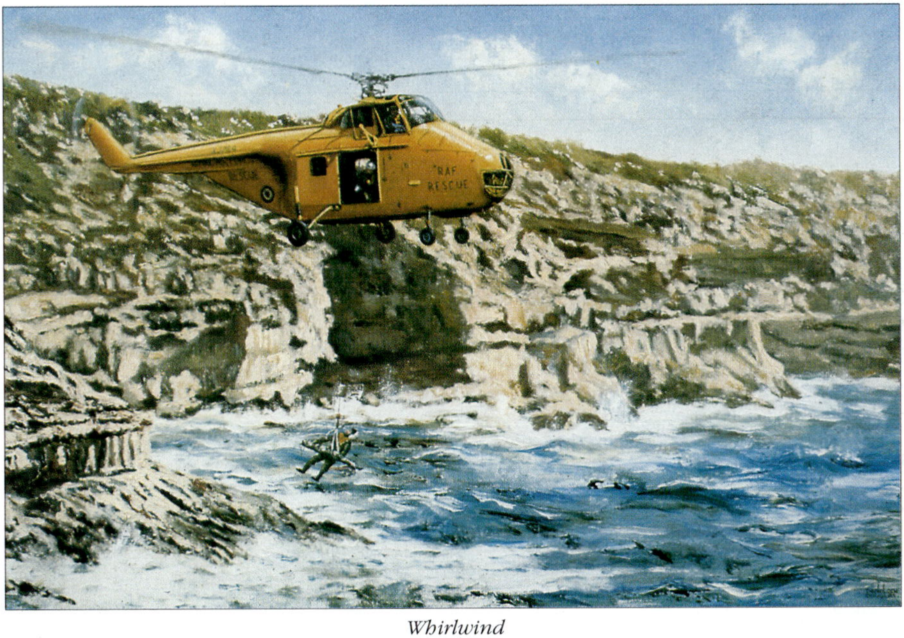

Whirlwind

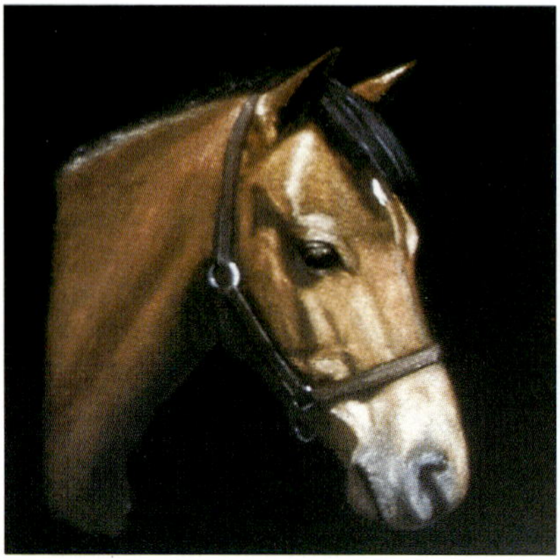

Horse

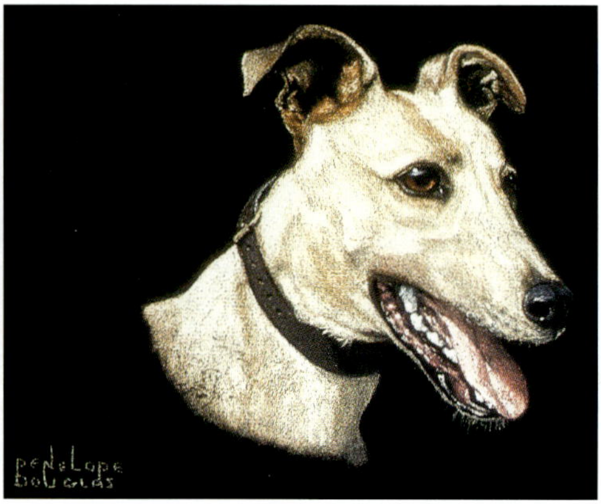

Greyhound

Portraits on black velvet

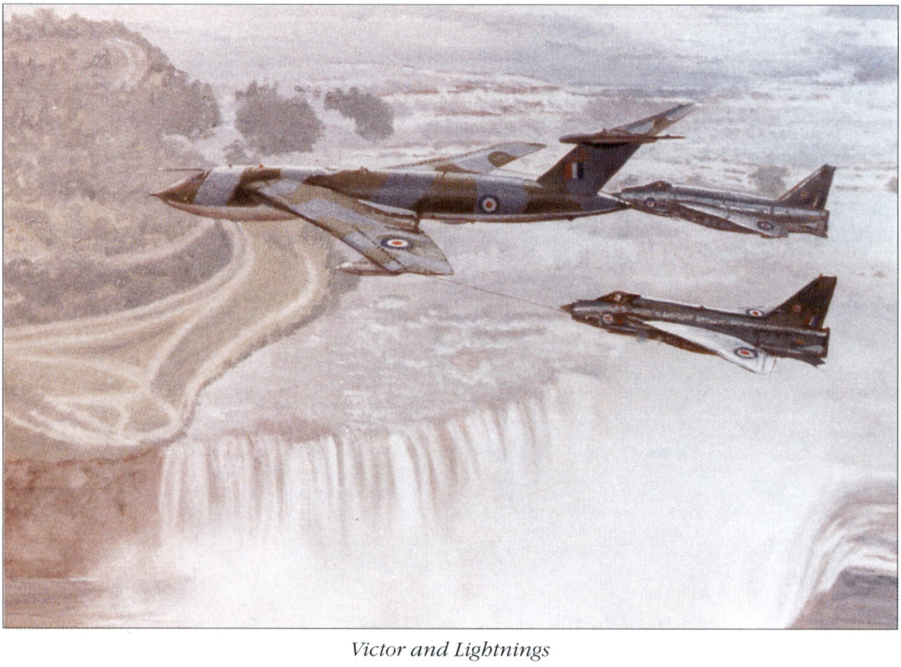

Victor and Lightnings

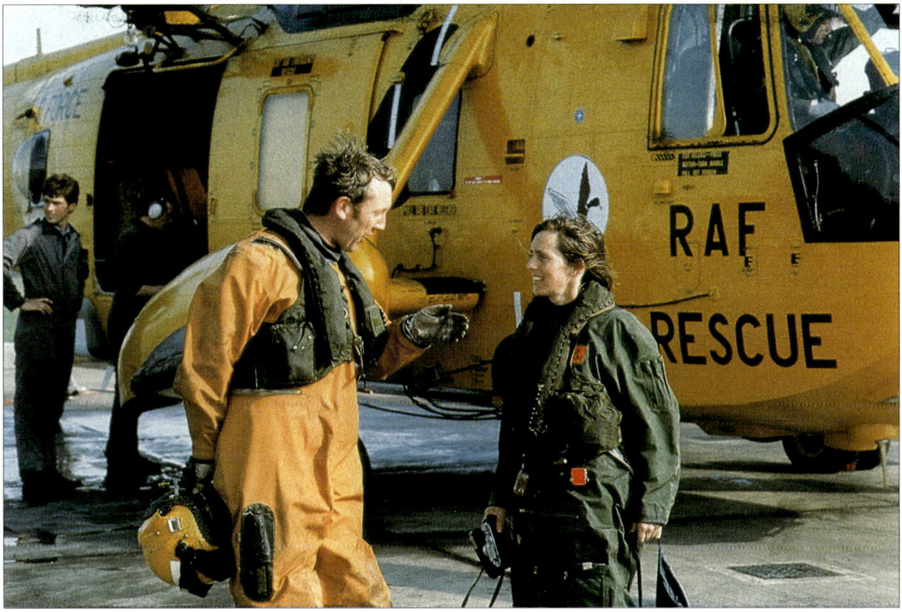

Mel Ward and self

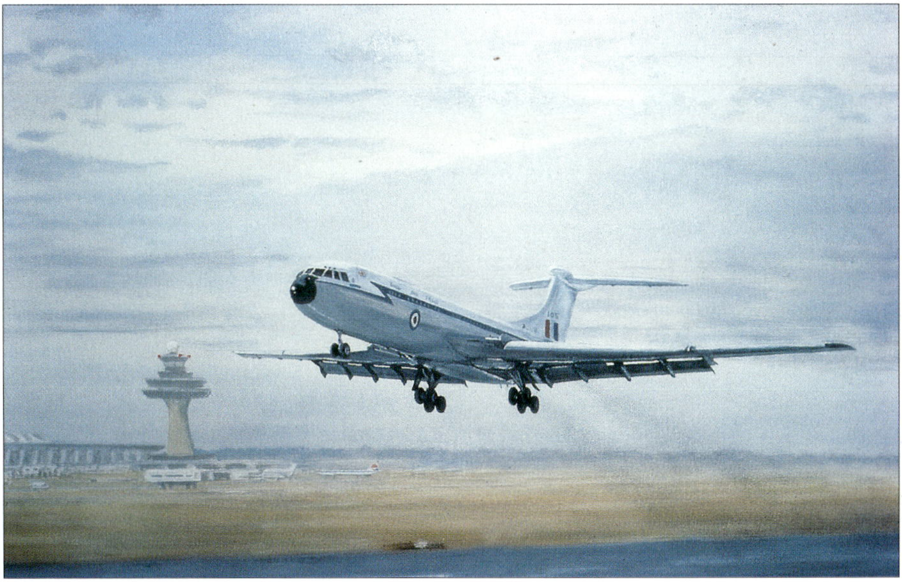

VC10

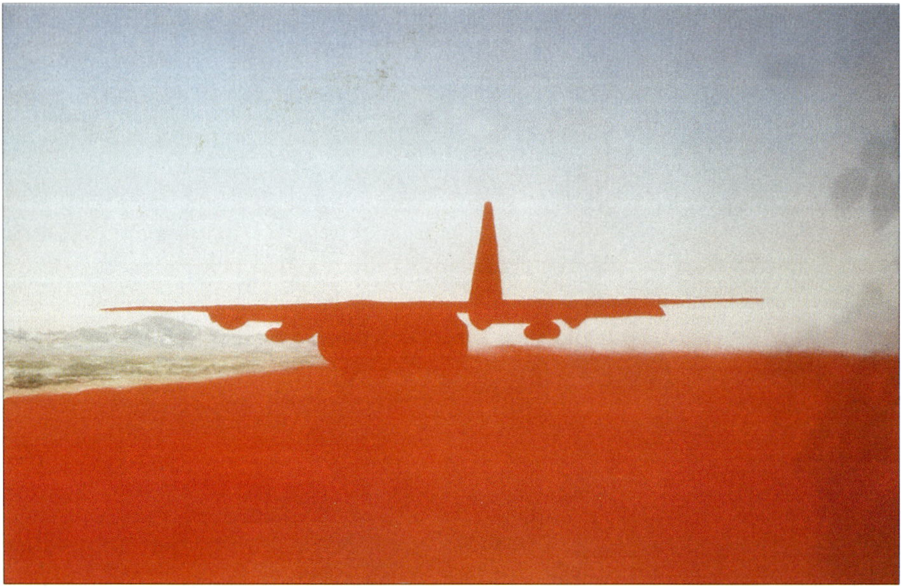

Red underpainting

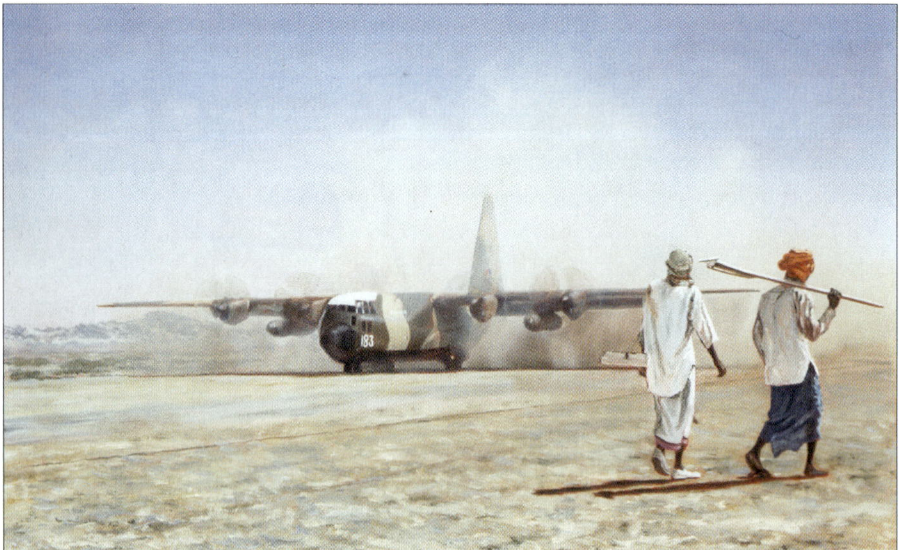

Hercules

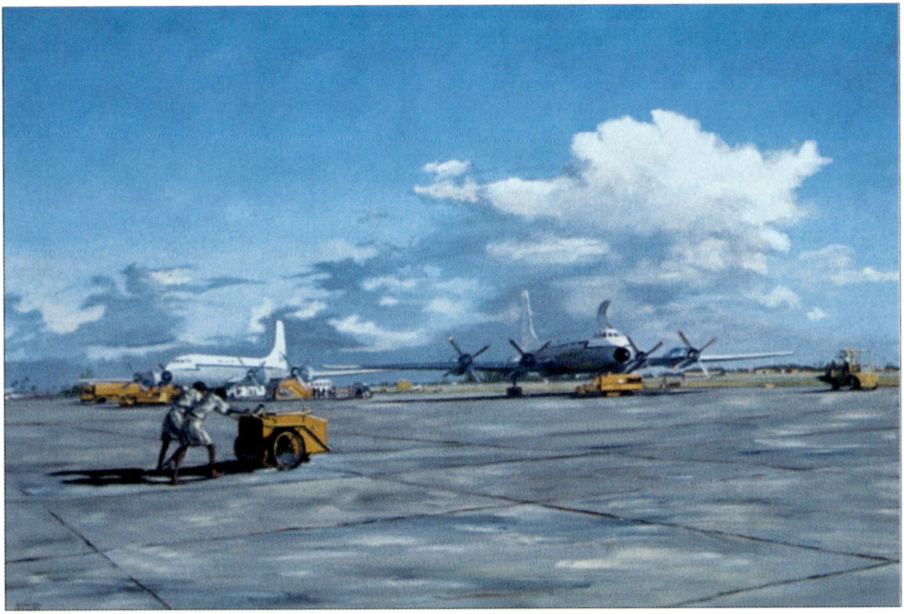

Britannia

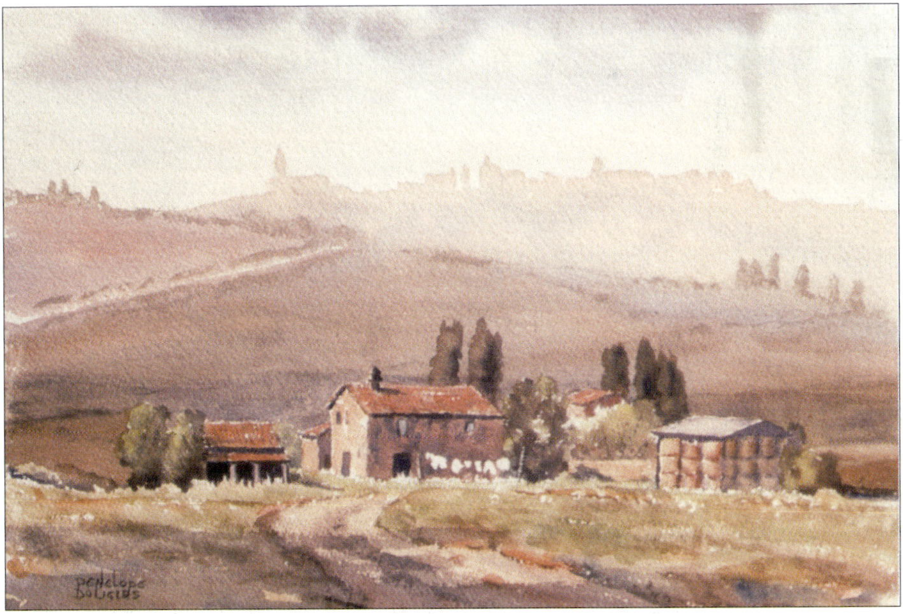

Tuscany (watercolour)

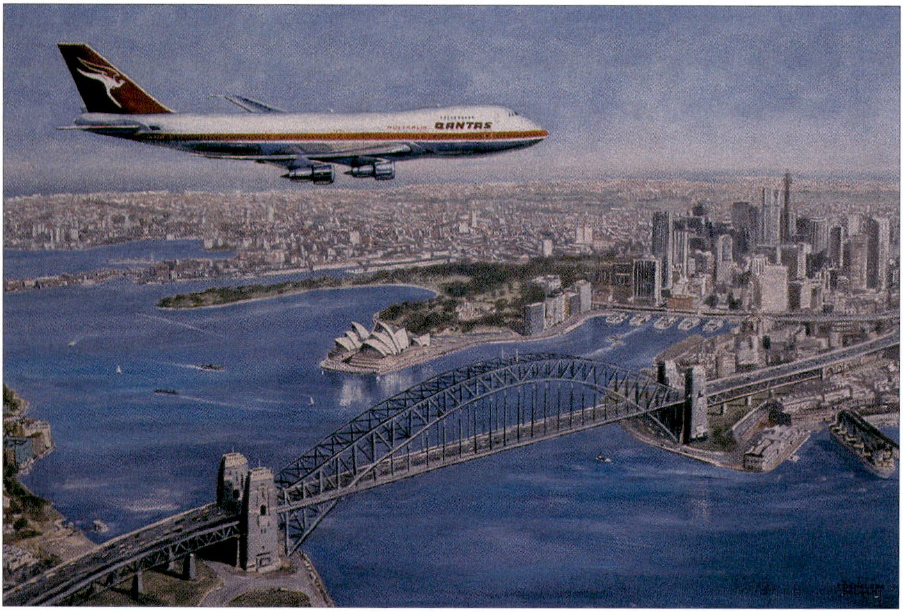

Boeing 747B

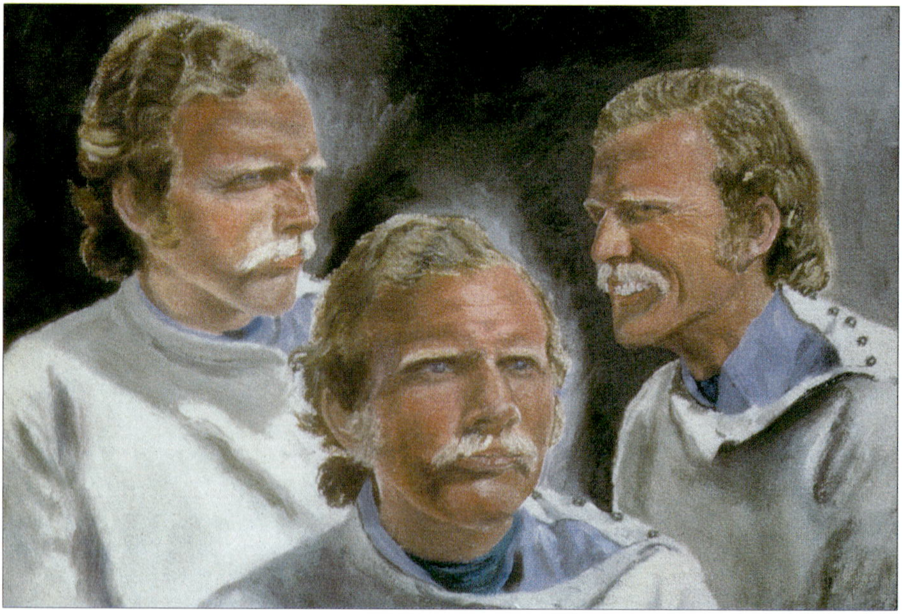

Peter Nichols

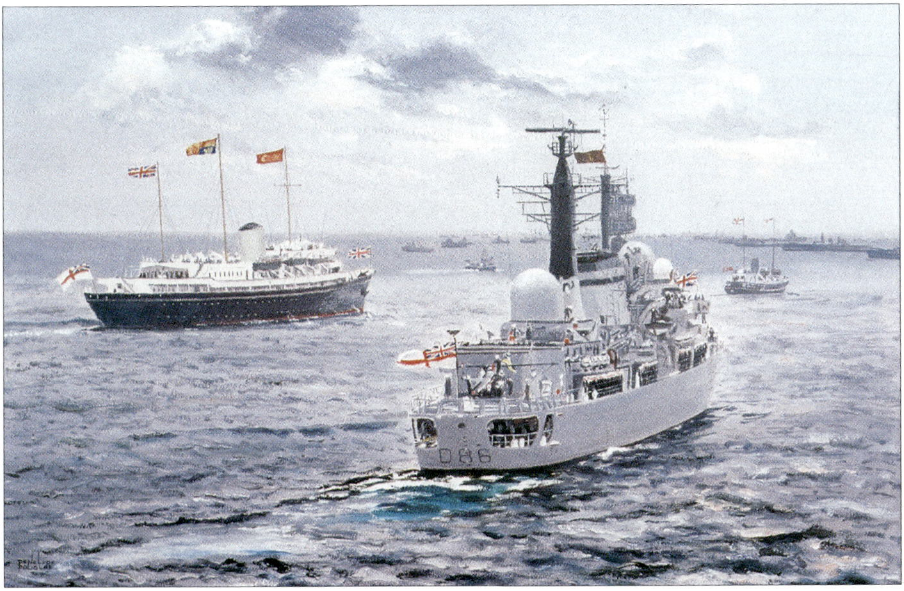

Britannia and H.M.S. Birmingham

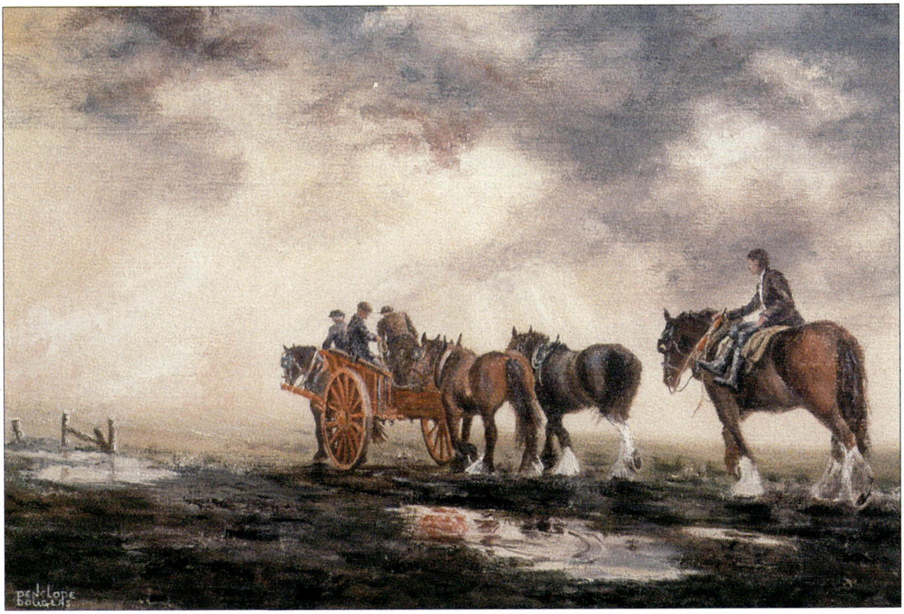

Homeward bound

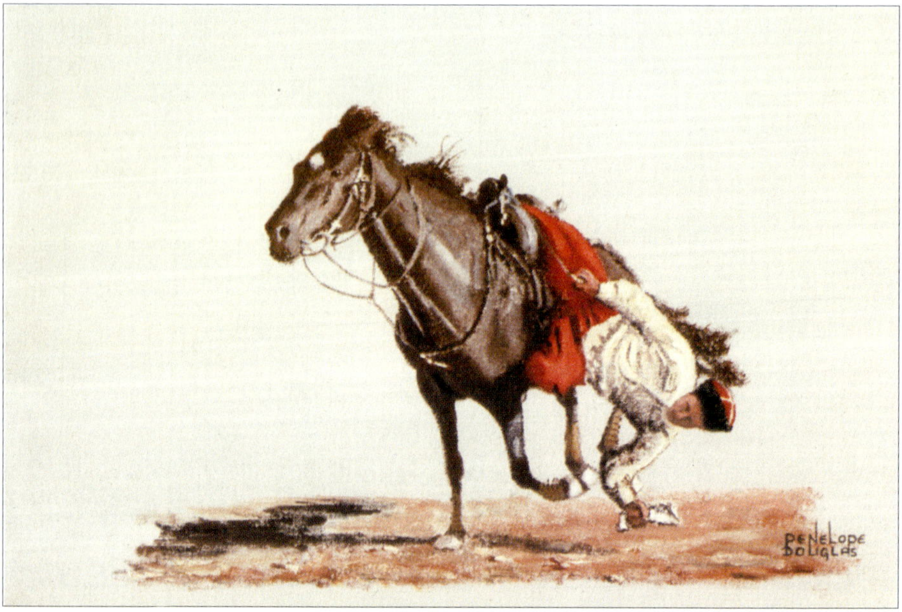

Cossack rider

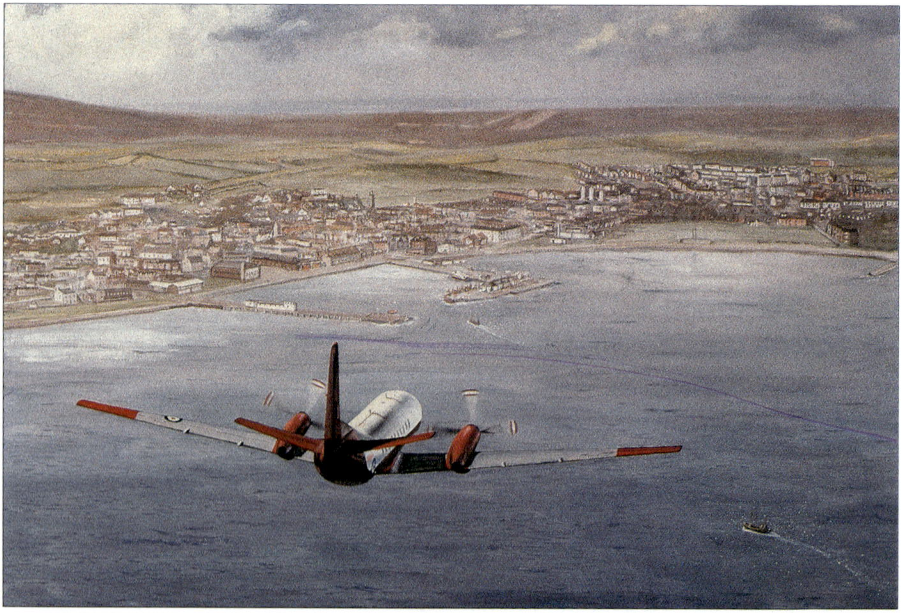

Andover

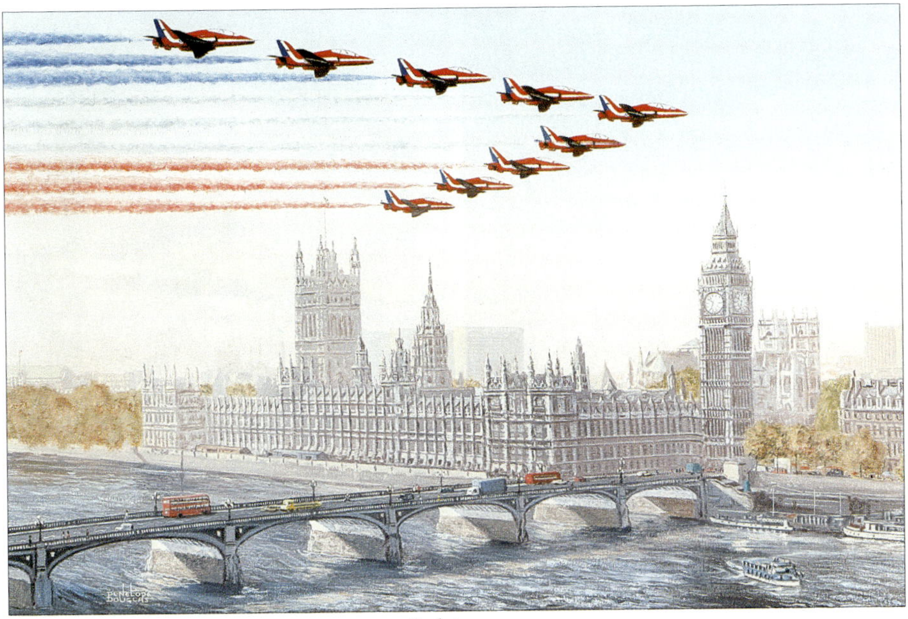

Red Arrows

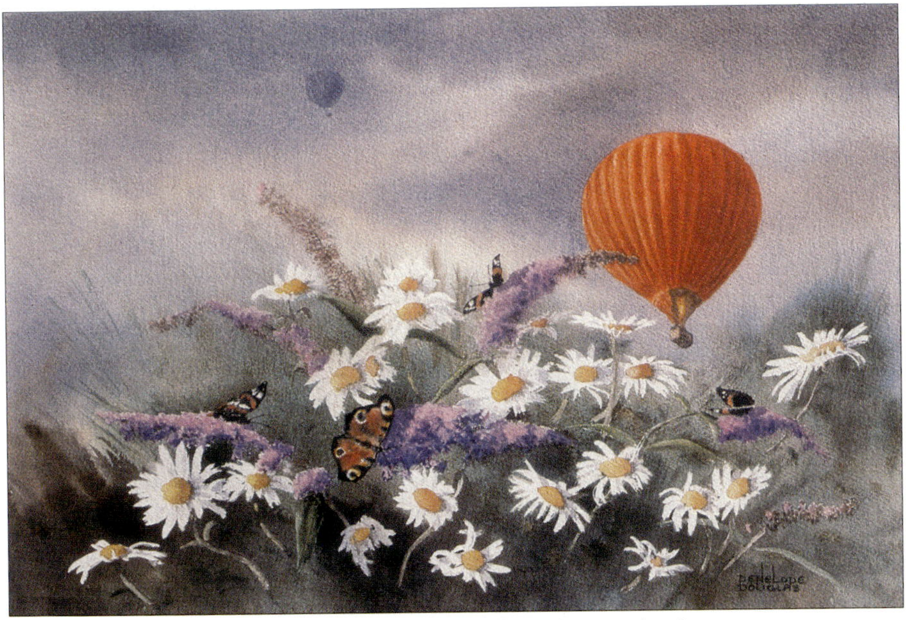

Buddleia, butterflies and balloons (water colour)

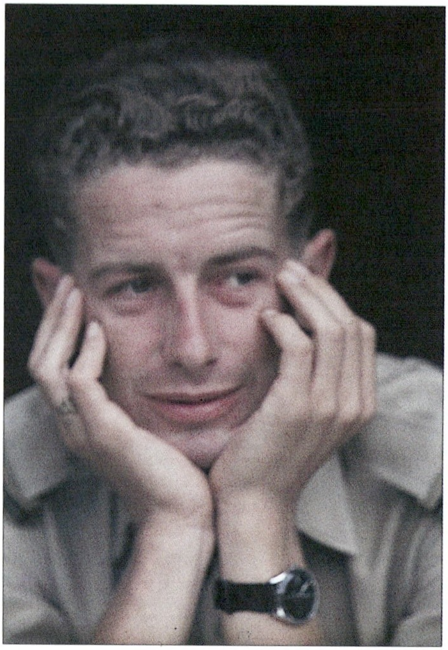

Peter Fish

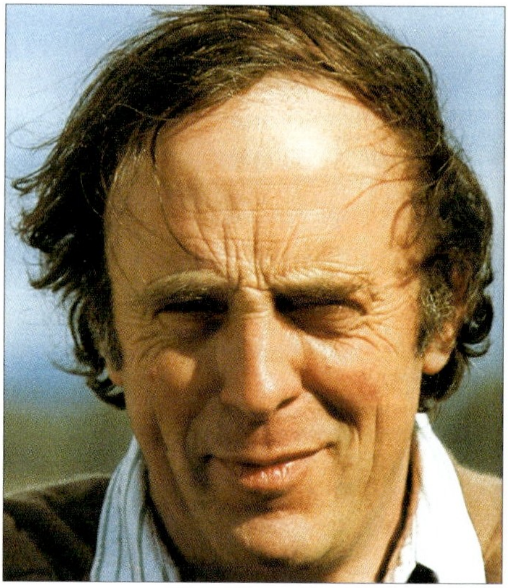

David Douglas

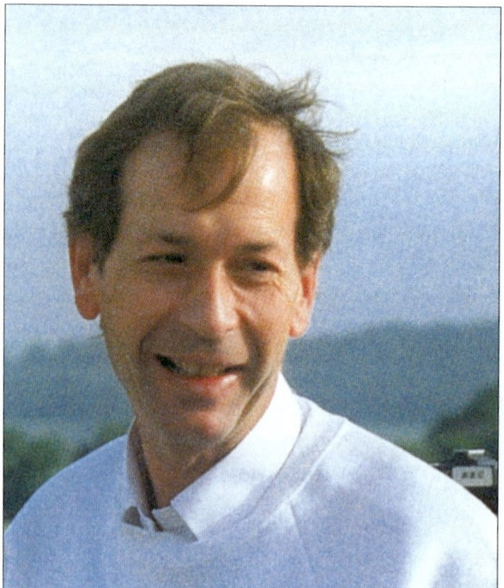

Tim Gauvain

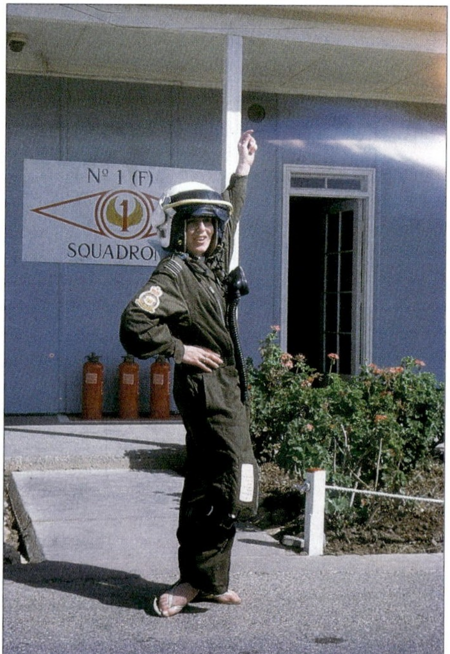

Self-Akrotiri

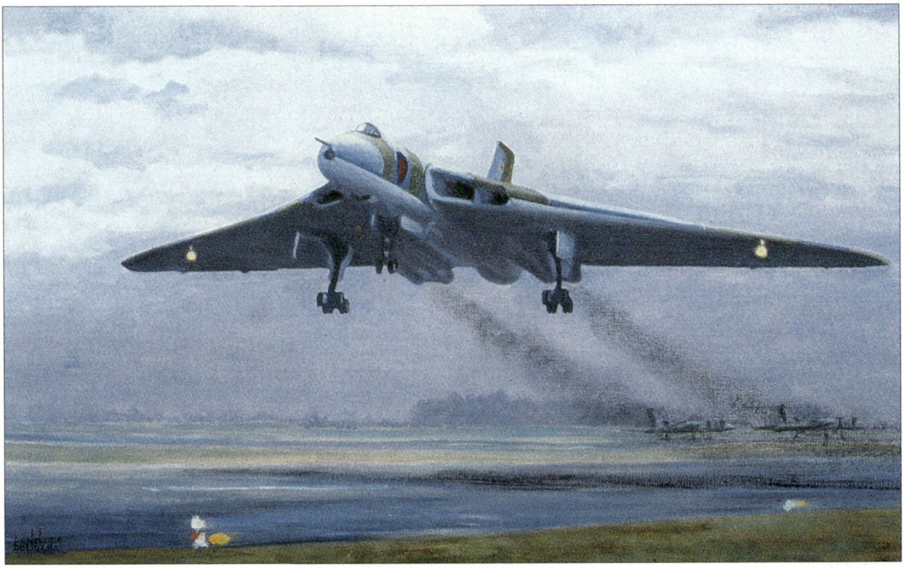

Vulcan – (raffle prize)

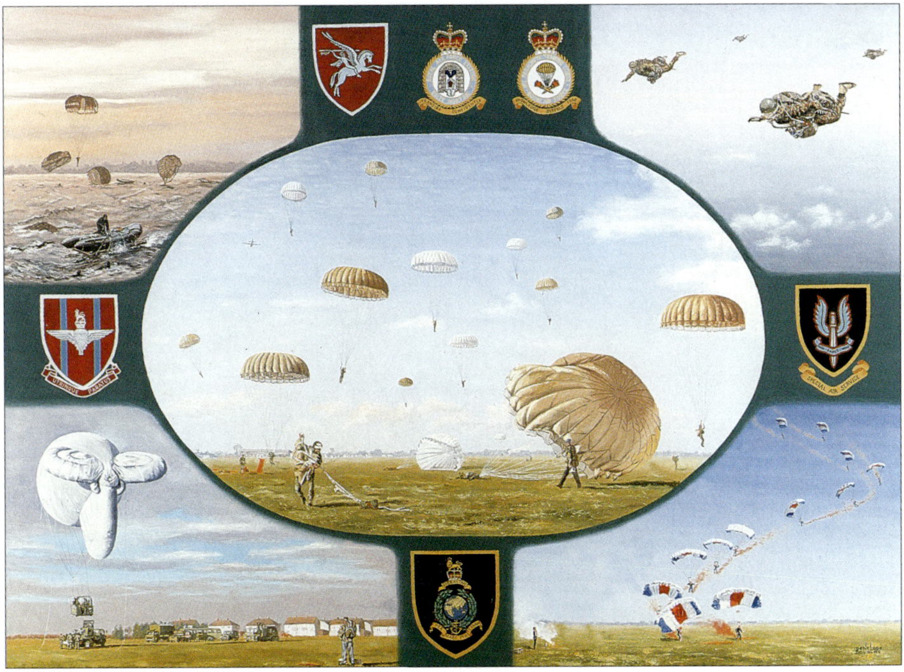

Parachute Training School

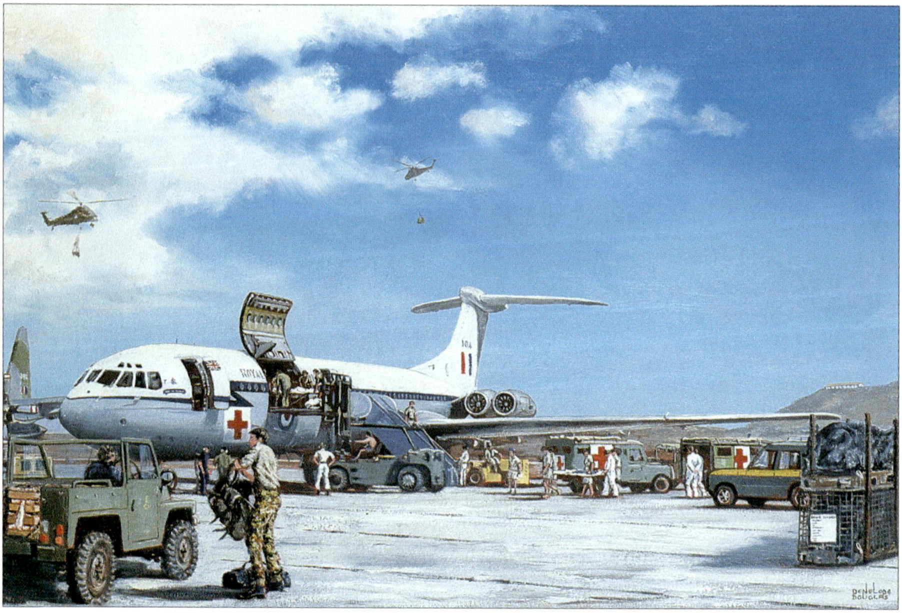

VC10

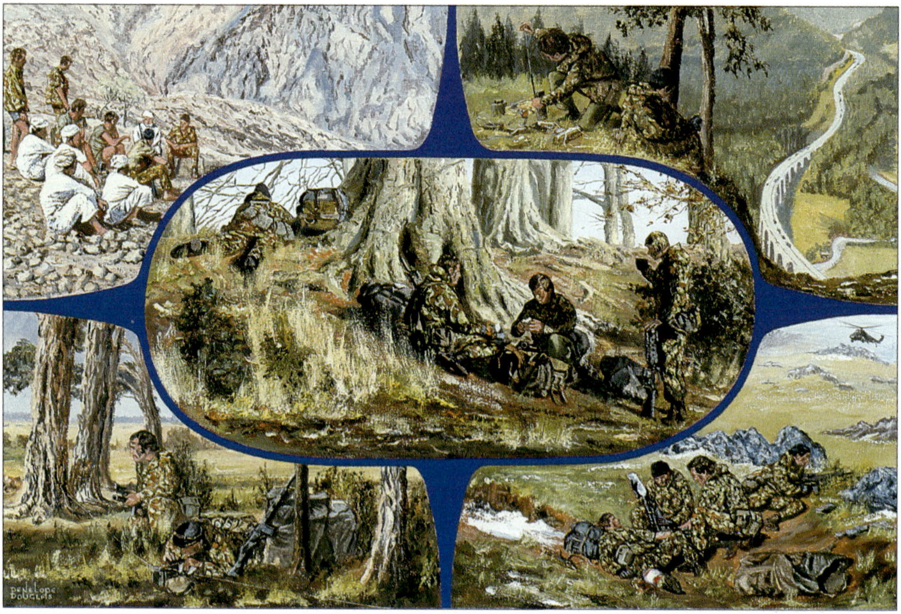

22 Special Air Service Regiment

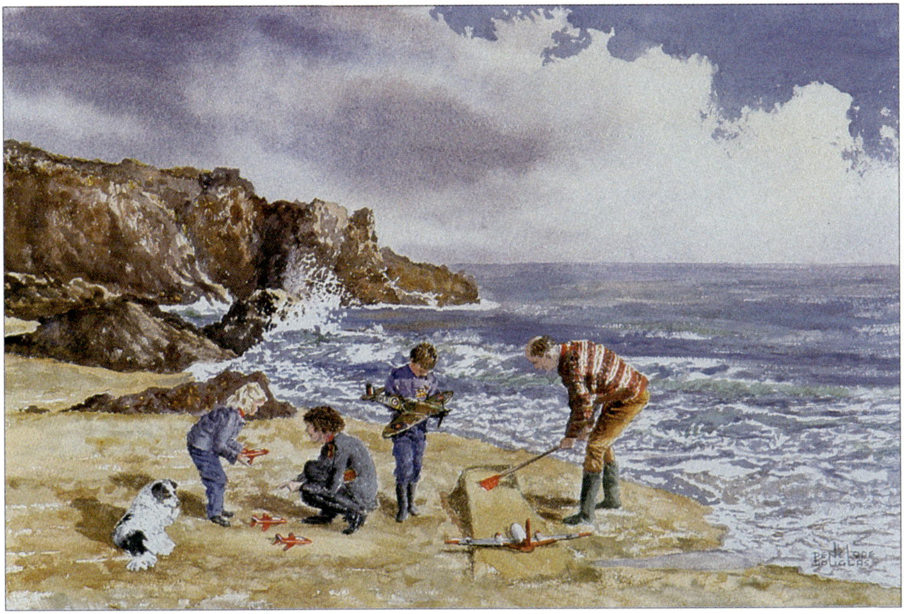

Sun, sea, sand and imagination (water colour)

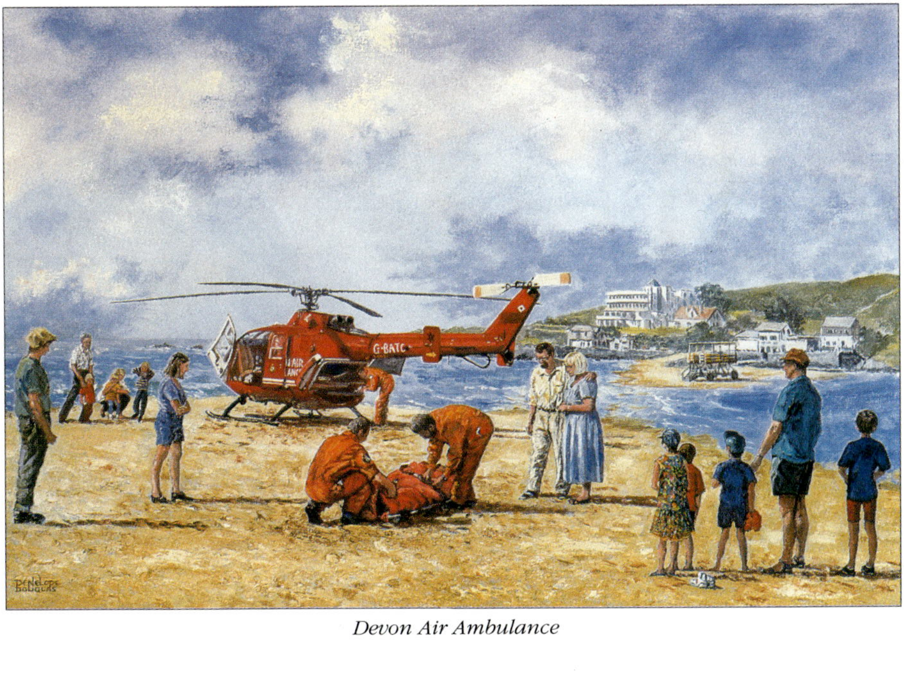

Devon Air Ambulance

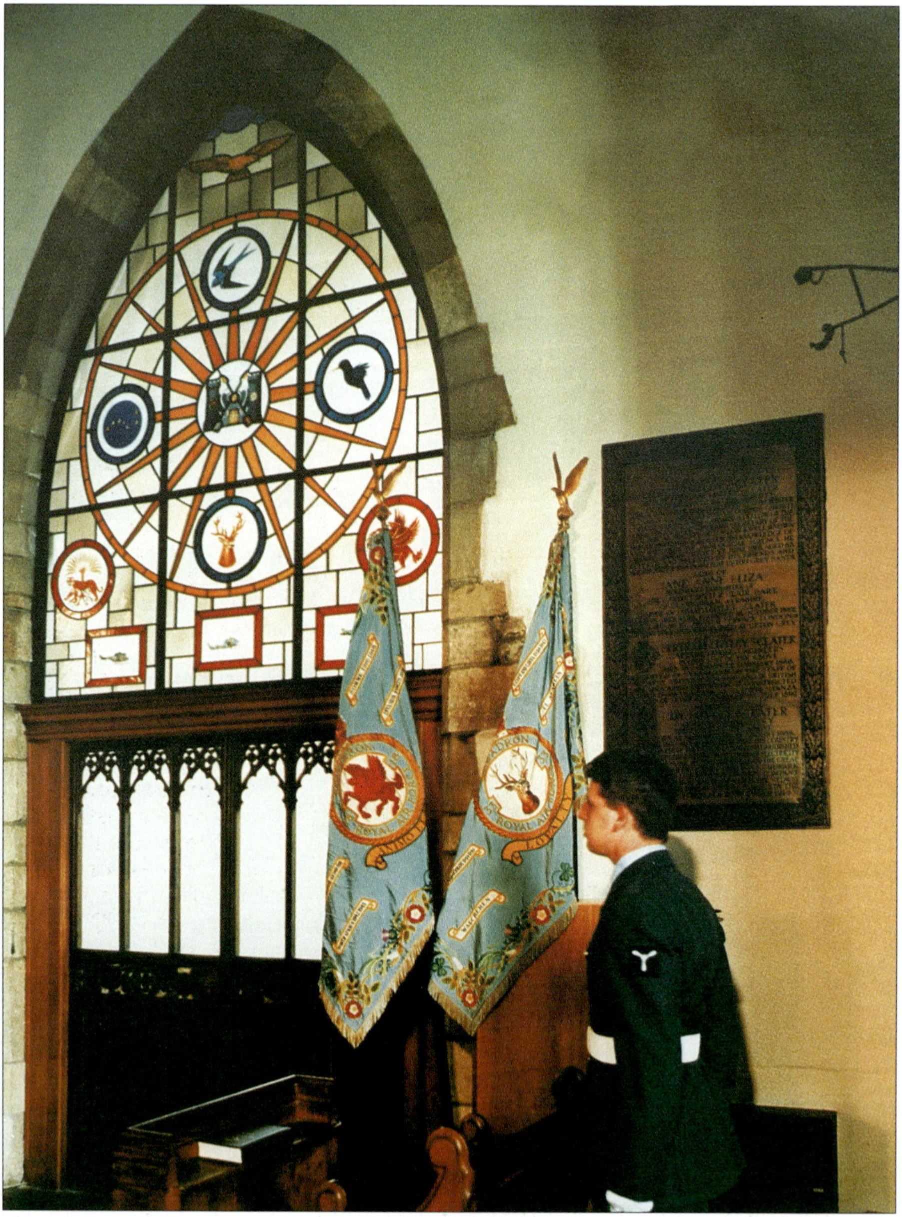

The Royal Air Force
Support Helicopter stained glass window – Odiham

CHAPTER 10

GIBRALTAR AND A FLIGHT AROUND THE ROCK

For R.A.F. Brize Norton's next commission, the Belfast picture was to have the background of Brize Norton. For security reasons, details of the aircraft I worked on were kept quiet, but I painted the Belfast with a helicopter being loaded into it. Again, I put three figures in the foreground, their reflections visible on the wet surface of the airfield. I was determined to be authentic, and asked the men to study their clip-board and be deep in discussion, and they became an essential part of the painting. I was not good at inventing figures, only content with seeing them for real.

There is the theory that when painting figures, all the heads should be level, whether they are close to the viewer or distant, whatever their size. There is an element of truth in this, providing the ground is level! However it doesn't always work. Before putting a brush to canvas, I plan the painting meticulously beforehand, and this is a quarter to a third of the actual work of producing the finished canvas. Figures had to have a reason for being in the picture and active where possible, shadows on folds of material, creating a round person and not a flat one were all important points to be encompassed.

Brize Norton were wonderfully kind and gave a reception for each painting when I delivered it. Usually this was a drinks party, and the station photographer took a record of the event, and it wasn't long after I had completed the Belfast painting, that Wing Commander Tony Richards OBE, C.O. of 10 Squadron wished to discuss the forthcoming painting of a VC10. They felt Hong Kong runway was the perfect setting for the aircraft as they wanted it taking off from the airfield, and Hong Kong's runway, stretching out into the bay, could be recognised immediately. But at intervals there is a clamp down on movements of civilians with the Armed Forces, or Service personnel, their reasons for travelling had to be justified. This was for both the expenses involved, and legitimate reasons given if there were 'Questions in the House,' and often involved those with the talent for taking part in sporting fixtures. On this occasion the Director of Public Relations Air Commodore Paddy Hine MBIM, turned down my flight that the Mess had requested. The Squadron were particularly disappointed, so was I, for they wanted their aircraft to be well represented. Much discussion followed including the information that they flew to Washington DC. Here I was extremely fortunate for earlier that year I had joined a close friend Andrew Ashenden for an unforgettable holiday in the States - we started in San Francisco, drove to Las Vegas (not my scene!) on to stay at the Grand Canyon out of season which was utterly peaceful and with snow round the rim made it wonderfully romantic and picturesque, then went on to Los

Angeles, from where we flew to New York for two days, Andrew stayed to work, and I went down to Washington for twenty-four hours - and quite by chance to finish my film, I had taken photographs of the distinctive dished roof of the airport as we taxied out for take off, and there was my material! The Squadron fully approved of the idea, so the painting showed the VC10 taking off from Washington.

Amongst several visits to Brize Norton airfield watching the VC10 taking off from the runway, on being driven round the perimeter track, we had to stop at the lights as an aircraft was coming in to land. It proved to be Concorde! Some of the civilian pilots were training, flying a circuit, and what an exquisite sight, Concorde almost stood up and begged as she approached the start of the runway, famous nose dipped, and to see her so close she was amazingly spectacular. What a bonus! With the VC10 painting completed, it was hung in the Ladies Room, and some time later when Princess Anne made an official visit, a beautiful display of flowers stood beneath the painting with an exceptionally tall apricot gladioli sticking straight up in front of the nose of the aircraft!

Brize Norton were heading for taking over as the R.A.F. Station with the largest collection of Douglas paintings, for the next to be commissioned from there was of the Argosy. DAN AIR, or 'Dan Dare' as the R.A.F. called the airline, flew me out to Gibraltar as the Argosy was used for checking the radar, flying low along the runway, and with the Rock of Gibraltar as a background, I was to go and get the material. At Luton airport, apart from the flight number, I had no ticket or papers whatsoever, but there were no problems, all arrangements had been made for me. What a compact and strange set up greeted me in Gib, the pan and runway, the main road going straight across this, and towering above it, the Rock, familiar from books and post-cards. I made my way to the Officers' Mess where I was to stay, a typical white painted building, paved patio outside with the sea lapping against the surrounding wall, overlooking Gibraltar bay.

The ETA of the Argosy was delayed until early evening, so taking courage in both hands, I joined everybody in the bar. I caused quite a stir! I was simply, female! Various people came and talked, one man a trifle tight insisting that I spend the entire evening with him, but I was waiting for the Argosy crew, aware I'd look pretty stupid if they preferred to be without me! Eventually they landed, Squadron Leader John Robinson 'the boss,' Dick and a couple of Petes! I was in their company for the whole of my visit and what company it was! I discovered I was officially, 'One female member of Argosy crew of Officer Status'! Again, laughter and stories, soft Mediterranean breezes, delicious food in the evenings in the Spinning Wheel, and with imported food, the tinned milk in tea or coffee that I remembered from Changi days. We went on to a 'thrash at the United Services Club' around midnight with dancing. With my love of this I didn't do badly with four partners! Pete had too much to drink that evening, fell asleep in the loo, and had to break OUT of the hall after it had closed, the description of his antics, hilarious! Much of the daytime was spent getting material of the Argosy as it flew the length of the runway.

The aircraft was the special radar and navigation aid calibration version. How was I to get the aircraft, person standing in the centre of the runway with theodolite, and the Rock of Gibraltar in one picture? Because of the height of the rock, the aircraft would be insignificantly small, so I felt it best to get all the material I could and sort it out later. As one of the crew I was told to report at the squash court early evening. I attempted to murmur that I'd never held a squash racquet in my life, but thankfully excuses were unacceptable! It was an order! I had been an atrocious tennis player, but found the lighter racket and faster game much more fun, and having been introduced to it, played for several years afterwards.

Sunday arrived, so did Panjo - a local - in Landrover, to take us up the Rock. He had the distinction of holding the record for driving a ten ton truck to the top in the shortest possible time! As we drove up the narrow, twisty roads, I wondered how! Access to the radar installations, therefore the very top of the Rock was reasonable for this particular crew, and the wretched policeman at the picket post would probably have been lynched had he not accepted me as aircraft crew! Looking dazed, he was heard to plead,

"You won't be more than half an hour will you?" And what a view! The runway and buildings directly down below were obvious from a sign reading, '1,300 feet to sickbay, 1,300 miles to London'! The Mess stood out; the bay with Royal Navy ships, yachts and smaller craft, Spanish mainland and the border with Spain. The British blow a bugle at dawn and dusk, and the Spanish, not to be outdone have something that sounds like a badly-in-need-of-practise dance band which makes a hideous racket on their side of the perimeter fence, about the same times each day! Weather was perfect, we had a sheer drop on three sides, and on the other several humps of rock stretching in line away from us like vast, craggy dorsal fins rising up from the ocean. Parts of these were water catchment slopes. Tangier could just be glimpsed through the mists of distance. Rock plants were tucked into folds of rock, pretty, delicate, crouched against the wind. On the way down we saw the guns, now a tourist attraction. The caves, originally storage for ammunition, held bats. These were the Schreiber's bat or Schreiber's long-fingered bat which have very long wings that fold back on themselves when the bat is roosting. Gibraltar has no natural predators such as foxes, but the yellow legged gulls have become too numerous, often forcing birds of prey down into the sea, so there is a rescue centre for these. The area is a staging post for many birds migrating south to North Africa. Towards the bottom of the Rock, houses were crammed together, typically Mediterranean, the colour of faded unbleached cotton, narrow streets with washing hanging out from windows to catch the breeze, steep steps linking the houses.

The following morning I was still struggling with thoughts as to how to achieve this impossible picture, the Argosy doing a circuit of the Rock, then flying low and level along the runway. It was infuriating, for weather clouded over and conditions meant I would have to get more material of the aircraft back at Brize Norton, but had all I needed on Gibraltar. I flew with the crew and it was while we were in the aircraft waiting for take off, that we heard about the two jumbo jets which had just collided in Tenerife. Inevitably much discussion followed. I stood behind the boss's seat, seeing Gibraltar from the air as we avoided flying in Spanish airspace which gave rather a strange pattern to our descent. Aircraft travelling from Gibraltar to Spain must fly via Tangier between the two, and there were endless stories of aircraft running low on fuel. Sitting in on the meteorological and crew briefing later, they were working out whether they could make England with strong head winds and full fuel load. The decision was probably Brize Norton, if not, St. Mawgan, Cornwall. They left ahead of me, I watched from the Mess. I was told later I had been seen hiding behind my camera! Although my flight had been cleared with Dan Air, they managed to find several problems, and it seemed much easier to fly out to Gib, than to get home again! The painting proved a pig to do with all the windows in the buildings, I was unable to show the very top of the Rock and do the Argosy justice, but the painting now hangs in the Officers' Mess at Brize Norton, and like the others, is three foot by four.

It was during many of these flights that I wrote my children's stories. In 1966 I had submitted several short stories for little children to Dean & Son Ltd. Many were accepted, 'Squirrel Secrets' was the first to be published in the Lucie Attwell Annual, others in the, 'Little Ones' Reader' Series - groups of short stories, each group a separate book under a different title - I wrote them annually. Deans were unwilling to publish more of mine than from other authors in the Lucie Attwell Annual, but got round this by printing some in my true name, others under the pseudonym Eliza Stopford - a shortened version of my mother's second name Elizabeth, and my own. On the death of Mabel Lucie Attwell in 1964, her married daughter, Peggy Wickham had taken on the artwork for the annual, illustrating it in a similar style to her mother and under the same name. I acquired the knack of writing for an artist, perhaps giving a description of a garment worn by an animal or soft toy character, with no mention of colour or pattern, leaving full scope for Peggy's imaginative illustrations which she thoroughly appreciated, and with pressure from her, in 1973 Deans produced my stories only in the Lucie Attwell Annual. The same went for the following year. Peggy contacted cancer soon after this, too ill to work on any more annuals, 1974 being the last to be published, and she died on 30th November 1978. She had two sons, now producing some of the original drawings as greetings cards, and figurines, and the illustrations of both Mabel Lucie Attwell and her daughter Peggy are still well remembered for their chubby, smiling, dimpled children, and their shiny, strap shoes.

It took me a while to get into the swing of writing for such small children, and I always threw the first two stories into the waste paper basket, for these merely launched me into the right frame of mind. Always on the look out for new ideas, I had written a story about No.1 Elf Harrier Squadron with the password of Kokkinelli and their various adventures, and although it was accepted by Dean & Son., to my knowledge it was never printed. Perhaps it was just as well! I had over seventy stories published, often using the names of children I knew, and those of adult friends who were reduced to the age of the young readers for the sake of the story!

CHAPTER 11

FROM ROYALTY TO ROCKING HORSES!

1977 - the year of the Silver Jubilee: for the Guild of Aviation Artists Annual Exhibition, I'd displayed a painting of The Queen and Duke of Edinburgh, called Royal Departure. I had been with the Press at Heathrow to see them boarding a VC10 for an overseas visit, and as the Royal pair walked past, the Queen did the equivalent of 'looking me up and down,' for I was the only woman. In the exhibition catalogue I was delighted to see a photograph of the painting.

Celebrations for the Silver Jubilee took place all over the country, especially by the Armed Forces, and I was extremely fortunate in having a Press Pass for the Review of the Fleet at Spithead. Seven miles of warships and other vessels numbering more than a hundred and seventy in all and over thirty thousand men, to be reviewed by The Queen from the Royal Yacht Britannia. The date - 28th June. The ships included the 43,000 ton HMS Ark Royal, nuclear-powered Submarines, the first two of the new type 42 class Destroyers, HMS Sheffield and HMS Birmingham, and the only ship to have been present at the 1953 Coronation Review, the deep diving vessel HMS Reclaim. The Merchant Navy was strongly represented, and the largest ship was the 277,749 ton BP supertanker British Respect. Organisations with close links with the Navy were present too, Royal National Life Boats, and H.M. Coastguards. An impressive list to say the least! Ships from seventeen other countries were there from the Navies of Commonwealth, NATO, CENTO, and EEC nations.

Mundane things like parking would prove impossible, so I went by train to Portsmouth, starting with the rehearsal the day before. It was when I was leaving that evening an amusing event happened, when I literally nearly bumped into The Queen! The Press needed to get their copy to the editors straight away, and when they knew I was returning to London for the night, I became a courier for one of the big national daily papers, given the money for a taxi to my flat when I reached London, but going via their Fleet Street office. Departing immediately, when I reached the railway station in Portsmouth, I discovered The Queen and Duke of Edinburgh were due to arrive by train at any moment, therefore the route up to the station was packed with crowds behind barriers, through which I was supposed to hurry! Not a hope! If I waited, I would almost certainly miss my train, and delay the speedy delivery to Fleet Street. I decided to brazen it out, and going directly to one of the Police I explained my urgency, and was told to walk up the road which was empty and cleared of people, down which the royal car would be driven, but to 'mind' as the Royal Family were arriving any moment! I scampered up the hilly entrance to the station, giggling to myself at the situation with the crowds on either side, the odd cheerful remark shouted at me, and was just about to go through the doors into the station when suddenly I was faced with the Royal Family about to come through the same doors towards me, so I melted back against the wall outside, … and had the best possible position from which to see them!

The day of the Review, the Press had been asked to gather at H.M.S. Vernon, where we were given a Press release. Because of Spithead's unique sheltered anchorage with access to the sea at both ends, fleets have gathered there for more than two thousand years. Roman ships from Portchester and Chichester, then later Alfred the Great's war vessels collected before leaving to fight the Danes. Queen Elizabeth I, in 1582 reviewed a Squadron at Spithead, and it is believed this was the first time yards were manned and salutes fired. In the time of George III's visit to Spithead, the Admirals and Captains wore the full dress uniform of gold braided tricorn hats worn over neat tie-wigs, a long kerseymore waist coat and fluttering lace edged sleeves beneath gold-frogged dark blue coat, white knee breeches, white silk stockings and silver buckled shoes. How wonderfully picturesque! 1853 brought about the first gathering of steam warships, including the first screw ships as well as paddlers. Reviews took place not just for royalty, but often in honour of overseas visitors such as in 1867 for the Sultan of Turkey accompanied by Queen Victoria and the Viceroy of Egypt. But on 23rd July 1887, a Naval Review concluded celebrations of Queen Victoria's Golden Jubilee, and now, 1977, I was about to witness the Fleet Review for the Silver Jubilee of Queen Elizabeth II.

A Gazelle helicopter flight over all the ships brought home to me the enormous scale of such a gathering. It was hugely impressive. What a shame that my father had died a few years before. He would have loved hearing about everything and talking about it, and part of me felt empty that I was unable to share it with him.

Joining members of the Press in one of the harbour craft, I was taken out to R.F.A. Engadine. She was the first helicopter support ship of the Royal Fleet Auxiliary Service and specially designed to meet the requirements of Naval training authorities in the flying, handling and maintenance of helicopters. R.F.A. Engadine did not carry her own flight, but the hangar on board was capable of accommodating four Wessex and two Wasp or two Sea King helicopters, and also had stowage for equipment and stores. In training, it was necessary for students to practice landing a helicopter on board ship, and they also took part in extended exercises against modern Submarines, and R.F.A. Engadine was essential for both.

We were given lunch on board, presented with such a magnificent spread, a real banquet complete with hog's head, that several of the Press photographers recorded it! Drinks had to be paid for.

The Review took place during the afternoon with several of the Royal Family on board the Royal Yacht Britannia, and this vessel was accompanied by the Destroyer H.M.S. Birmingham, R.F.A. Engadine being the third ship as this trio sailed between the lines of ships. It was an immensely moving sight, awe inspiring, the light on the water adding a wonderful silver sparkle to a glittering event. Finally there was a fly-past of Naval aircraft. As usual, people seemed to have been fantastic, and on board R.F.A. Engadine sailing between the many ships, I became lost in thought of how incredibly fortunate I was to be there. Once again I felt an enormous pride in being British. My thoughts went to my father. He had been Chaplain to the boy's training ships from 1926 to 1931, the Warspite, Worcester, Arethusa and Cornwall, and Chaplain to the Missions to Seamen. His brother, my uncle, Commander Stopford C. Douglas R.N. had served as second in command on H.M. Sloop, Alert, was later in command of H.M.S. Onyx and the First Submarine Flotilla and in command of a "Q" ship, followed by being appointed to the staff of Admiral Sir Lewis Bayley who was at Queenstown in command of the combined British and American fleet, and finally he became Deputy Chief Inspector of the Life-boat Service. I was on board a ship at Spithead; my uncle had been buried here. The description of his funeral in September 1928 makes interesting reading:-

'In accordance with Douglas's own wish, he was buried at sea from a Life-boat. The coffin, covered by the Union Jack, and carrying his sword and cap, was taken to Ryde Parish Church. Eight Life-boatmen in jerseys and life-belts carried his medals on a cushion. After the first part of the funeral service had been read ... . the coffin was taken on board the Yarmouth Motor Life-boat, which, with the Bembridge Motor Life-boat in attendance, proceeded, in perfectly cloudless weather, through Spithead. The battleships Benbow and Renown, and the Aircraft Carrier Argus, dipped their colours in honour of the dead as the Life-boats passed, and the crews stood to attention. The Committal Service was read by the Rev. E.C.Douglas (my father), and the body was committed to the deep about four miles S.E. by S. of Bembridge Point. Flowers were strewn on the sea, and a green flare, the Life-boat signal signifying 'All safe, coming home' was burnt.'

Now, many years later I too was at sea, celebrating the 1977 Silver Jubilee.

I painted several pictures of the event, the choice governed by my using the best material I had gathered. The Frigate Hardy was one; a canvas of the submarine H.M.S. Superb went to the Royal Navy Submarine Museum. As a result of a painting of R.F.A. Tidespring, I was sent a superb photograph of her sailing under the Golden Gate Bridge, and a large oil of H.M.S. Birmingham escorting the Royal Yacht now hangs in Birmingham at the Nautical Club. Without doubt, the Silver Jubilee Fleet Review had been a momentous occasion.

The Royal Jubilee Review of the Royal Air Force took place at R.A.F. Finningley at the end of July. Perhaps it was wrong of me to compare this alongside the Fleet Review, but to state the obvious, firstly comparisons are odious, secondly the noise level of a ship under way and aircraft overhead are vastly different, and thirdly it is hardly of vital importance whether the Press are fed or not! As regards the R.A.F., I had taken the Press information that 'refreshments would be provided,' literally. However during the lunch period, by the time I got to the refreshments reasonably early on, all sandwiches had been finished and no more were forthcoming! Drink was free of charge! The superb menu provided on board H.M.S. Engadine had set a standard which had rubbed off on the way people behaved, with the resulting excellent attitude and good manners. Those wanting drink, paid for it. The R.A.F. seemed to be the reverse. Many of the Press were hungry and irritable, and like myself had driven some considerable distance and been on the move for many hours in order to reach Finningley well before dawn. With drink free, several people were well 'under the influence,' and the whole day left me dispirited, and disillusioned. Perhaps I was behaving like a spoilt brat to have such thoughts, but although I got some flying material, I found the day had failed to stir my creativity and imagination for painting, and none of it was recorded on canvas by me. For a multitude of reasons, it was an utter anti-climax.

At one of the past Guild of Aviation Artists exhibitions, I had heard members talking of Contra deals. My family had been in Australia since 1976, and with these in mind, I worked on an oil of a Singapore Airlines Concorde on its first arrival in Singapore. I was not at the event so it was done deliberately from imagination. with Concorde on the tarmac and a celebration lion dance in the foreground. Having completed it I approached Singapore Airlines, and succeeded in exchanging the painting for a free flight as far as Singapore. A business-like man, I was informed by a friend, would probably have clinched a deal for an extended return flight through to Sydney, but I found that sort of thing difficult to pull off, and felt lucky to have succeeded atall! The painting was exhibited in London at the next Guild exhibition, marked NFS.

And so to rocking horses! The Trade Toy Fair took place at Earl's Court that year, and John and Mary Labouchere - I had known John since we were about ten - had a stand for their beautiful, traditional, yet glass fibre rocking horses, based on an original Victorian horse. John asked me if I would repaint the canvas 'stand' or backdrop. I worked on four enormous canvas sections using emulsion paints, and changed the previous backdrop of a toy shop interior, to a town that could have been in a Western film. The whole canvas became two walls of the corner stand, was eight foot high, and twenty-four foot long. At the end of a month's work I had the saloon, the bank, Mary's hats coats & corsettes, and a drugstore! It was battened on to wooden rollers, looked impressive when installed on site, but even better with the various rocking horses in front of it. I joined John and Mary doing duty on the stand, and we had a hilarious time as he had produced a remote controlled horse on wheels, with doll rider looking extremely realistic in breeches, jacket and riding hat. Mary and I would put the horse in the middle of one of the aisles, John took the controls to the balcony floor above, from where he could look down into the centre and control the horse, which to complete the humour, had an old fashioned Klaxon horn cleverly concealed on it! John would line the horse up behind somebody, sound the horn making them turn to see where the extraordinary noise was coming from, and understandably, nobody expected a mobile horse, even less one that formed a strong attachment to a total stranger and then followed them! Unobserved we watched the reaction, some people were very amused and enchanted by it yet unable to see from where it was being controlled, while others became acutely embarrassed, walking hurridly on with the little rocker keeping up with them quite effortlessly! On the sidelines we were helpless with laughter! Not surprisingly, the week's Trade Toy Fair passed very happily, and at night those working on the rocking horse stand, dossed down in sleeping bags on my sitting-room floor.

To return briefly to my previous visit to Cyprus, while there I had been commissioned for a painting of a Lightning by a pilot's wife, as a present for her husband. Distressingly, he was killed when his aircraft crashed. The painting was still requested, and as his widow lived some way from me I was given an introduction to Tim Gauvain, also an R.A.F. pilot, and his wife Sandy, who would take the painting up north and be the go-between, and they came to play an important part in my art life.

They introduced me to Michael and Lell Popoff who lived near Grimsby. I travelled up to Lincolnshire to stay with them for a commission. Michael farmed, owned a Zlin - a small aerobatic aircraft - and wanted a painting of it. I spent the most amazing week-end with them, Michael glancing at the sky and saying casually,

"I've got half an hour to spare. We'll go up and have a look at Grimsby!" The Zlin was parked just beyond the farm buildings. I was seated behind Michael, had never been in such a small aircraft before, was immensely excited and had my eyes opened to what flying is really about. During these sorties I got the background of Grimsby harbour that Michael wanted. The material of the Zlin itself was acquired by my having a flight in another light aircraft, while Michael flew alongside banking and turning for me. I had a wonderful time, several flights with him, even seeing swallows flying level with us and much higher than I expected, and as a thank you to them, reproduced as a small painting, a tiny sepia photograph of Michael's father giving a Cossack performance on horseback. The old photograph had been taken of him riding at a public display, leaning over from the saddle at full gallop to pick up a handkerchief from the ground. Lell knew of the treasured old photograph, I painted it in the correct colouring but felt it would be most effective if I left out the crowd of onlookers, so didn't paint any background whatsoever, leaving the canvas white. Michael knew nothing of it until he came to collect the Zlin painting, and at sight of the unexpected gift he was so moved, he cried. It gave enormous pleasure, and later became one of a pair when I matched it with a commission of his mother doing dressage on a magnificent stallion, white as snow and very showy.

David Shepherd, who had given me such valuable help and encouragement long before I ever imagined I would be painting aircraft, gave one of his wildlife and steam engine talks in Norwich and stayed with my mother and me for the night. We got home late that evening after his talk show, and when I ran through a selection of available food, David chose three boiled eggs! I remember the pleasure of that time at home, for the three of us talked into the small hours of the morning, much of it memories of childhood days during the end of the war.

I was soon on my travels again, taking up my Singapore Airlines contra-deal, and this time Australia beckoned early in 1979, and in order to justify both the expense and the distance, I flew to Darwin and went south by bus - a twenty hour drive or so - to Alice Springs, talking with the driver for much of the journey, learning all I could about the country. From 'the Alice,' I flew to Ayers Rock - they still had Dacotas in use - was a typical tourist, watched the movement of the sun changing the colours on the rock from brilliant rust-orange to deepest indigo. As was the fashion for those who were both fit and interested, I climbed it in the coolness of dawn, and once I had reached what I thought was the top, the rock became less steep, and I was amused and surprised to find a painted broken white line that led climbers along the undulating route to the very highest point. As it was identical to the white lines down the centre of a British main road, it seemed incongruous up there.

East of Alice Springs I spent a few nights with a charming family on a ranch in the shadow of the MacDonnell range of mountains at Ross River. Visiting Australia had not appealed to me very much, it was my family that drew me there, and I had been shocked to discover that I could travel around a thousand miles down the Stuart Highway to Alice Sprints with low, scrub trees either side of the road and no view or change of scene for literally hundreds of miles. But at Ross River the landscape was extremely picturesque and with stunning colours. I had chosen Ross River because I could go out on horseback while there, and even though the only other person to ride was a total beginner and curbed me, my mount, Ironbark was an ex Ringer's horse, responded to any aids immediately, and I was sent off on my own cantering along the side of the river with Ironbark neck-reining round scrubby bushes, responsive to the lightest of touch. It was sheer heaven! As children, one of our two ponies had been trained to neck rein, so it had become perfectly natural to me. I am not the bravest of riders, happiest on a horse I know well, but it was one of those truly magical times, and Ironbark and I were totally as one. I was in my element and loved every second of it!

We also had several drives into the bush in an old bus, walked long distances, and on one of these quenched our thirst by drinking with cupped hands from pools alive with wriggling tadpoles! Where there's life the water's safe to drink! We were surrounded by wildlife: beautiful large butterflies that danced and fluttered almost close enough to alight upon me, kangaroos and rock wallabys, and birds from the butcher bird - so named because they collect food in a larder - flocks of native green budgerigars, and the grey backed galah cockatoos with pink breasts, that seemed to fly in groups in formation, one moment all showing greyness, the next pink, reminding me of the Red Arrows! In the evenings Gill Green gave us talks on both the life of the Ringers on the cattle ranches, and Aborigines. He had such a fund of stories I inquired if anybody had written a book about the stockmen. He replied that he had collected all the material and wanted to do so, but had never got round to it. (Some months later I wrote and asked if I could return and work on a book with him. I had no reply, nor from following it up with a Christmas card. But I got a letter from him eventually saying that he had contacted Multiple Sclerosis and was very unwell. The news saddened me greatly. They were such a lovely family, and I had helped the teenage daughter with her painting, a subject she was taking for an exam, and in the few days I had stayed there, I had become very fond of them.)

Back at Alice Springs, with work in mind I got material of the Royal Flying Doctor Service, and saw two patients brought in to the base by air before being taken on to hospital. Both were Aborigine, collected from remote outback areas.

Continuing my journey by bus via Adelaide and the mining town of Broken Hill, I arrived in Sydney and saw the family at last, David, Sally, and the three children, Katya, Justyn and Mark.

My brother's work was making commercial films, plus an excellent documentary on garlic, and as I wanted to get material of Sydney harbour, bridge and opera house from the air, add a 'jumbo jet,' and attempt to secure a commission from Qantas, he had arranged a flight for me in one of the television channel helicopters. Being such a vast country, these are used often for filming news-worthy subjects. His secretary, also Sally by name, was to be included as my P.A.!

"What! You must be joking! I've never had one of those! What on earth is she expected to do?" She came, clipboard in hand! Whether our play acting fooled anybody I don't know, but at intervals, when given information, I would ask her to make a note of it, the pair of us playing our parts to the full! The scale of Sydney harbour was vast, it was wonderful to be seeing it from the air, the weather glorious, and totally unbelievable to be hovering there, requesting, and being given whatever angle I wished of the opera house and any other landmark. We must have been airborne for at least half an hour and with my P.A. politely doing what she was told, naturally it went straight to my head! My old Leica worked overtime, and confident I had got superb material, I got an interview and a commission from Qantas!

Back in London, as a result of my experiences 'down under' I was invited to do a radio broadcast with the British Forces Broadcasting Service, and also met Anne Howells who interviewed me for, 'Woman's Hour'.

I painted two large pictures, two foot by three, of a 747 'Jumbo jet' in flight, with Sydney opera house, the famous bridge, and much of the harbour shown below as the background. Qantas had a choice of which they wanted as their commission. I did not expect them to purchase both, but was interested in their discussion and recognition of the various buildings I had produced in the pictures; the painting they chose not to buy was turned down because since I had completed it, the Qantas building had been increased in height with an extra floor built, so the picture was inaccurate! Oh well! You can't win 'em all!

Happily, I painted a canvas of the Ross River area, the water reflecting the brilliant blue sky overhead, the sandy banks and soft grey-greens of the gum trees, the strong purple-dark shadows, and the red earth which was such a part of the red centre of Australia, all filling me with the utmost pleasures and memories.

CHAPTER 12

A CLOSE SHAVE AND A PHANTOM ARTIST!

R.A.F. Brize Norton commissioned a painting of an Andover, 115 Squadron, again for the Officers' Mess. The aircraft was the special radar and navigation aid calibration version, and had taken over from the Argosy, and the Squadron wanted it in flight, lined up for the runway. I thought it would be a more unusual painting to show the aircraft from behind with the runway ahead. Getting material of the Andover was fairly straight forward but great fun, with the Squadron pulling out all the stops to help, so they arranged a flight for me in the aircraft with another Andover flying ahead of us. With my superb view from the flight deck, looking out ahead, the sun was shining on one side of the fuselage of the Andover in front and slightly below us, casting perfect shadows that would allow me to show the shape of the aircraft. It proved a successful, unusual and rewarding sortie.

As background they wanted the airfield of Machrihanish, Scotland. Again we got airborne in the Andover and flew north to Machrihanish. The weather refused to oblige with sun, it was grey and misty and not the conditions in which to achieve good photography, especially from a flight deck. Cambeltown was in the foreground, the runway in the distance, and some-what distraught at the worsening murky conditions, quickly I got all the details I could before the weather closed in and we headed back for Brize Norton. As we flew south, fog formed below us, somebody had tucked up the country in a cotton wool blanket for the night, taking care not to smother all spires and towers above a certain height, leaving these peeping up through the fluffy quilt. Brize Norton closed before we got there, so we headed away from it, flying north-west to one of the few airfields still free of fog, on the Isle of Anglesey.

The place was extremely busy. Expecting 'one female crew member,' R.A.F. Valley had kept the last room in the Officers' Mess available which happened to be in the men's quarters. The rest of the crew had been booked into a local hotel, and we were all together as these arrangements were given to us. At the same time, as I was to stay in the Mess I was handed the normal kit issue for crew members who have been diverted, for naturally none of us had anything with us for an overnight stop. On being handed the plastic box, intrigued I opened it straight away, to find a towel .... a razor and shaving cream! The ribald remarks and laughter I received from the crew were unrepeatable, but at least amongst all the teasing one of us had what was needed, they leapt at the chance of razor and shaving cream, disappearing triumphantly to the hotel with it, as having been allocated accommodation in the town, none of them would have a diversion kit. I returned it all next morning as expected, and as I handed it in solemnly, the razor blunt and every bit of shaving cream used up, I and the crew couldn't wait to see the expressions on the faces of the orderlies! I had been woken around 5.30a.m. with a very welcome cup of tea and,

"Morning sir!" I replied in my softest, most feminine voice,

"Thank you very much," and imagined him doing a sleepy double-take half way along the passage as it dawned on him that the voice had been unmistakenly female, AND in the men's living quarters! Out by the aircraft dawn was breaking, the sun attempting to peep through nature's net curtains, a magical misty morning, one for walking with a dog across grass and leaving a trail of dew drenched footprints, or being down by a river with the mists hanging over the water when all would be silent ... but R.A.F. Valley reverberated with noise like an air show, as the many aircraft which had diverted there roared away to their scattered destinations.

The canvas commissioned was three feet by four, and was officially handed over to the Officers' Mess at a drinks party put on for the occasion, the Squadron more than satisfied with the painting. Later, a photograph of it was published in a book called, 'Brace by Wire to Fly-by-Wire, 75 years of the Royal Air Force 1918 - 1993'.

Having slept in the men's quarters at R.A.F. Valley, I deteriorated further for my next commission, and was reduced to a mere ghostly figment of the imagination, when I received a letter which began, 'Dear Phantom Artist,' ... The upshot of this delightful correspondence was a flight to Germany, to R.A.F. Wildenrath to join Tim and Sandy Gauvain, Tim being the boss of 19 Squadron, flying ... Phantoms. He had asked for a painting of the aircraft taking off, and once again I stood at the side of the runway with the ground literally vibrating as the aircraft thundered past. I was deafened by it, could see the afterburn glowing, and felt exhilarated by my closeness to such a noisy subject, and the smell of the fuel as the aircraft punched its way into the distance. The painting was to depict the aircraft fully armed, and I had temporary Station Passes in order to see all I needed including the weapons. The R.A.F. photographer took some pictures of me sketching the nose wheel of the Phantom, then had to re-do these, as classified material had been included in the first photographs.

Recently I was asked what I felt about painting pictures of aircraft and weapons that are built to destroy, to be used in war. I found it a difficult question. Obviously the perfect scenario is that they are never used for the purpose for which they are designed. To be in the unique position of watching our Armed Forces at work is enormously special to me, and with this involvement I feel immensely proud and in awe, and a kind of reverential fear for both man and machine.

I very much enjoyed staying with the Gauvains, and Sandy, as 'Female Voice', was writing articles for Zulu magazine, and published a two page spread on my paintings, illustrated with photographs, and really 'did me proud!' I met men from both Phantom Squadrons, and found it fascinating that each group had a different character, one giving the impression of being a trifle laid back and rowdy, Tim's appearing more dedicated, quieter and more dignified. Was this the influence of each boss or pure chance?

Tim was an exceptionally good organist, and through this link I was introduced to Ray Hubble, the Station Padre, who surprised me by asking whether I would undertake to design a stained glass window for the Forces church. He felt I was an appropriate person to approach as they wanted both Spitfire and Phantom aircraft worked into the layout. It would be installed at the side of the nave, the design would be in the centre (two smaller clear glass windows on either side,) and was about ten foot high and three foot wide, the top being slightly arched. It was to be made in Germany by Herr Peter Thomas. So, when I returned home, there began a series of letters from Tim and Sandy starting, 'Dear Phantom Artist,' signing themselves Hildegarde and Klaus, and correspondence from Ray with details of measurements for the window. The latter were horribly confusing. Reference to light measurements and the number and size of horizontal bars, and figures galore, sped to and fro. My father, when Rector of Tittleshall in Norfolk, had a window reinstated in St. Mary's Church by the renowned firm of King, in Norwich, so I visited them and discussed my window. If anything this made the confusion even worse, for I was paddling in a pool which had great depths to it, and probably shouldn't have got my feet wet in the first place!

To produce the cartoon (not unlike a dress pattern) was a lengthy, absorbing challenge! I was told it had to be done on paper to the exact size of the window and in black and white only, with a second smaller version to show the colours. I incorporated the dove of the Holy Spirit towards the top right-hand side of the window, designing it so that both wings were outstretched, beak down on to the breast in the centre. I couldn't do the more traditional position, because it would have ended up looking like a tail chase with the Spitfire, which was slightly lower and towards the left. Material for the dove was no problem, for at the time my family kept a variety of the most beautiful true fantail pigeons, all prepared to pose for their favourite artist! Apart from the dove, none of the symbols to be included in the design had any religious significance, so from the dove, I put thicker leads horizontally and vertically, forming the cross of a crucifix, not obviously so, but to be noticed if bored with a sermon! Slightly above centre was the Station crest. Towards the bottom stood a Phantom aircraft outside a HAS (hardened aircraft shelter,) with navigator in the back seat, pilot standing by the nose of the aircraft, and aircrew in attendance. At the very bottom was an oblong horizontal shape into which would be put the wording, 'In memory of the few'. The whole design was linked up with a random pattern of horizontal and vertical lines giving shapes of squares or oblongs, a few with coloured glass, most of the background being clear handmade glass. I had learnt at King's that these shapes, being irregular in size, would blend into the background and emphasize the main symbols. Behind the HAS I put some shapes of soft grey clouds, grass of pale green in front of it. With the window being made in Germany, and Ray on the spot, I suggested that he see the pieces of glass and therefore the colouring, and check that he was happy with it, before the whole thing was leaded together, but with Herr Thomas working some way from Wildenrath, I don't think this happened. All correspondence between Herr Thomas and myself was in German, and as I didn't speak the language, I had invaluable assistance from a German couple, Hermann and Brigitte Treutler, who lived in the same village in Norfolk as my mother, and who were a great help with translation.

The Ministry of Defence flew me over to Germany for the dedication, the Bishop being on the same aircraft. Well before the ceremony Ray took me proudly into the church to show me the window, obviously thrilled with it! As we walked up the path, I wondered how I would feel about it. At sight of it I was horrified and appalled! It was awful! I couldn't believe it! For one thing the clouds behind the Phantom looked like huge heavy boulders, the grass in front was so dark it was almost black, and the colouring of the camaflage on the aircraft was way out on the colours I had given, which should have been copied. The thickened lead for the cross was missing due to it having been made the same thickness as the rest, one of the oblong shapes I had put in colour was installed in clear glass, and the 'W' at the end of the word 'few' was much heavier than the rest of the letters. I could have wept! I felt deeply ashamed and disappointed, inwardly questioning whether a different design on my part would have looked better, or whether ...

For once I kept quiet! This was obviously the best thing I could have done, for the window was made, installed and about to be dedicated. Nothing could change it now. Several hours later when I perhaps unwisely, mentioned my views privately to Tim - thankfully played down, a very mild version of what I'd felt - he was both surprised and perhaps a little hurt, and rounded on me sharply telling me that I shouldn't be so critical of myself! The point was everybody loved it, and there was just total delight all round. I had praise from every direction, inwardly miserable as I felt that in no way was it justified. When people said,

"You must be terribly proud," I replied,

"Well everybody seems enormously pleased which is very rewarding."

The window was unveiled by Air Marshal Sir Peter Terry, Commander-in-Chief of Royal Air Force, Germany, and dedicated by The Right Reverend G.S.Snell, Bishop to H.M. Forces. That evening I had the privilege of watching the ceremony of Beating Retreat at Rheindahlen for The Queen's birthday, starting with a fly-past, fanfare by the ceremonial trumpets of the 1st Battalion of the Royal Welch Fusiliers, display by the Fusiliers and Massed Bands of R.A.F. Germany, and bringing the day to a wonderful and memorable end, a dinner party with Sir Peter and Lady Terry and guests. (As I write, I understand Wildenrath will close as an R.A.F. Station, and there are plans that the window will be brought back to the U.K. and installed again somewhere suitable.)

Our British weather is full of surprises, and during the night of 29th March 1980, winds of over fifty-five knots swept the North Sea, conditions of near freezing temperatures and thirty foot waves, and at dawn the country awoke to the horrifying news that an oil rig, the Alexander Kielland, had collapsed in the Ekofisk area, in the worst oil rig disaster ever, with the loss of well over a hundred lives. Over forty craft of all kinds, British, Dutch, German, Danish and Norwegian, aided air support and searched the area for those who survived that terrible night. There were incidents of extreme bravery, including Flight Sergeant Mike Yarwood with the Search and Rescue Helicopter from R.A.F. Boulmer, who twice jumped into the waves to pull somebody to safety. On one occasion he had to detach himself from the line and swim to a boat, staying until the helicopter had guided a rescue ship to its aid. As a tribute I decided to do a painting.

Collecting the material and piecing it together was much like working on a jig-saw puzzle. The R.A.F. SAR Squadron were a great help. In order to have the sea in the picture beneath the helicopter, I needed to paint the Sea-king from slightly above, looking down on it. Dick Jeeves, a superb photographer with Eastern Counties Newspapers came with me on a flight in the SAR helicopter based at R.A.F. Coltishall, as he felt my mission was worth reporting in the local newspapers. Soon after we got airborne, some of the electrics failed and we returned to Coltishall immediately, but at the second attempt, we headed out to the Norfolk coast near Cromer.

Here they winched me down on to the top of the cliffs so that I could get photographs of the helicopter flying along the beach slightly below me. There was definitely a funny side to this. The winchman, Flight Sergeant Melvyn Ward was with me, and although I was to be winched down on to dry land, for the flight I had been kitted out in an immersion suit, an all-in-one garment with boots attached, in theory the neck seal fitting tightly. It would have been fine for a large six foot man, but at five foot two and slightly built, the rubber seal had little connection with my neck, and even two pairs of socks failed to fill the void inside the boots! These must have been at least a size ten! It was not until I was hanging from the winch line that I began to see the comical side, for the weight of the boots took them down away from my feet which dangled somewhere around the knee area, and the huge boots hit the ground some considerable time before I did! Having attempted to gain slight control of my balance, I clumped and stumbled around the top of the cliff in my mammoth feet, and one way or another succeeded in taking a series of photographs of the chopper, Mel passing on to the pilot my requests for the desired angle and height that I needed for the painting. The few onlookers who had gathered to watch, must have been perplexed why one of the crew appeared to be an undisciplined sozzled achoholic! I was strongly aware how a man on the moon might behave, and once I lost all self-restraint and fell, rolling down a slight incline and covered in sand until the ground levelled out. It was almost impossible, and hilarious! Mel, chortling over my absurd behaviour, grabbed several folds of material and hoicked me upright. Dick Jeeves had got some 'worm's eye' photographs of my coming down the winch wire, and some 'bird's eye' ones of my being winched up, all of which appeared in the newspapers under, 'An aerial close-up for artist Penelope's next work.' It was a very strange sensation while Dick was being winched up, to be immediately beneath the helicopter as it hovered above me while I waited for my turn. Sand was blown everywhere but directly below the body of the helicopter I was in a sheltered pocket. Later, Mel Ward was again in the newspapers as he was given the bravery award of the Air Force Cross for helping to save thirty-two lives from a burning tanker. The crew of the ship had been foreign, but Mel had volunteered to be lowered on to the deck of the ship despite the hazards of fire, smoke, burning oil and gale force winds, had calmed and organised the rescue of the crew, some of whom were lifted to safety to the helicopter, others picked up from the ship's lifeboat by a nearby rig support vessel.

The second piece of the jig-saw involved visiting the oil rig support ship when it docked at the quay in Great Yarmouth. She was helping to find survivors that night, and I wanted to know where the lights on the vessel were placed and the angle, therefore what area of the sea would have been picked out by them. Thirdly I joined the crew on board an R.A.F. boat at dusk, and out at sea we met up with the Sea-King as I needed to watch the aircraft at night with its lights on. Standing in the bows in my orange oil skins, (my sailing clothing,) the chopper crew apparantly gave me the nick-name, 'The Orange Captain'! The crew of the R.A.F. boat were a great bunch, and I took the helm for part of the way back, another new experience, and fascinating to try and judge how the boat would react and try to keep on a steady course towards the distant lights of Lowestoft. The painting was completed, and showed part of one of the severed oil rig legs floating on the surface, the oil rig support ship with its lights catching the Sea-King, and down below, two men in the heavy seas illuminated by the helicopter and about to be winched to safety. I had never painted a night-time scene, and most of the canvas was literally as black as night, giving greater significance to the lights on both helicopter and ship, and the area illuminated by them.

After the painting was finished, 'Pebble Mill,' the television programme from Birmingham, asked me to join them for one of their mid-day programmes when they covered the story of the oil rig disaster and the rescues by the crew of the Sea-King. The helicopter was flown to the grounds of the Pebble Mill studios, Mike Yarwood and the crew were winched down, and were interviewed during the programme. My painting was shown as an artist's impression of the appalling conditions in which they had worked. Bob Langley, the interviewer, was convinced he would forget my name when he showed the painting - 20 × 30 inches - to give me the credit for it, and hastily referred to a piece of paper clutched in the palm of his hand! I had prints made of the picture, something I had never tried before. It was a total misjudgment that anybody would wish to be reminded of such a tragic event. Disasters don't sell. Financially it hit me hard and taught me a lesson. I exhibited the painting at the Guild of Aviation Artist's annual exhibition, and to my delight, found the story of my getting the material for the painting written up in the Peterborough article of the Daily Telegraph. With over two hundred paintings hanging in the exhibition from which to choose, being singled out as one of only two paintings mentioned was a delightful surprise. Years later, when I met and became friends with Jane Birkett, I discovered her brother, was, Peterborough!

The Headquarters of No.ll Group was based at R.A.F. Bentley Priory, Middlesex, one of the main buildings had been emptied of contents in order for the floor to be treated, and had gone up in flames. As the Station had featured largely during the Battle of Britain, it was in the process of being rebuilt when I was commissioned to do a painting of it for the Officers' Mess there. Unknown to the C.O. Air Vice Marshal Peter Latham, a second painting of the same subject was to be presented to him. Material had to be partly from old photographs, as with restoration work under way, much of the building was covered in tarpaulins. The Station was well known for the magnificent cedar tree close to the buildings on either side of which was a Spitfire and Hurricane. It was a splendidly calm and peaceful subject, and I spent many an hour seated on my stool in the dappled sunlight cast by the cedar, painting. I was taken down to the 'hole', the area of safety under several feet of concrete, from where the Battle of Britain had been controlled. This had often been reproduced for scenes in war-time films, so looked familiar. I was asked to write some words backwards on a Perspex wall, as the WAAFs would have done during the war, words that would be read the correct way round by the 'top brass' seated the other side of the huge map of Great Britain, round which WAAF's would work, showing by models the position of each Squadron at that moment. I found this backward writing remarkably easy, though many did not - presumably just the way my grey matter was distributed! The Mess painting, two foot by three, was being presented to the Officers' Mess by Frank Hayter who was a Vice President of the Guild of Aviation Artists, and unveiled by Sir Peter Gadsden, Lord Mayor of London. It was a black tie affair to include dinner, and a very grand evening. I bought a new dress in a blue-green crepe, had my shoulder length hair done for the occasion, and then panicked as Yvonne Bonham who was invited as representing the Guild, got very late collecting me in London, murmuring,

"I wonder what the best route is?" and I thought we'd never get there in time. However by the skin of our teeth, we made it, just! What an evening it proved to be! I felt a glorious mixture of elation at my achievement and self-effacement, the painting was received with great delight by all, and Peter Latham and his wife were enormously pleased with their surprise presentation of the second canvas. The two paintings were worked from slightly different angles.

Painting is usually very solitary work, but an official reception for the hand-over of a picture made it very, very special, one of the perks for the hours of lonely secluded work that goes in to producing a painting. Later, I received a letter from the President of the Guild, Frank Wootton, who had seen the painting and made some very complimentary remarks.

Sir Peter Gadsden had invited me to the Mansion House, and a few weeks later I went, reminded of Alice in Wonderland as I knocked at the doors which were so vast they seemed to dwarf me, and was given a personal tour of all the main rooms by Sir Peter. They were indeed, beautiful, and I was delighted to be shown round by the Lord Mayor himself, a generous gesture.

R.A.F. Brize Norton featured again, seeking a painting of the Tactical Communications Wing. Landrovers are always lovely vehicles for pictures, chunky, their soft tops often sagging and bleached by the sun, and there were plenty of excuses for painting them with this subject. In order to get everything depicted that they wanted, I put the terrain as a hill, enabling me to work upwards in the picture and not purely into the distance. I enjoyed working on it, not only because of the Landrovers, but as the vehicles were camouflaged, plenty of other canvas around as well, with both men and vehicles amongst the trees. Technically I had a great deal to consider - anything that glinted would be unheard of - badges and clothing had to be correct, rifles would have been within reach if they had been put aside while equipment was dealt with, but with the painting finished, the C.O. Wing Commander Bob Stickland was so delighted with the picture, he asked for prints of the original. This was the first time I'd had copies requested, so after much thought on the best way to do this, I gave TCW a quotation for the lot, adding that they could decide their own selling price for each print and handle the marketing. I would get them made and deliver them. It worked beautifully.

The Red Arrows have given various displays over London, and as I wanted to show them flying up the Thames as a birthday tribute to Her Majesty the Queen Mother, with the Houses of Parliament in the background I sought permission to look at the latter from the roof of the County Hall. It was granted, but I was entertained by having to sign a paper first, that I would not hold them responsible either if I threw my possessions onto passers by beneath, or if I chose to commit suicide by doing a Tosca and flinging myself from the battlements! I worked up there for some time, very pleased when finally I returned to some warmth, for it was a beautiful but chilly autumnal day. I then went to see the Red Arrows which were in the fascinating stage of training for the usual three new pilots who had just joined the team that year. No displays were being given at the time, and they were flying with half the formation - the formation sliced lengthwise - and it was very unusual and strange to witness such a crack team flying part of a formation with one team member way out of line, struggling to catch up and get into place. But it didn't stop me painting them because as artist, I could tidy up a formation in the same fashion that I could erase telegraph poles to improve on a landscape! The power of the brush! A short time after the painting was completed, the R.A.F. Benevolent Fund printed it as one of their Christmas cards, which sold so well that it was repeated the following year. I also had a letter from Rackhams, Birmingham, one of the House of Fraser Group, saying they wanted both the painting and me in their Manchester store of Kendals, for a publicity day when all the pilots would be there wearing their scarlet Red Arrow flying suits. The painting went up to Manchester ahead, displayed in the window for a week or more, plus a huge poster for their, 'British and Proud of it' promotion, announcing it was the, 'First public showing of the R.A.F. Red Arrows Oil Painting by Miss Penelope Douglas G.Av.A, to be exhibited at the Guild of Aviation Artists ... Meet Miss Penelope Douglas here on June 1st, who will meet the Red Arrows in person.' The last sentence read as if I had never come across the pilots before!

I also visited the firm of Ingham Day in Birmingham, who felt very enthusiastic about making a jig-saw puzzle of the painting. They were so keen they decided on a one thousand or fifteen hundred piece jig-saw on top quality card, and I felt very elated as it would help my finances a great deal. However hopes were dashed, for later, they informed me that after long and careful consideration they had decided not to bring out a new range of puzzles that year. Although we were in a recession I was most disappointed. I wondered whether they had changed their minds about using my painting, and the recession was merely an excuse.

During work on these recent commissions, once again I had exhibited in Norwich. My prices had gone up steadily over the years, and I was interested to learn that a painting bought by a couple near King's Lynn, who had chosen it simply because its colouring toned in with their newly decorated walls and not for any other reason, presumably having had the house redecorated a few years later, had sold the painting to a gallery near Holt. Discovering it for sale there, I found its price had increased and was not far off what I was now charging for the same size of canvas. The question of when to put up the fees was always a delicate decision. If put too high, I might lose some commissions. Inflation, therefore all my expenses had to be considered. On the whole I judged it alongside the number of commissions I had ahead of me. If these were too numerous I became swamped by the anxiety of trying to catch up and I didn't like to keep people waiting too long for an order, so it seemed a good time to raise the fees and shorten the list slightly; yet I needed a certain amount of work in front of me and a rough estimate of my income and expenditure and leave time for any contingencies. It was never easy. When exhibiting there were always extra expenses, hire of the room, percentage of sales to the gallery, printing of catalogues, and many smaller extra costs. The Guild of Aviation Artists took twenty-five percent of all sales, so in London I put up my prices accordingly.

In Norwich I had about fifty (new) paintings on display, receiving half as many again in commissions, a very successful week. When it was over I started work on the orders, packing in the hours and by the time these were completed I was exhausted and feeling very stale, which was unusual. I had been working desperately hard over a long period of time. The nervous energy spent on dealing with commissions, meeting deadlines for those who wished to give orders as Christmas or birthday presents, and all the organisation and travelling involved had taken their toll. Painting was not a job where other people could have helped me with the work. For some time I felt devoid of imagination, enervated, worn out, and reached the stage where I never wished to see a tube of paint again! Feeling as I did, without any doubts or regrets whatsoever, I decided I had no option but quit on painting altogether. I had simply had enough of it. I was fully aware that I'd had a wonderful life from many of my commissions, especially those for the Armed Forces and it seemed unappreciative almost selfish, but the decision was made. In my favour it has to be said that art is creative, and any energy or wish to be inventive and original had deserted me completely.

If I was expecting sympathy and understanding from my friends, I certainly didn't get it! My decision was met with blank astonishment. Many of them tried to persuade me that of course I'd continue painting, but I truly couldn't see it happening. I fobbed them off by saying that perhaps I'd return to it one day, but if honest with myself, thought it was highly unlikely. Fortunately no more commissioned work came in at that point, perhaps because it was January, so on that I was spared a decision. I didn't mean to be ungrateful for a marvellous time painting, but ... I quit. The relief was colossal!

CHAPTER 13

BONE DOME FOR A CANBERRA

In my flat in London I felt a wonderful freedom! I had no studio there and had been working in the sitting-room which was far from ideal. Due to having a lodger to help with expenses, my work had to be cleared away by the time they came back in the evening. Released from these slight pressures, the joy of all painting gear packed away for good was almost overwhelming. Although I was debilitated and drained, in some contrary way I felt a surge of renewed energy for things afresh, and was now at liberty to take any path I chose. I wanted to make Christening gowns, as friends, Gillian and Dick Brockbank, had paid a fortune for a Christening gown from The White House in Bond Street, London, for their baby daughter, Rosie, and if I could produce a gown of that standard, then why not make them for The White House. My first sewing at the age of seven, was to pinch one of my father's large white handkerchiefs and embroider a daffodil in one corner - a horrible screwed up mess - and present it to my mother as her birthday present! I had been taught dressmaking in my teens, making many of my own clothes which proved much cheaper than buying garments, and enjoyed tailoring classes in London. In order to sew the Christening gowns I bought several baby patterns and a pleasing choice of white materials, ribbons and tiny pearl buttons, and after a few months had six gowns finished with bonnets to match, beautiful, old-fashioned, all fully lined and the type of gown that would hang for miles beyond the baby's feet! Having completed them, I was told by a friend 'in the know' that The White House had their own manufacturers, not accepting work from outside.

Sewing was a good contrast from painting, though was just as creative as I mixed patterns and sewed to my own designs. This period lasted about five months. Towards the end of it, I had a visit from Paula Davies of the Daily Telegraph to do an article about me. The photographer came too. But I couldn't believe the approach I was given from somebody working for such a respectable newspaper - perhaps it had simply not been her day!

"Can you tell me your age?"

"No," I smiled politely, "I often get asked my age, but I don't feel it has any bearing on whether I can paint or sew."

"Well I shall find out!" I thought to myself that surely she had something better to do! "Do you have a lodger who's a lover that you're sleeping with?"

"No," still polite, but my smile was fainter.

"Well many people do."

"Do they." I made this a polite statement, not a question.

One more query of that sort and without doubt I would ask her to leave. Daily Telegraph! Not a daily 'rag' that might have written that sort of article. I was extremely surprised and angry too, but if she had been trying to get a rise out of me I kept my feelings hidden to myself. However having asked the questions she had, she settled down, though when I read the article which I hasten to say was a good one, when she referred to me as, 'This reserved, sweet-faced woman ... ' I read more into it than most people might have! Afterwards I thought perhaps I should have inquired whether she was sleeping with her photographer! The picture in the paper showed me with the Red Arrows painting and a Christening gown.

In the flat next to mine lived Rosemonde Nairac. Also artistic - she created many of the designs for Rosenthal's porcelain amongst other talents - we were both working at home and had much in common. It was during one of our many discussions that she came up with the idea of doing drawings for children, one for each letter of the alphabet. She suggested I write a sentence or so for each letter that would enable her to use her imagination for the illustrations; it could be funny and especially, nonsense. Warming immensely to the idea, I picked the letter 'F', but the more I thought about it the more I wanted to write it in rhyme; then to let the rhyme be long enough to tell a story; finally I felt it should have as many words starting with that letter, as possible. It must not be purely an alliteration for that would make it difficult to read fluently, and of course we would try to get it published! The letter 'F' progressed well, two fat frogs, Fred and Freda, who were afloat in a clog - why a clog? Well it happened to rhyme with frog ...

And frequently their task
With fruit and food and flask,
Was to feast 'till they were full,
And give the oars a pull.
Freda liked the fried fish,
It was her favourite dish.
Fred fancied frozen food,
It put him in the mood
To function on his flute,
While Freda played the lute.

and so it went on. Rosemonde worked on the most enchanting drawings of these two frogs, sailing happily, one playing the flute, the other a lute, giving them beautiful expressions ... which would soon change as the story unfolded to the hazardous fortunes of these two charming characters. Having done these illustrations in rough, work mounted up for her plus the realization that there were still another twenty-five letters to be done, and she chose not to pursue the idea, giving me full encouragement to continue if I wished. Illustrating children's stories was definitely not for me. It needed a tremendous flair, imagination, and skill with the pencil, and I knew my limitations. The wording however was different. I had become engrossed with it, got a tremendous satisfaction on making the stories for each letter rhyme, and loved every second of thrashing around with words and making them work for me. My father would have relished doing this with me. The dining-room in my childhood home, had one wall which was entirely books.

Not a meal went by - and these were family meals, no television distraction - without my father leaping to his feet to look up either the spelling of a word that had occurred in conversation, or a quotation, or tell us the history of an event or a person. It happened with such regularity that it was part of our lives and never questioned. It did however leave its mark, and when all my own books were packed away during moving house, it was the reference books that I longed for more than any others. To return to the Rhymes of Rubbish Through The Alphabet, I worked on it with utter contentment until I had completed all twenty-six letters. A tadpole from Tasmania was a trampoline expert whose tail became severed from her body when she fell from the tightrope, but by the end of her story 'she convalesced with tonic and a trip to Tenerife, and returned to trampolining to the public's great relief!' 'A maggot from Mauritius with a Mona Lisa smile manufactured millinery of a most bewitching style, some were mustard coloured with mink or monkey trim, or had mock marigolds or mulberries arranged around the brim' - contacting mumps proved hilarious! 'Josephine was a jellyfish with a jovial, jaunty air' but a judo loving lobster jumped upon her, and in court, 'the journalists were jotting down each good judicial point, while the lobster jerked his muscles and flexed each and every joint'. Although I have sent them to one or two publishers, so far I have not succeeded, ... but I DID enjoy writing them!

Although I had not painted for about ten months, unknown to me something was stirring in that direction within me, so I was particularly receptive to the beauty of Blagden and Chew Valley Lakes and the entrancing scenery around them, perfect to encourage a little landscape painting! I was visiting Gwen Kirton in Chew Magna, near Bristol, I had never painted that area and felt the urge to get at my brushes again. Gwen suggested casually that I do a few paintings and put them up in her home, and she would invite a few friends in; they could be for sale, and the small percentage to her would be a great help as she needed a new portable heater. It was on! Feeling much restored, and with my 'batteries recharged,' I worked on a collection of small paintings, and bought the sherry that would accompany the social exhibition. Some of the pictures were bought by the Managing Director of South West Water, who asked me to do further paintings for the company. After seeing these, South West Gas commissioned a large landscape for their boardroom. Not surprisingly I was delighted and keen to be back at work again!

I was invited to do another television interview for the B.B.C. Look East programme which became entertaining in more ways than one. Ian Masters, who would be talking with me, was a foot taller than I was, and the producer felt because of our difference in height, a walking interview past a row of my paintings was unsuitable. There followed ridiculous antics by Ian walking along with knees bent, suggestions that he remove his shoes. I said I could wear my shoes inside his and be an inch taller! The paintings were set up on easels, several were dog portraits, Ian giggled a 'heel' and 'sit' at me during rehearsals, and we and the technicians were laughing so much that any interview seemed impossible! One of Ian's questions was to ask if any particularly entertaining incident had happened to me, so I told him about Masirah and that there wasn't a man there who didn't want to rape me and that if I knew that I'd be all right. Ian liked it very much, and decided this rape story should come towards the end. The final rehearsal started and all was going so well the producer gave us an extra thirty seconds. In the world of television and radio that is a long time. We did a proper take, all went smoothly and then our allotted time was up.

"We didn't get our rape in," I reminded Ian. He gave me a very good reply! Although it was not included in the actual broadcast, the crew had deliberately kept the cameras rolling! How we ever managed that interview seriously I still can't fathom!

The Royal Air Force bring out First Day Cover issues at intervals, and I was asked to do a painting for the envelope of the 40th anniversary of the first flight of a British jet aircraft, the Gloster Whittle E 28/39 "Pioneer." On 16th January 1930, Frank Whittle filed the application for his first jet propulsion patent, visiting the Gloster Aircraft Company factory in 1939. His invention - taken up by the Chief Designer Mr W.G.Carter, collaborating with Whittle - drastically altered the evolution of the aeroplane. The background for the aircraft in flight, was to be R.A.F. Cranwell as this had been chosen for the Pioneer's first flight, mainly due to the hard-top runway. To paint this was a fascinating glimpse back in time.

Time also interested me through taking horology evening classes in London, though I was not by nature, much good at mini engineering. An American I met at these classes asked if I would do portraits of his two teenage children, and although it was not a subject I was at home with, I accepted. I had several sittings with them and completed the paintings, each on a separate canvas. Feeling that the daughter had come off better than the son, I duly delivered them. The parents felt the opposite, mainly because the daughter - a spoilt little madam - had changed her hair style since I had started work and made so much fuss that she didn't like the portrait, I thought it easier if they just bought the one, an arrangement which suited them. It put me off painting people - I could do without the hassle! I had none of these problems with animal portraits!

I hoped to be working on an aircraft painting again and it wasn't long before I received another commission, and found myself sitting on an aircraft seat in a crew room, receiving instruction before a flight in a T4 Canberra of 13 Squadron, who were based at R.A.F. Wyton.

To the uninitiated, it goes something like this:-

Right, parachute first - four straps to feed into a sort of 'box' the size of a small, flat, round margarine tub at the front of my waist, the lower ones from each hip to be passed through a loop, brought up between my legs and clipped into the box by twisting the front of it until the metal ends of the straps slit into their appropriate slots. Two shoulder straps fit into the upper part of the box. You twist the front of the box one way to insert the straps, and the other way and squeeze to release everything. The parachute straps are lighter in colour, so I know which are which. Tighten the shoulder straps first, then the ones from each hip, and the result is a parachute harness which I would virtually be seated in if needed. Next the dark straps of the seat, also fitting into their own box which should lie below the parachute box. There are two blue webbing, thinner straps that are passed through a ring on my flying suit just below the knee, and cross diagonally up under the webbing hip straps of the ejector seat harness, and the metal part of the hip straps pass through the loops on the ends before clipping into the box.

"What are these for?"

"To stop your legs flailing about as you leave the aircraft." Yes of course, and passing them diagonally would also keep your legs together as well as pulling them close underneath you on exit. The hip straps must be tightened, then the shoulder straps. The ejector seat box undoes with a lever and proves much easier to undo under instruction, than the parachute box. Next I am shown where the oxygen fits, then that there is a bar with a push nozzle on my left not unlike a car brake, that would release the seat and allow me to lean forward to pick my camera up should I drop it! A similar device on the right would raise the seat up or down before the start of the flight, and I would need to take my weight off the seat slightly in order for it to respond.

"If you eject, pull the ring that is between your legs vertically upwards HARD. Don't just expect it to work with a gentle pull that moves it an inch or so, it's got to be pulled right up 'till almost level with your shoulders. Then there will be, possibly, a second or two delay before you automatically leave the aircraft." With this, similar loops, double ones for each hand are above each shoulder behind and above my head, though the lower loop for ejecting would be easier to deal with, and I shouldn't need to resort to the top ones. Once in the air, two small parachutes would deploy after a second or two, stabilizing the seat and stop me swinging wildly about.

"If you've ejected at over ten thousand feet, then you will continue to descend on those two shoots with the seat attached to you."

"How will I know the height and not separate from the seat too soon?"

"Only separate from the seat when the trees come rushing up towards you. You will fall faster with the seat and it will keep you warmer. It's twenty degrees below zero up there and you don't want to get cold." I agree, smiling, but wondering (not unlike Winnie the Pooh!) at what point trees could be considered to be rushing, and when fairly stationary!

"Now," my instructor continued, "if the trees are rushing up to meet you . . . ."

"DAD."

"Quite right. There's a D ring here on your left hip, pull it!" I do so, struggling a little and needing both hands to get it to respond. The D ring comes out on a metal cord about eight inches long. "Now move the clip on the box of the ejector seat harness." I do so and the harness falls away. "AND (the A of DAD) finally the second D ring which will open the parachute you're sitting on."

"Fine." I remembered the DAD from a previous flight.

"You will need to lean forward and push yourself clear of the seat, and doing so will help to release the parachute. You shouldn't need to do any of this as it should all be automatic from leaving the aircraft." Finally I am shown the safety pins that lock the seat from operating when not in the air. "Don't leave your seat after the flight until both pins are secured, one locking the loop between your legs and the other is the one behind your seat. Enjoy the flight Miss!"

The next port of call is to fit my out with a flying suit. Five foot nine is the smallest.

"I think you'd better get into it out by the aircraft," says Tim Tucker generously, looking down at my five foot two. Next, bone dome. After much effort they find what is considered the smallest. It swamps me! Somebody advances with a large screwdriver! Help!

"I'll tighten these ties which will pull the criss-cross webbing inside the bone dome tighter until it is resting on the top and back of your head, and it will raise the bone dome up off your shoulders." The men are enjoying this! The screwdriver comes into action. He tries to rock the bone dome, tightens it a little more, and I stand up feeling awkwardly top heavy!

"Now the mask." Ghastly childhood images of gas at the dentist come to mind. They clip it on, a black rubber mask covering from the bridge of my nose down each cheek to below my mouth. "Come over here Ma'm, and we'll make sure you can breathe properly and it's working and you can take the pressure in the aircraft." I follow them to a large black machine affair rather like a metal board with various dials on it. They attach my oxygen tube and put me on oxygen by pushing the mask tight (in theory) by pulling a lever down on the front. I can breathe easily. "We'll just simulate the cabin under pressure," I continue to breathe easily.

"I've got a gap under my chin," I explain, "and can get all my air through that!" I was sorry I'd spoken! They advance on me and tighten various chains and bits and pieces until I am unable to breathe other than from the panel in front of me. I watch a little button flash a white line at each breath.

"Now we'll put the cabin under pressure and increase it."

"I ceased to breathe completely," I explain on being released. I'm scared!

"Normally you try to get a big breath IN when you're short of air. This time you've got to force the air OUT." We go through it again, but I don't seem to be able to get any air other than permanently in. It feels suffocating and frightening.

"Does this happen automatically in flight?" I ask doubtfully.

"No, only if there's a failure of cabin pressure." I pray there won't be!

Next they try the radio. Can I hear them? Yes. Can I hear a slight whining? Yes. Can I hear one higher in pitch? No, definitely not. I am asked to take my bone dome off, needing help to undo the chin strap and mask, the removal of both ears being very high as it is winched off my head.

"Yes, it's faulty. We'll fix it." Next, flying boots. My shoes are not considered suitable.

"Size four and a half!" exclaims the man in disbelief. "We've got size eights. Tim hastily comes to the rescue as his are sevens. He fetches them plus two pairs of socks. Gloves also much too large. To hell! I'm ready!

Next I had to report to the medical centre. Good, I thought, I'll know how my heart is, blood pressure and everything. Thoughts came to mind of offering a pint of blood in Akrotiri, men fainting all round me, and being told they couldn't take it as my pressure was too low. The medical went like this.

"Have you ever flown in an aeroplane?"

"Yes, I have."

"Are your sinuses clear and are you free from a cold?"

"Yes".

"I'll just look down your ears; hold your nose and swallow." I am pronounced fit to fly!

All is fixed for the flight tomorrow. My nerves are taut, probably because I can be airsick, and especially with the knowledge that under certain cabin conditions the art of breathing seems to be non-existent! I enjoy the company during the evening, followed by a lousy night's sleep. Next morning I have a fascinating visit to the photographic department and the use of a stereoscope - a device by which two photographs of the same object or area taken at slightly different angles are viewed together, giving an impression of three dimension with depth and solidity as in ordinary human vision - over terrain in Italy. During this, signals are rushing to and fro frantically between 13 Squadron and the HQ Strike Command as permission for me to fly has never been sought! Authorisation is granted immediately.

"Do you often fly civilians in a Canberra? I ask.

"No, very seldom. It's just not considered a suitable aircraft." The answer pleases me enormously!

Time to go. I fetch my camera and take my travel sickness tablet. In the Ops room we study the maps. We are flying from R.A.F. Wyton to the Southampton area, to try and see if, from the air, we can pick out the old airfield where 13 Squadron were formed in 1915. Air corridors over Southampton are usually extremely busy, but today seems to be an exception. After a call of,

"Aircraft's u/s," as a screw has been lost, it is tracked down, and an hour late, we walk out to our transport. I stumble a little, and remind myself that I must allow for six inches of boot out beyond my toes! "We can't find the keys," somebody shouts cheerfully. Oh God - not another delay!

We reach the Canberra. Tim is there to help, ready with my flying suit.

"It should go on over your boots." I hope he won't see my hands shaking. I clamber into this outsize suit, the crutch flapping between my knees, grinning I haul it up where it should be, kick a leg to show movement, and let the crutch fall back to my knees again. The crew's expressions say quite clearly that they are highly amused and are enjoying the antics of this small member of the crew enormously! I put the life jacket on getting plenty of offers to help me do it up.

"I've never dressed a girl on the airfield before," announces somebody gleefully. They stand back to admire the finished product, the soft rolls of flying suit gathered round my calves and prevented from descending further by the huge boots. I tighten the velcro round the sleeves, tugging up the extra foot of length to my elbows. (I can never understand why men say they find me so sexy when I'm dressed in their clothing which is far too big for me!)

"Oh I forgot," says Tim cheerfully, "you've got a dinghy below you. It will hit the water before you attached to a line. Just yank at it and the box will burst open and it will inflate - there's a handle on it somewhere saying, ' pull'."

I watch from the tarmac as the right hand seat of the Canberra is forward in place, to allow Dick, the navigator to climb through the door (if you can call the hatch that!) into the back. My seat is then moved back by one of the aircrew, and it tips forward at the same time, allowing the captain, Dave, to climb through into the left hand seat, then my turn to get into the right hand seat, still back and tipped, beside him and strap in. I'm strongly aware of the familiar smell of an aircraft. I don't find it easy to get all the straps really tight - wish I have the strength of men's hands - Tim does contortions until everything is fine, I am clamped in place. My bone dome is handed to me, oxygen mask attached, I flatten both ears and prize myself into it, Dave connects the oxygen tubes, the white line flashing, and I am breathing! Finally gloves, and lastly my Leica. I give a thumbs up sign to Tim as he steps back away from the aircraft, and one of the aircrew tips my seat upright, and moves it forward into place. I've watched a Canberra being started up, and there's quite a bang when the cartridge explodes, but inside, I feel the slight throb as first one engine starts, then the other. Dave goes through the pre-flight checks and we taxi along the perimeter track, the dual controls moving between my knees. What a position to be in! Fantastic! My heart is thumping, adrenalin pumping! We line up at the end of the runway, further checks, and Dave tells me if we have to eject, he will say, 'Eject eject eject!' Dick will go first, and I am to wait until I hear the bang of his ejector seat, then go next.

"Or failing that," he grins at me, "I shall have already gone and it will dawn on you you're in the aircraft alone!"

We have slight radio trouble as we take off, exciting, so exciting, faster and faster, the trundling sound and jiggling stop, everything smooth, we are airborne! We bank round, climb to about two thousand feet and head south east.

"Where the hell are we?" says Dave. We study the ground below. "Dick, is that Cambridge on our right?" Dick does some quick thinking and says it might be, later confirmed as we pass over Newmarket. We seem unable to pick up Alconbury on our radio as they are busy with an exercise, so find another wavelength instead.

"This is Charlie Charlie Delta three eight - we're travelling at a height of two thousand feet and would like to head south towards Clacton ... " They ask what we are. "Canberra."

"Charlie Charlie Delta you have permission to continue ... " Compass bearings are given, and we go up to three thousand feet for a while. The radio is giving nasty whining noises, Dick unable to stop it. I can speak by moving the switch on the front of my oxygen mask, but I'm asked to turn it off when not speaking because of the noise of my breathing. (At least I'm doing so!) How fabulous this flight, and how wonderful water looks from the air, so sharply visible, full of reflections, and how beautiful the twisting snake of a river, the shape of a lake, so alive! Clacton doesn't look very exciting - remember not to holiday there! We head out over the sea, looking for land to the south.

"How deceptive, I thought I'd seen it ages ago," I comment.

"You get bands of light on the water that look exactly like it. There's Manston airfield,"

"I have a friend who has a house built on the top of the cliff," I tell him.

"We'll head out and keep round the coast and see if we can find it for you. Manston looks dead, not a thing happening."

We bank slightly again, joining the coast east of Brighton, where I pick out Tricia's house, then piers and various buildings I recognise. Chichester cathedral really stands out, ... and wow, look at all the estuaries around Portsmouth ... think of the money in all those swanky, private yachts ... there's the dockyard, quite a few Naval vessels around, looks busy ... I am getting uncomfortably hot in this aircraft ... the cabin has been controlled at a cooler temperature earlier, but beads of moisture are forming, or as Dave puts it,

"We've got snowballs coming in." Now come on, I think to myself, you are NOT going to be sick! Pull yourself together and concentrate on what's down below. We discuss whether we have found Gosport, but the old airfield seems incredibly difficult to find, I take several photographs, there's a bit of empty grass which might be it, or is the new airfield built right over the old one?

"We'll go round again for you Penny." I try not to notice the angle of the wretched aircraft or how uncomfortable I feel. We study the ground intently, and circle it a third time. Finally we straighten out and head east, away from our planned route due north through heavy air traffic and busy corridors as our radio is playing up badly and we would be in severe trouble if we had a radio failure heading through that area. In fact the only way they can talk atall, 'an esssential,' they explain laughingly, later, is by cutting me off completely. Dave and I drop our oxygen masks for a bit. They remind me both oxygen and cabin have a funny smell, I return my mask aware, as before, more of breathing out - funny how this set up makes me aware of breathing, when normally I never am, except perhaps panting after exercise or something. I am feeling almost unbearably hot, am in total silence, extremely uncomfortable, and this flight is becoming an endurance feat. Dave signals me to reach forward to move one of the controls for him. I put my hand on various buttons, watching his face after touching each, until his expression changes and he puts a thumb up. I push the lever over, expecting it to stay there. He signals for me to repeat it, this time I hold it there, then I feel the pressure changing on my head, my breathing begins to be a struggle as I feel everything tightening - God I admire these men who do this as a full time job! He signals 'that's fine', and I release it again, cooler, more comfortable. I just mustn't be sick! I watch the land below. The sky is magnificent, we have a sunset, sometimes the wonderful, soft colouring hidden by some cloud level with us. I can feel the air and atmosphere, it is breathtakingly beautiful! Boy, it's SO beautiful! Soon we begin to lose height, flaps down, undercarriage, the lights of the runway ahead, and suddenly, at this lower level I have the radio again - some loose wire has connected! I glance at the countryside below, no sun down there as it has slipped below their horizon, but up here we are treated to an awe inspiring sight. The sun is balanced on tiptoe on the horizon, sinking as we watch, the whole sky filled with rose-pink softness deepening to cloudless crimsons and purples that coalesce and fuse into the shadowy lightless upper sky. Then the sun slips from our horizon too as we head in to land, the landing lights standing out clearly in the dusk. The aircraft rocks imperceptibly in the slight wind as we continue our descent, then we creep over the end of the runway, very gently fly level with it, lower each second until we touch the tarmac. We taxi along the perimeter track, finally coming to a stop, guided by one of the aircrew with their 'ping-pong' bats. We release our oxygen masks. I sit tight, knowing the first thing I must do is to put the pins into the ejector seat.

"That's fine Penny, you can climb out now." I do so - air, lovely fresh, chilly, evening, FRESH air! Oh, it feels SO GOOD! Smells so good!

In the crew room I am greeted by Tim, who sees a smiling, happy woman appear! Gleefully they inform me that in our absence signals have been whizzing to and fro with Strike Command, and it seems 13 Squadron have got their flight plans changed successfully, and will be joining me in Akrotiri for the whole of my Tuesday to Friday visit in Cyprus next week, rather than just overlapping. Laughingly I tell them I'm renowned for having several husbands attached, and we look forward to meeting up again. Of the various possibilities for the Canberra painting, our flight proved that no old airfield was obvious enough to give background for the picture, and Cyprus is chosen instead.

The warmth and balmy atmosphere of the Mediterranean was wonderful on arrival at Akrotiri, especially after the gloomy November days of the U.K. As I got out of the aircraft I could almost smell the oranges! The background for the painting was decided - the amphitheatre. The setting was magnificent, for it is situated right on the coast, and on a previous visit, I sat there listening to a classical music concert, looking down on the ocean, all quite unforgettable. Plans were made for me to see the amphitheatre from a helicopter, and also the Canberra in flight. They insisted I should see both together, and couldn't understand that to see each separately, would be fine, and I would put the jig-saw together. It was all rather fraught. For one thing it was essential I was trigger happy with the camera and therefore needed to change the film while in the chopper, all of which took precious moments.

For another, because of their insistence that I see both together, the Canberra was against the sun which was hopeless, but in spite of being somewhat hustled by the winchman, thankfully I managed to get the material I needed, reminding myself that as I had been given a flight out to Akrotiri for just that reason, if necessary I should speak up if things were wrong, and not sit back and fail

The painting was presented to R.A.F. Wyton, (the crew took excellent photographs of my home in Norfolk on one of their flights,) and hangs in the Officers' Mess, and invited by the C.O. Wing Commander Tony Terrett, I thoroughly enjoyed a final visit there in December for the Disbandment Parade and Reunion of 13 (PR) Squadron.

CHAPTER 14

GORGEOUS, BILLOWING PANELS IN THE SKY

Funds were being raised for the new extension of the R.A.F. Museum at Hendon, and I was asked to paint a picture of a Vulcan bomber taking off for R.A.F. Waddington, near Doncaster as a raffle prize for No 1 Group. Weather for watching the Vulcan from the side of the runway was dismal, though the sight of such a beautifully designed aircraft and the thunderous crescendo was both breathtaking and deafening! In spite of the smooth sweep of the wings and the graceful, triangular shape which I had so enjoyed painting, shown in flight over Pathos, the three quarter front view gave quite a different impression, and it struck me as an obese hulk! Yet it still appeared graceful! Perhaps because the weather was so appallingly gloomy, my material seemed equally gloomy, so the result was a fairly dramatic painting, the aircraft dominating the whole canvas. It was very well received and was to be second prize, sandwiched between a Thomas Cook Holiday and a Sanyo 3030 Rack Hi-Fi! The Station Commander, Air Vice Marshal Mike Knight CB AFC BA RAF and his team gave me very good support and I had a great time there, with the painting given much publicity.

Among the Officers I met Group Captain Colin Preece OBE AFC RAF, and it was after getting the material, he asked me if anything had gone wrong in my work. I told him the story of High Wycombe and the Victor tanker refuelling the Lightnings over the Niagara Falls.

"And what happened to the painting?"

"It was banned to the back of the studio cupboard," I replied with both shame and frivolity, "and I haven't looked at it since." He then came out with the most unexpected statement I could have imagined,

"I was flying the Victor! I'd love to buy the painting!" What an extraordinary coincidence! Of all the various disasters that had happened, it was pure chance I had picked that one! Colin also asked for a second, similar painting as a presentation gift, so after all that had happened in the past, I found myself painting it again. The Vulcan raffle prize was won by Squadron Leader Mike Holdsworth who was stationed at Alconbury, and he wrote to tell me he was going to present it to the R.A.F. Museum.

Back in Norfolk, one of my more significant telephone calls was to the local Police.

"It's Penelope Douglas speaking, from Barnham Broom. I'm an aviation artist, and I'm ringing to let you know that I've got two helicopters landing in the field opposite the house on Tuesday morning!" What an amazing message to give!

The Army Air Corps had commissioned a painting, and suggested that instead of my driving to Cambridge for discussion, they literally drop in on me with both Scout and Gazelle. Two choppers! Unbelievable! My family, David, Sally, and the children, Katya seven, Justyn six and three year old Mark were visiting from Sydney, and as if arranged for their benefit, the date for the chopper's arrival was during their week in Norfolk. I had been asked to inform the Police, so if anybody rang them to say a helicopter had come down and presumed it was in trouble, the Police would have prior knowledge. It really was exciting! Nobody local could have failed to realise something was happening due to the racket and echo from the arrival of both aircraft. They made a pass over the house and landed a short distance from it. After the business had been dealt with over coffee, the crew put all three children in the Gazelle and we have happy photographs, Katya wearing a headset.

Arrangements were made that I should meet up with them in the Stanford Battle Area near Thetford as I wished to show the role of the Army Air Corps, and as the song says, 'Her mother came too!' She watched everything from the car, seeing me working with both choppers and the men on the ground with their weapons. It was special to see the pleasure it gave her, for normally she would not have been with me. The painting went well, and included some of the beauty of the countryside - one of the most arid areas of Great Britain - with the wonderful shapes of the pine trees included on the canvas.

From choppers to parachutes! No 1 Parachute Training School was based at R.A.F. Brize Norton, and a painting of them was requested for the Officers' Mess, to join the other pictures. After the initial visit to PTS, I drove to Weston-on-the-Green to meet up with them again. At six-thirty with the sleepy mistiness of early morning sunlight, it was a strange and eerie sensation being out on an airfield with various men dotted about at random - rather like planting bulbs when they say you should just scatter them with no particular pattern - all was silent and still. A flare was lit, marking the DZ (dropping zone.) A Hercules droned in the distance overhead. Still silent at ground level, up above distant figures could be seen appearing from the aircraft, round parachutes opening automatically above them, the crack of sound as each became fully inflated inaudible to those of us down below. As the figures drifted downwards, the silence was broken.

"Put your bloody legs together!" Instructors on the ground suddenly came alive, watching student's descent and guiding where necessary, shouting instructions upwards through megaphones as those jumping became lower. Students landed, rolled awkwardly, struggled to their feet disintangling themselves if needed, parachutes were gathered, snatches of conversation coming to me as the students passed.

"Piece of cake!"

"Fantastic!"

"I'm not fucking well doing that again!"

"Mine got twisted. Had to kick my legs to sort it out."

"No problem. Hope we get another jump in."

"I was shit scared, but it was bloody marvellous!"

The ambulance on standby collected a student with a sprained ankle. It was their first jump after the initial training period at Brize Norton.

This subject had so many facets to it, the best solution, and a new idea for me, was to do the main painting in the centre of the 3′ × 4′ canvas, with a smaller picture in each corner. Badges were also to be added and at least the canvas seemed large enough to try such an idea.

What a satisfying subject parachutes are! Gorgeous panels of billowing fawns, greys and browns, and once the student had landed they took on marvellous shapes as they started to collapse - hopefully the canopy not the student - deep shadows and sunlight essential. My concentration was intense, for at P.T.S. was a painting where the artist had got the wind coming from two different directions, and I mustn't make the same error. Mostly these first jumps took place just after dawn in very light winds, so a 5.0a.m. start from London for me to get there on time, often frustrated by the jump being cancelled as winds became fractionally too strong for men who had never jumped from an aircraft before, or who had very little experience. I spent over a hundred pounds on fuel. I learnt the hard way. In future the first visit to a Station, and delivery of the finished painting would be free, other trips, so much a mile. This had the effect that people would think twice before inviting me down for nothing in particular! This was my living, and expenses were mounting horribly on this painting, and I should have been more businesslike. I was also getting the material for five separate pictures on one canvas, so a great deal of work was involved. In the four corners of the canvas, one would show the barrage balloon, the other three the ultimate in parachuting, the display team of the Falcons, the Special Air Service, and Special Boat Squadron.

The balloon takes about five men, is made of rubberized Egyptian cotton with an aluminium surface to reflect heat and light. After two hundred flying days it is thoroughly checked. It costs around a thousand quid to inflate, the cost of the balloon over twenty thousand pounds. I was invited to go up in the cage hanging beneath it. Why is it that I seem to cause so much amusement when I'm in an outside flying suit or as in this case, I was staggering across the airfield with full parachute and reserve chute weighing over half my weight, NOT in order to jump - it doesn't particularly appeal - but should the main cable break, the balloon will gain height and set off across country! There is only one way down! We rose slowly to about eight hundred feet with an instructor, and several students about to make their first descent. I saw real fear on their faces. I gather it is easier to jump from an aircraft on a static line (one that automatically inflates the parachute as you leave the aircraft), than from the intimidating stillness and silence of a balloon. Much like the old wartime films, the funny stories and light hearted conversation of the instructor, and the hilarious comments in return had me rocking with laughter, the whole thing a big act to banish terror! All but the instructor were parchment pale. Jump they did!

Material of the Falcons was straightforward, very colourful with the red, white and blue of the oblong nine cell chutes, and in just the way an artist can remove a television aerial in a landscape with a house in it, so I could tidy up a Falcon who was slightly out of line! These were experts, supremely confident, very impressive, and able to land on their feet on a sixpence, (or, for the under twenty-eights, a one pence piece!)

The Special Air Service were to be shown freefalling from a great height. One of the P.T.S. instructors posed for me on the ground on his stomach, legs and arms all raised slightly as if he was free falling. Being a stickler for accuracy I was not entirely happy, so was given details for getting in touch with the Regiment. Their response when I rang had not a second's hesitation.

"Come and see us." I went! Had I not done so, the painting of them would have been inaccurate, for with a four man patrol I would have painted them too close to one another in freefall. I left the barracks with all the details I needed ... and ... a commission from the S.A.S.! I would return!

As with many of the paintings for the Armed Forces, there are times when I see, learn or hear restricted information. I respect this: if I didn't, I might not have been allowed to continue working with them. Should there be any doubt, none of it appears in this manuscript.

Poole Harbour, where the Royal Marines are based, was where I was to meet up with the S.B.S. for painting a water descent, some of the S.A.S. jumping with them. The S.B.S. are the water experts of the Special Forces, so I was to get material from a landing craft. As we got under way, heading out into the bay, Gemini boats kept us company, their manoeuvrability astonishing, those handling these small rubber craft just standing casually in them as if quietly in front of a fire on a winter's night! I would have been seated and hanging on for grim death, for some of the angles they reached would have had me terrified of being plunged into the sea! With the water descent, the first thing to leave the aircraft was the pallet on which was an inflated gemini, and in it, engine, fuel, ammunition, stores, supplies, clothing etc: equipment giving total independence. The S.B.S. watch it leave the aircraft, and only follow it providing its chute has deployed. They land as close to it as possible, cut the rope that holds gemini to palette, and climb aboard the inflatable. They are dressed in black wetsuits and look horribly evil! Many more men than a four man patrol were jumping into the sea that day, and I was very amused and surprised when one black clad figure suddenly appeared from the water and slithered his way over the side of the landing craft without warning, much like a James Bond film, grinned and said cheerfully,

"Hallo Penelope!" He was one of the S.A.S! Once again, they had all been the greatest of company to work with. Prints were made of the painting for P.T.S. and the following year it was reproduced on the back of the Falcons' brochure. I was given a superb photograph of them which all had signed.

This painting of P.T.S. included many figures. Once again it was vital to get the anatomy correct, and the light and shade on a figure making the person as accurate as possible. All were active, each person involved.

CHAPTER 15

WINGING IT, LONG, TO WIDEAWAKE

1982 had our television screens and radio broadcasts filled with news of the Falklands. With members of the Press from all over the world, I photographed the Vulcan that was to bomb the runway at Port Stanley.

War, is by nature, hateful, disgusting and repellent. It was an extraordinary sensation to see it on the small screen, seemed like an invasion of privacy, and I felt fearful that the public were being given too much information and therefore endangering our Forces. Like thousands of people, I watched mesmerized and horrified as the war escalated. Ships that I had seen serene, peaceful, dressed overall with sailors lining the decks at Spithead, I was now following with daily news bulletins: H.M.S. Antrim, the Sheffield, Arrow, Glamorgan ... witnessing in the privacy of my home, helicopters flying through palls of thick choking blackened smoke in the rescue of survivors from ships that had become blazing infernos. It seemed horrendous. Yet I admired enormously the sheer professionalism of our Forces. The Harrier with its unique VIFF (Vectoring in forward flight), proving to the world its supremacy stratigically. There is no doubt that amongst other things, the outcome of the Falklands war improved and updated equipment and strategies.

Although I was to go down to Ascension Island, a private commission for Colonel Robert McMeekin of the United States Air Force came first. My mother had suffered a stroke, thankfully not hospitalized, and I had been combining nursing her with completing the P.T.S. painting. As she was recovering, Judy Balfour took over from me while I flew to Washington. Bob McMeekin, like Tony Balfour, was a pathologist, visited the U.K. regularly, had bought a painting of mine at the R.A.F. Museum, later discovered Tony and I were cousins, and invited me 'across the pond' to work on a picture of his own personal light aircraft, a six seater Beechcraft Travelair D95A, built in 1964. Bob wanted it shown on the ground at Kitty Hawk, North Carolina, with the family beside it, so, in this tiny aircraft, we were to drop in there on our way down to Georgetown, South Carolina, where various members of the family were meeting up for a fortnight's holiday on the coast at Myrtle Beach. Bob and his wife Bebe were in the front seats, Robert junior of seven weeks between them, behind the front seats Harriet aged two alongside me, Matthew aged four in the back.

On arrival at Kitty Hawk we looked round the Wright Brothers' museum, exhibits included a full scale reproduction of the 1902 glider, and the 1903 flying machine. Outside were two sheds, replicas of both the hanger and workshop with living quarters. Markers showed the length of the very first manned, powered flight - on December 17th 1903 - a distance of one hundred and twenty feet. Piloted by Orville Wright, the machine driven by twin propellers working a thirteen horsepower motor, the flight lasted for twelve seconds; the second flight a hundred and seventy-five feet, the third two hundred, and the fourth eight hundred and fifty-two feet. Well! Those few yards of swaying flight, airborne for the first time started something! How the world has shrunk as a result! Next we flew on to Georgetown, then drove to the house, rocking chair on the veranda, the peaceful rhythm of the ocean close by, the smell of salt and sand. The beach was outstandingly beautiful, and seemed to stretch for miles unbroken. I was thankful I had a swimming costume - a bikini would have been considered shockingly brazen!

My day started with a long walk along the beach, sometimes finding sand dollars (sea biscuits - urchins,) the overpowering beauty of the sunrise over the sea, watching the pelicans formation flying a few feet above the waves and so comical, then painting most of the day, making enormous treble-decker sandwiches for everybody at lunchtime, and joining the family after working, during the late afternoon. They were super company, and after the anxiety over my mother it was wonderful, welcome relaxation. In ten days the painting was finished. I had stipulated I was not to be disturbed by the children in my bedroom cum workroom, for Harriet would have turned the paints upside down and ruined my wet painting in less time than it takes to mention her name, a small determined, delightful thug, and Matthew would have helped!

I made the following notes in the aircraft as we set off back to Washington, stopping on route for fuel:-

We're flying at nine and a half thousand feet, doing a hundred and fifty knots on route from Georgetown to Montgomery airport near Washington. We've just had the most fantastic climb from the runway, threading our way upwards through a mass of cunim with a cloud base of about four thousand feet, Bob flying by sight as well as instruments, picking a path between clouds that is wide enough for our tiny aircraft. This is REAL flying, and it's tremendous! A pause, while I signal to Harriet to suck her thumb, relieving the pressure on her ears. Matthew is already asleep in the back, a release for him - for all of us - as with Downs Syndrome, he doesn't understand that during the flight we can't just open the door and let him out! His feet are resting against my canvas with its protective hardboard: commission completed, I feel I've come to know every inch of this Beechcraft! Bob has flown this to Alaska, Mexico, the Caribbean and all over the U.S.A. He is a flying instructor too. But oh boy! Just look at those clouds! They tower around us. Our aircraft is minute among them, so tiny and dwarfed, and we are like a fly among wedding-cake tiers. We've a large cunim in our way: Bob banks gently to port, our wingtip nearly touches the cloud as he finds a way round. We are now off course, so he watches for a gap through them to starboard ... we find one, and ... here we go! How do you describe something like this! It's a bit like flying inside a knobbly ice box! I can see blue sky at the end of this tunnel of cunim ... I'm glad I've got my dark glasses on as it brings shape to the clouds that would otherwise be lost in the glare. I'm amazed at the lack of turbulence when we're so tightly surrounded by such vast and towering cunim. Harriet is asleep too. Hopefully, as she's had half a tablet, she won't bring her lunch up this time! I smile at my first introduction to the flight, with yells of protest from Harriet as she was strapped into her car seat in the aircraft,

"Get me out of here!" Well who wants to get into something that's going to make you sick? I could sympathize! I had tried to distract her as we taxied for take off, and she had turned to me conversationally and said,

"Yer've gotta wing out yer winda!"

"Yes, you've got one too! Two wings!"

There's a cloud up there towering above us that looks as if somebody's taken a knife to a pile of icing sugar and smoothed out the top. Bebe suckles her youngest, her beach hat propped against the window to keep the sun off the baby's face. What visibility we get in this aeroplane! We leave the magnificent cunim behind and I hand Bebe a 'diaper' as 'Baby Brother' burps up his last few ounces. Suddenly the engine note changes, and we yaw from side to side. Bebe turns to me and signals all is well. Bob grins,

"Just one of the fuel tanks draining: I didn't catch it in time." The colour returns to my face! We refuel at Rocky Mount as planned, and after another half hour's flight at two to three thousand feet, we land at Kitty Hawk. There is the huge monument to Wilbur and Orville Wright that I have put as the background in the painting, a massive, solid, eighteen metre chunk of grey-white granite. I am lost in thought about that very first hesitating flight, the cheers of the men running alongside, especially now after our magical path around and between those cunim. Wouldn't that first flight, in length, take place INSIDE a 'Jumbo'? The first flight was a hundred and twenty feet, less than the length of a soccer pitch; the second flight was a hundred and seventy-five feet. The length of the shell of a 'Jumbo' is just over two hundred and thirty feet, so yes, those first two flights ... Time to go ... we take off and climb to just over two thousand feet, returning to Montgomery airport with a magnificent view of Washington below us. I recognise the Jefferson Memorial, the Washington Monument, the Pentagon ... can't find the White House ... must be somewhere in those trees ... what a fabulous flight it's been. What an experience!

A few months later it was time to concentrate on the next flight with the R.A.F. These opportunities for travelling, particularly overseas, were exciting, inspiring and wonderful. My family had not the funds available to holiday together. The only one I recall, when we were united, was a camping holiday in Norfolk, in a cousin's orchard. I remember turning a plate of blackberries and custard accidentally in to my lap. We were visiting from Rochester, our home at the time, and another vivid memory is of my brother and I going riding at stables on the outskirts of Norwich, we missed the bus afterwards so we hitch-hiked home, though the driver of the empty taxi we travelled in, refused to go beyond his base, and we had to walk the last mile which meant crossing Mulbarton Common, where I had to piggyback my brother as he was frightened of the cows grazing there! We must have been under nine years of age at the time. My father's addiction to work, coupled with the low clergy stipend, narrowed the annual break to his taking three Sundays off when we children were in our teens and at boarding school, and my parents had these two weeks visiting us in Dorset and Gloucestershire from Norfolk, with their caravan. This was in summer and coincided with Speech days. They told me they once had a week-end away during the war, when they took a room in a hotel on the sea front at Brighton. Little did they realize one of the guns defending the country, was positioned on the roof. At night I was hauled into bed to lie safely between them as the noise was shattering. Undaunted, every time the gun fired, I cheered it on loudly, unaware I was reducing my unfortunate parents to nervous wrecks! Although I took the experience in my stride, it left me with a hatred of sudden noises and loud bangs which is still with me. Perhaps because of unbringing, I have neither been one to have a regular holiday, nor go abroad often. An overseas break was never an annual event, but when the funds allowed it on rare occasions, was as relished and appreciated as the flights I had been enjoying with the R.A.F.

These working flights were seldom straightforward. I was travelling to places that were unfamiliar, often with people I had never met, with the anxiety that I must achieve collecting the necessary material during my visit, without fail, but I made the most of each opportunity, and was extremely grateful. On this occasion I was to fly to Ascension Island, commissioned by 10 Squadron for a painting of a V.C.10 bringing casualties back from the Falklands war.

We left Brize Norton mid morning, I was listed as crew and on the flight deck of the V.C.10 in the jump seat for take off. What a privilege! The main body of the aircraft - seats face the tail in R.A.F. transport aircraft - had eighty passengers, and freight, including a pallet of life rafts for an R.F.A. ship. Mrs Fergerson of eighty-two had been flown to the U.K. to have a hip operation, and was excited at the thought of seeing her home in Port Stanley again. A large inflated penguin sharing her stretcher had been autographed by hospital staff, the best message, 'No climbing Tumbledown Mountain for at least a week.' After six hours we landed at Dakar, French Senegal which was unbelievably filthy, where we refuelled, a quick turnaround, and took off into the setting sun, stunning colours including a rainbow, and three hours later we could see the distant lights of Ascension, the runway, and for me, the excitement and pleasure of being on the flight deck for so long. Air Movements were in an inflated Harrier hide, most of the 'buildings' tented and temporary. I collected my case and was taken by Landrover to the bungalow I would be sharing, situated beside the beach, and my mosquito-netted bed which I reached around 1.0a.m. after drinks with Gerry Bunn, the C.O. of 10 Squadron. Furnishing was sparse, curtains hanging on by a third of their hooks, but I was here! Having seen the vast cockroaches, I hoped none of them were feeling affectionate enough to find their way under my mosquito netting to join me in bed! There are limits!

Ascension Island, situated about five hundred miles south of the equator, was an essential link in the eight thousand mile route between The Falklands and Great Britain. In 1982, by the end of April, Wideawake Airfield had become the busiest in the world and had over eight hundred servicemen there. Years ago, 1815, the island became a refuge for seafarers and was claimed on behalf of George III to prevent the French using it in order to rescue Napoleon from St Helena where he was exciled. The Americans had built the airfield on Ascension Island during the Second World War, a more modern runway built in 1956. Ascension's main role was as an international cable and wireless station, and the tracking of missiles and spacecraft launched from Cape Canaveral.

Usually there were about twenty-five flights arriving at Wideawake Airfield each month, but the total in 1982 was over three and a half thousand, almost entirely British. The majority of these movements were by helicopters, carrying men and stores to and fro from Task Force ships.

On my first morning, I was picked up soon after seven by John Best, a navigator on Victor aircraft, and also at sea - the Admiral's Cup, and with Peter de Savary on the Victory in the America's Cup. On the airfield we watched the R.N. Sea-Kings winching supplies out to the ships; with no harbour and a thirty foot swell, it was the only method of transferring everything from beer to bandages, sardines to sensitive material. The sky seemed to be full of choppers, most with stores slung in nets beneath them, a continuous conveyor-belt of coming and going. I was unable to go out and get material on the V.C.10, for the Americans running the base had not been briefed about me and wanted to know, 'what that God-damn woman was doing on the airfield!' It was maddening to see the VC10 in the distance, know she was shortly to take off, that I was missing vital seconds when I could be working, and that the next flight was in a couple of days time. On the American base amenities were good, meals were excellent. Many of the accommodation units were known as Concertina City, with walls similar to the bellows of my piano accordian. These units had arrived as folded packs, extending to make improvised accommodation and office units, and were superior to tented lodgings.

The Uganda was moored in the bay and I had an opportunity to paint history, but then found the helicopter flight that I had been assured was possible in order to see the ship, was cancelled because apparently I didn't file tidily under any specific category for the paper-work, and nobody knew what to write on my 'blood chit!' Politics and the endless change of arrangements as one man pulled rank on another made me irritable, angry and frustrated, thwarting my hopes of achieving any paintings, and increasing my anxieties. However, John took me off to show me the island, superb company, fun, and looked after me magnificently!

Ascension island being volcanic, seemed a lunar landscape, just like living in an enormous lumpy ashtray! In a Landrover we drove up Green Mountain. Being the highest, it is wrapped in sufficient mist for plant life to grow around the top, lush trees, flowers, bamboo and cacti, like custard topping a Christmas pudding. I was amused by John's snow-white trousers which would have looked more in place on board a ninety foot yacht than walking up Green Mountain, but he looked equally immaculate at the end. The radar unit at the top had superb views over the whole island. In the early evening we went swimming in a salt water swimming pool, joined by Ruth - she and I were sharing the bungalow together - she was an aeromed or nursing sister on an aircraft.

That night Ruth and I walked along the beach, joining a group of the men to see the green turtles nesting. To have arrived on Ascension at the one time of year when this happened was a wonderful bonus. I felt incredibly lucky to watch these huge reptiles purposefully hauling themselves up the beach for reproduction, the wide pattern of tracks marking their route from the sea. We gathered round to watch, almost silent, speaking in hushed cathedral voices lest we disturb her. She was over a metre in length and would have weighed in at about two hundred and fifty pounds, and could have been sixty, seventy or even eighty years old. Well above the highest tide line, she started to excavate the egg chamber, the saucer shaped scrape dug with hind flippers, amazingly dextrous, and then she excavated a deep hole - arm's length - before she stayed apparently motionless with the back of her shell poised over it. As she laid her eggs we could hear them dropping, hardly see them, until her task was completed, the number of eggs around a hundred, filling the hole to about six inches from the top of the nest. She moved to scoop a flipperfull of sand to cover them quickly, and for a moment they were quite visible, the size, shape and colour of ping-pong balls, but with a leathery surface and slight give to them. Then she started the laborious effort of covering all traces, using her front flippers forwards like somebody diving from a springboard, then drawing them back, the muscles in her flippers flexing to make them extremely efficient shovels, flinging the sand with such force that we had to retreat if too close behind her. In covering all traces of the egg chamber, she had cleverly produced a dummy scrape from the removal of sand to conceal the real nest, and then exhausted, started on her way down the beach to the sea, a slow, gruelling arduous task. One lad climbed onto her back for a moment or two. She moved forward as if unaware of the extra twelve stone weight. There is the legend that they weep with emotion and exertion; perhaps they do, but maybe it is a natural response to the amount of sand that must get into the eyes as they scoop it to and fro. This may have been her first egg laying visit, maybe she had already done so a fortnight before, perhaps again a fortnight later, probably five visits in all. The incubation would be seven to ten weeks, the eggs developing in a temperature of twenty-four to twenty-six degrees. If the temperature dropped below a certain point, all the baby turtles would be male, if higher in temperature, they would be female. One thing was certain, in about sixty days a mass of tiny hatchlings would erupt from the egg chamber, taking two or three days to reach the surface, a group effort, their body fuelled by the egg sack. Then, guided by the moon and the light of the stars reflected in the surface of the sea, the hatchlings would run the gauntlet to make their way to the water, those hatching out at night surviving better than those facing the daylight raids of frigate and other birds, crabs, lizards and fish, an extremely hazardous trek. It is believed that during this journey down to the sea, the tiny turtles absorb information that enables them to return one day to this very same beach, in order to lay their eggs when they had matured in thirty or more years. Green turtles are the only breed that migrate great distances, and some of those who nested on Ascention Island had been tagged, and found fourteen hundred miles away feeding off the coast of Brazil. Perhaps too, these beaches on Ascension Island might not face the problems of contruction and development, and also the pollution. I wouldn't have missed watching these turtles nesting for the world! My touch of the David Attenboroughs!

Next day I was able to get material of aircraft generally, and if politics reared its ugly head, it only meant my flight out to the Uganda had been cancelled again by the Station Commander. I never met him. Perhaps under the circumstances, it was just as well! Understandably I was torn between my impatience with him that he alone had put a stop to my getting material for a painting that would have had a place in history, and being aware that Ascension Island was extremely busy, he was ultimately responsible and had far more to do than concern himself with some wretched artist. One of the chopper crew had taken my camera when visiting the ship, but the results were far too dark to make out the necessary detail. Finally, when Uganda had sailed and was well out of reach, he gave me permission for a chopper flight! Frustrating, and too late! In the Sea-King I sat in the left hand seat, and with sacks of mail slung underneath the aircraft, we did a mail run to the four ships at anchor, a really worthwhile job and one of tremendous importance to the men. Then on for a tour of the island, hovering over the volcanic craters, everywhere a million shades of greys and browns from the terrain; the craters had fascinating names like Table crater, Spoon crater, Broken Tooth, Devil's Riding School, and Devil's Cauldron.

After we had landed, I had the knowledgeable company of Peter, an Army Major who took me along the coast and showed me the Wideawake or Sooty terns and their young. The airfield is named after this beautiful black backed tern which was so entrancingly graceful in flight. Later, Peter took several of us north of the only town, Georgetown, to Comfortless Cove, aptly named because in the mid 1800's, yellow fever victims were put ashore and abandoned from passing ships, and their graves and headstones were a sobering sight. So infectious was the disease that nobody would risk going near those suffering from it, the Marines used to take food along the beach, ringing a bell when they left it, moving away before the sick fetched the nourishment. Comfortless Cove was aptly named indeed. Then on to the northern coast to English Bay, the only cove where anybody dares to swim because of the wicked currents and undertow around the island, just watching the swell of those seas frightened me to death! Frigate birds and Sooty terns wheeled overhead.

Back at the bungalow, I was in serious trouble as unbelievably both my Leica cameras appeared to have jammed. Ruth was great, for I dived under my bedclothes to make an instant dark room, while she piled rugs and anything she could find on the top, and groping beneath the pile, I discovered one film had been faulty. I managed to detach it so thankfully I was back in action! Ruth and I spent another night watching the turtles, sleep seemed superfluous. Turn around time for a turtle laying her eggs was two and a half hours, and for a V.C.10 at the height of the war, forty minutes!

I was due to leave next day, and at long last would see ambulances parked beside the V.C.10, patients, mostly stretcher cases, being taken up on the hoist and fitted three deep in the aircraft, a flying hospital. They had arrived from the Falklands on a Hercules, been put into a huge inflated tent like a Michelin man, out of the sun, then not long before take off, were carried to the ambulances on route to the VC10. Time was of the essence, and while those on the flight deck were running through their pre-flight check, I photographed frantically from every imaginable angle, rushing up the steps to the aircraft for my flight home just as they were about to be rolled away. Ruth was working on board and grateful that I could help for there were many injured men to attend to. One man had a heavily bandaged hand as he had been fixing a sling on to the hook under a chopper, had not handled it properly and his thumb had gone up with the load. Ouch! Another was Major Stephen Hambrook, Royal Engineers. He had shown Margaret Thatcher round the Falklands - her visit had just taken place and she had a caravan with 'all mod cons' inside a Hercules to get down there and back - and within hours of her departure, he had lost a foot in a landmine. I spent much of the flight getting him cups of tea and listening while he told me what had happened, how he had asked his companions not to come to him in case the same fate awaited them, how he rolled back towards them, his mangled foot and boot hanging apart from where it should have been, his strapping it up and morphine, the wait for the chopper ... Ruth told me the injured had a need to talk. At times he was in such pain, speech was impossible, cramp often in the foot that was missing. He had refused morphine during the flight or any other painkiller as only without them, could his determination to greet his wife on his crutches and not on a stretcher, take place. He was a remarkable man, so full of guts, and if he was an example of a British soldier, what a marvellous race we British are!

The picture, underpainted in scarlet, was one of the most successful I worked on, reproduced as cards and prints for 10 Squadron, the latter presented to V.I.P's who flew with the Squadron, our Government, overseas personnel, and ... Royalty! It was also published in John Blake's, 'Flight, The Five Ages of Aviation', illustrated by members of the Guild of Aviation Artists. John is also a Founder Member of the Guild, exhibits his paintings regularly, is a Freeman of the Guild of Air Pilots and Navigators, and amongst his many interests (which include being the chief commentator at Farnborough Air Show,) finds time to write books on aviation history. To quote from the book, 'Penelope Douglas paints a number of Royal Air Force subjects in refreshing variety. Here she has admirably conveyed the atmosphere of efficient action surrounding a hospital aircraft ... Even among professional members, paintings of animated ground subjects as convincingly handled as hers are sufficiently scarce as to attract immediate attention.' Thanks John! A second painting was published in Jane's 'Aviation Review.' One thing is certain, I could never have produced those paintings without that flight to Ascension, and witnessing, first hand, a hospital aircraft.

CHAPTER 16

PRIVATE DOUGLAS - LEAN, MEAN AND DANGEROUS!

22 S.A.S. wanted a painting that showed a four man patrol in the centre, and round the outside the four individual skills that make up the patrol, all on one canvas. Languages - the background was the Middle East, soldiers and local men talking together; Demolitions - two men having set charges, watching the destruction of a bridge from a distance; Medical - putting up a drip for an injured soldier in the Falklands, and Signals. Working with PE - plastic explosive - for the demolition picture, I made a complete fool of myself, forgetting I was with experts, and when the charge was set I beetled away as fast as I could instead of moving slowly with the men, and the sight of my white face peering from behind a bush, they found hilarious. I got teased unmercifully, luckily managing to see the funny side too! As already mentioned, I loathe sudden, loud noises! With the medical part of the painting, joining the men for a lecture, I had my heart and pulse tested, and both must have been going like the clappers from the understandable nerves, not only of being picked out, but from my determined struggle at trying to put up a drip!

I had all the help I needed to get the material for the picture, stayed in the Officers' Mess, had the greatest of fun, at intervals wondering if I really was with such a crack Regiment or whether it was all makebelief. I got my leg pulled and many a laugh, caused them amusement too, and will never forget one evening watching the Clint Eastwood film, 'Every Which Way But Loose', because the comments of the men during it were hysterical! Of what I saw, learnt, heard, and took part in - sometimes taken completely by surprise which is part of the way the S.A.S. operate - inevitably all that I keep to myself. I have no photographs of the painting in my portfolio as it avoids people asking questions that I am not prepared to answer. Prints were made of the painting, and through discussion it was decided the five pictures should be divided up by a thin blue line, the colour of the S.A.S. belt. Later, they wished to change this to the colour of their fawn beret, and got a local firm to reprint over the blue line on every print. I never saw the results, but on one of my visits I repainted the dividing line on the original canvas. Being the unit they are, with the reputation they have, I felt very honoured at being with them, especially with their confidence in me and their trust that I could and would 'keep my mouth shut'. Without doubt they were a terrific bunch to work with. During my time with them I was included in all social events at what was then, Bradbury Lines, (now changed to Stirling Lines after David Stirling, who started the S.A.S.) and thoroughly enjoyed these occasions.

Having painted the individual skills, a second commission was for troop skills. I was to go overseas with the S.A.S., to the Middle East, but it was cancelled an hour before I was to leave home, for various reasons, one being that on documents the word 'artist' had been misinterpreted as 'reporter', causing chaos. However, arrangements were soon made for working with the Regiment, again overseas. Then the fun began! It would mean being with the soldiers for seven weeks, and flying from the U.K. with them in a Hercules. Now, as I had discovered on a previous occasion, there is a bit of red tape at the Ministry of Defence which says no female civilian may fly in that aircraft. Approached by the S.A.S., the R.A.F. remained steadfast to the rule book, and absolutly refused to let me anywhere near a Hercules. The S.A.S. were determined to get round this, and rang to say. … I was to join the Territorial Army! Private Douglas on parade? As instructed, I rushed up to London to the correct department for enlisting, faced with a Major who looked desperately ill, was pale green in complexion suffering from a horrendous migraine. The sight of me was almost more than he could face. I felt desperately sorry for him, but no, I couldn't come back some other time. After a prolonged effort to deal with the essential formalities, ashen and weak, he said,

"We usually get papers through within six months. Will that be all right?" In this situation I wondered how I had the audicity to reply,

"I'm afraid not. I need them fairly quickly."

"When do you want them by?" Poor man! I hated to do this to him. I took a big breath,

"Next Thursday!" I gave him six days!

This was followed by a whistle stop tour round various M.O.D. departments, and finally when all essentials had been completed, at the Duke of York's HQ I signed on the dotted line, swore my allegiance to my Sovereign and country, signed the official secret's act, and there I was, officially, 'A MEMBER OF HER MAJESTY'S ARMED FORCES, in the Headquarters Intelligence and Security Group (V) and attached to the Special Air Service Regiment,' my Service Number WO474697. All this had taken just over one week! No wonder I pinched myself! HARD! I also had to have a medical from a Colonel at Knightsbridge Barracks, and had been briefed by the S.A.S. what I could say in reply to any questions, which was basically no information whatsoever! The Colonel asked,

"Who are you with?"

"HQ. Intelligence and Security Group." To my amusement, this had the reaction that he not only looked at me admiringly, but shut up like a clam! No further questions followed while I was examined. Finally he risked speaking again,

"I know I mustn't ask you anything, but is your work mainly physical or mental?" What a georgous question! Ridiculous images flashed through my mind. What should I reply?

"Both," I said firmly, feeling once again like Winnie the Pooh demanding honey and balloons! It transpired he needed to give me a special ear examination if I would be parachuting, but this was not needed. The outcome of all this frantic to-ing and fro-ing was, I could now officially fly in a Hercules! The S.A.S. had, as they intended, dealt with the situation.

I knew I would be working with such a superb Regiment about six weeks before departure, and realistically felt it was vital that I should be as fit as possible. I would be the only woman with many men, and didn't intend to embarrass them or myself unnecessarily, so started a fitness programme, building up over the weeks, swimming for half an hour daily, walking just over twenty miles the first week, and between thirty-five and fifty a week towards the end. Any clothes that I needed, I purchased in quiet colours, mostly soft khaki greens, I packed an incredibly well cut brilliant yellow swimsuit and a couple of long skirts, 'just in case' and had nightmares wondering if I had got any of the things I would actually need! My main essentials were sketch pads, cameras and enough films to last the whole trip. At the Hereford garrison, I had been kitted out with army clothing, combat gear - the camouflage jacket and trousers, two pairs of each, jungle hat, also soft leather gloves with padding over the knuckles that turned out to be the best driving gloves ever. As it was unheard of that a woman should be needing all this within that particular Regiment, it was all accompanied by ribald remarks, laughter, and great entertainment!

"What size?" They looked my five foot two up and down while I stood helpless with laughter over their antics, "Ghurka size!" they announced as it echoed back through the stores! I was given a checklist for personal things, but as this started with shaving kit, (not again!), and mentioned shell dressings, rifle cleaning kit, parang, and paracord, it was more disconcerting than useful! Candles! Candlelit suppers? Hardly! Face veil? The image of beautiful figures on horseback, sidesaddle, with top hats and veils came to mind. What was an OPS waistcoat? Should I have drawn morphone × 2 before leaving?

When I reached the Hereford Garrison the night before departure, the Colonel asked what my mother thought about my destination.

"She doesn't know. You asked me not to tell anybody unless it was absolutly essential. She knows I couldn't be in better hands, and that is all." I hadn't intended to impress him, but I had clearly done so. I was told I could send her a postcard later on. Amongst other things the Colonel briefed me on, he added,

"You must realize Penelope, that unless you stay with the men, you will get raped. There is no doubt on that whatsoever." That was another sentence I shall remember until I die! The reason was that the Germans, if they chose, could book a holiday from their country which could include arrangements for sex with the Africans, all booked and paid for in advance, consequently many African men took it for granted that any woman who was white, would want sex with them, and were quite prepared to take it whenever there was an opportunity. (While in Kenya, in many of the bars and nightclubs, African women were encouraging their young daughters - many in their low teens - in prostitution. With Aids prevalent and on the increase in Africa, it was not surprising that later in the year, the Armed Forces were no longer permitted to take R and R - rest and recreation - after a tour in Africa.)

We were to fly from an R.A.F. base, and as it seemed sense to leave my car there ready for the return, I drove in convoy with my bright red Vauxhall Chevette tucked in between official coaches! It seemed incongruous and being on my own in the car I felt strangely detached and rather lonely. What the hell was I doing here? I had been anxious as to whether I would even be accepted by the Squadron I was going with. I had only met one or two of them briefly, the Officers, a small number from working on the previous painting, and felt an uncomfortable mixture of tremendous excitement and great apprehension. The Colonel had got to know me a little, and had said although the whole arrangement was unheard of and had never been done before, that is, anybody going on detachment with an S.A.S. Squadron, let alone a woman, that I would have no problems. I tried to reassure myself.

We took off, the aircraft packed, the Hercules got hydraulic problems and we returned to the base, to take off five hours later. Once airborne, within five minutes from being stationary at the end of the runway, we were given the signal that seat belts could be undone, and immediately men seemed to be moving everywhere, prowling like big cats, slinging hammocks and getting comfortable for the long flight. It was obvious that they knew exactly what they were doing and had no intention of experiencing any more discomfort than was necessary. Many had the Walkman music, some slept, some read. Talking was out due to the noise of the engines, cotton wool or ear defenders were much in evidence. I had neither. The seats were a nylon square, metal bar under the knees, webbing backed, and very soon, extremely uncomfortable. I was seated not far from the front door where it was too dark to read. Freight was packed in tightly, so I couldn't stretch my legs forward atall. Time hung heavily. The loo, a canvas bucket with a flimsy flapping curtain round it was half way up the side of the fuselage, and well ... best not to drink! We stopped on route in Crete for the night. I was stiff and tired. It looked so neglected, scruffy, untidy, dirty and dusty, building going on everywhere, and such a contrast from the U.K. On the next leg of the flight I was invited by the R.A.F. crew to use the top bunk on the flight deck with the luxury of being able to stretch out and read. We were flying at twenty-four thousand feet. Seven hours later we landed at Nairobi, for us no customs or passport control, and as a temporary Service member, several of us stayed in a country club, where I fell into bed arguing with a mozzi.

Arrangements had been made that I was to stay with Robin and Biddy, who had gone out from England to farm, had been in Africa for a long time and farmed dairy cattle and coffee. It would be easier for me, for when not working I would be with local people and enjoy the opportunities it would give me, and much easier for the soldiers who could wander from tent to tent starkers without bumping into a woman!

We all left Nairobi and from our base, I was taken on to my host and hostess, calves tethered round the farmhouse to keep the grass short, flowering shrubs, and homely atmosphere. Biddy's widowed mother, Ma B, of eighty-one lived in a stilted house in the grounds, she was charming, tough as old boots, had had both hips replaced, and her husband Sir Donald

Bailey (born in 1901) had designed the Bailey bridge. I felt I'd gone back fifty years to an old colonial set-up. I was told the African servants steal, though not those closely connected with working in the farmhouse. Antique furniture adorned every room, beautiful china, and my hosts, unbelievably had three Alsations, a terrier, two Boxers and ... seventeen labradors ALL IN THE HOUSE! (Could that be termed 'a protection racket'?) Next morning I was woken by Neongeza an African servant, and given breakfast, thick cream with Kenya coffee, then had a hair-raising drive into the local town with Ma B who couldn't see a thing, and I did her shopping for her while she sat in the car. Biddy had disappeared to run a horse three day event, Robin returned from the farm for lunch. With cattle, he was crossing the local Sibu with Guernseys, trying to produce an animal resistant to local disease and tolerant of dry conditions. He found this more satisfactory than the Sibu X Fresian and was complaining that he thought one of his cattle had been stolen.

The S.A.S. Major, (who I shall refer to as Boss) fetched me, and we went off in an opensided, hard topped Landrover, had roast impala with landowners some distance away, and drove through the bush for a while, a quick 'recce'. On return to the farm, the missing cow had been discovered with a broken leg, having caught it in a root both ends of which were firmly in the ground, on her way down to the river to drink. She had been missing for two days. Robin and the Africans had got her on to a trailer and back to the farm, the bone which was sticking out through the skin, all a gory mess, was put back in place, and Robin plastered it up, pumped stress vitamin B into her, and within half an hour she was on her feet. This was farming in Africa!

With the S.A.S. we had Gazelle helicopters flown by the Royal Marines, so for work, I was collected direct from a field above the farmhouse, usually the Boss was in the aircraft too. What a way to commute! Every African on the farm stopped work and gathered to watch the chopper land, collect me, then take off. The soldiers were now 'dug in' miles away out in the bush, brilliantly camouflaged, and we joined them.

Much of the time I was working, but when not doing so I joined Biddy and Robin, so I led two completely separate lives. In spite of Robin's care and the antibiotics, the cow got gangrene, he shot her, the African boys skinned her in the garden, and the meat used for both human and dog food, nothing was wasted. In the evenings I used to walk down by the river, plus Orlando, a particularly attentive Labrador, who, Biddy informed me, would tell me if the leopard was about! At the week-end we joined Biddy at the three day event, and after it was over Robin invited me to go with him in the Landrover to take an African, Henry to his house which was some distance away. It had rained, conditions were appalling, every inch of the driving Robin was steering into a skid or out of one, the track was alongside a lake which had hippo in it and were notoriously dangerous, Robin arguing that he was not prepared to drive another foot, and Henry replying again and again that his hut was just round the corner! Our return, bouncing through pot-holes and slithering back along the track had us and the vehicle covered in mud. Accommodation for the three day event was entirely tented - we were very relieved to get back - and learnt a puff adder, very poisonous, had been killed by one of the jumps. All those I met seemed public school types with a colourful range of four letter words and minds like sewers! I was aware that I was missing being with the S.A.S. - Biddy and Robin refered to them as 'my lads' - and their quiet friendliness, and was happy to get back to the farmhouse and work. The army kit, most fitting into a belt round the waist, included a water bottle and a curved mug affair the size and shape of a case for field-glasses. During work, they would stop 'for a brew.' Small but efficient cookers had water boiling quickly, and because of being constantly on the move, one brew would be made for each four man patrol, and it would be passed round. When it was handed to me, I took my drink and passed it on, later told,

"When we handed you the brew and you shared it without hesitation, we decided you were one of us!"

The S.A.S. are immensely private, not wishing to be recognised or known. Apart from one soldier who inquired curtly where the photographs were going to end up - he relaxed as soon as I said the Regiment would have them - I did not get the hostility from them that I was half expecting, and after a day or so, none of 'my lads' seemed to object to my sketching or photographing them. This meant I could relax, get to know them, and as time went by I grew into their ways and habits more and more. I certainly had no problems, was totally accepted by the men. Once, when we paused briefly during moving through the bush, I raised myself upwards to take a photograph, & got a hiss from behind me,

"Get your bloody head down Penny, or you'll get shot." I was becoming more a soldier and less an artist! Being out in the bush we saw game galore which I really appreciated. Mostly they looked in excellent condition. We disturbed a giraffe right beside the track, and seated in the Landrover level with its knees, its height took my breath away! I learnt there had been an accident yesterday, when Africans with tractor and trailer had been out in the bush, one of them riding on the tow bar had fallen, the trailer wheel going over him. With great confidence in the British Army, knowing we were nearer than anybody, the Africans asked for help. The medics had been checking their kit, went straight to the scene, rendered first aid, put up a drip, and got the chopper diverted there, getting the injured man to hospital in Nairobi. Without us, his chance of survival was nil.

Out in the bush, on exercise, work went well for all of us. I fired a GPMG (General Purpose Machine Gun), could see the tracer going, even ricocheting off distant rocks. When we spent the night working as well as the day, I had only barest essentials in my back pack with cameras. Stars were brilliantly bright, one of my lads knew names of constellations - how amazing it was to look at millions of stars and when somebody says,

"You see the group there ... ." pointing to the Heavens, that you KNOW you are all looking at the same group of stars! I could understand ancient man thinking the sky was a vast dome. Southern Cross and the Great Bear could be seen in the same sky. One amusing incident, I was supposed to climb up onto some rocks on a given signal, to photograph immediately with only a few seconds in which to do so, found the rock too high for me as I tried to get a foothold to climb quickly, and next moment I felt hands under my thighs, and I was up! For food we had twenty-four hour rations that took up very little room or weight to carry, but with the addition of water for dried menus, produced a relatively tasty, substantial meal. My bedroom, when work finished towards dawn, was a four ton truck! My fitness enabled us - me too - to cope with everything though it didn't prevent us feeling tired after a long session's work. During the night, lion could be heard roaring. I watched dawn break and the sun rise from the ridge, down below were some African mud dwellings, their cattle and goats, all surrounded by a thorn hedge.

Boss, and what I shall call Deputy Boss and Boss Three joined me for supper in the farmhouse. Boss Three had been with one of the S.A.S. expeditions and had climbed to the summit of Mount Everest. Biddy and Robin were away, Neongeza, dressed in white, went to town starting with shutting all twenty plus dogs out of the room! The oldest dog, much loved by Biddy, was incontinent one end and sick the other, often in the middle of a meal, which would have taken the top off the evening! Nassar, the African cook provided a delicious three course meal, and (instead of meals on our laps in the sitting-room,) Neongeza prepared the dining-room table with all the silver and best crockery! Clearly he intended Memsahib should have the best with her three men! Neongeza waited on us and never stopped beaming throughout. I sometimes put my hair up - after the usual bath with brown water in which I was unable to see my limbs three inches below the surface - and wore a long skirt. We had several of these evenings, a welcome change and interlude from the harsh conditions and work, were served a really scrumptious meal, a treat for us all, and for me particularly, listening to superb conversation. If Biddy and Robin were out rather than away, they usually returned around one in the morning - the pack of dogs would roar into the room - then whisky all round for my lads and a change to more general conversation.

One time Caroline arrived, a friend of my hosts, who had trained many of the animals for the film, 'Out of Africa' - Robin had an extras part though I never discovered him - Robin and Biddy were away, Caroline confided that it was time the old Labrador met a peaceful end, she knew that Biddy couldn't face dealing with it but would be relieved, for the quality of the dog's life had become appalling. Mogadon, she decided, giving the old fellow about a dozen tablets. As I was always up before Robin and Biddy, to meet the helicopter, I knew it would be my lot to find the old dog dead next morning, so I didn't sleep well that night. Because of the mess he made the dog slept in the porch. As I opened the inner door quietly at dawn I heard his tail thumping with joy! He had suffered no ill effects whatsoever, if anything seemed considerably fitter and less full of arthritis than before, and Biddy never knew about it!

One of the extraordinary things of being picked up for work in the Gazelle, was hearing the medley of songs on the radio, that I can hear on Radio 4 in the U.K. around six in the morning. It seemed so incongruous to be flying over the African bush listening to that familiar link. Of the three Marine pilots, one had been nick-named the 'Cardboard box' because although a good pilot, he flew entirely by the rule book. Another pilot was a natural, often taking his own course, flying lower, following a river bed, so with the latter, we saw much more wildlife, and had more fun. Word filtered back to me that my lads were delighted to have me with them, and were glad I was a female, therefore non-competitive. Certainly I felt totally at home with them all, if anything picking up some of their habits and lifestyle during work, and still becoming more like them. Had I been a noisy, bumptious, full-of-myself woman, I would not have lasted a minute! Although they knew the reason for my being with them, I don't think MY past, or work, came up in conversation atall. I didn't mind a bit but it was unusual I suppose. Everything worked together very well, such as my going to Nairobi with Robin and Biddy for a week-end, then picked up by one of my lads for the return journey, on our way to join the rest of the Squadron.

Although it was common knowledge, I had not appreciated that the British had a presence in Kenya all year round in the form of one Regiment or another. The terrorist uprising of the Mau-mau during the 1950's when Kikuyu tribesmen had tried to end colonial rule and drive white settlers out of Kenya, had not been forgotten. What I had not expected was the deep rooted fear and obvious unease of the settlers thirty years later. Due to the African safari rallies, many, like Robin and Biddy, had kept the radios that they had used at rally check points, and these were used every morning to white friends in other outlying settlements, ensuring all was well with everybody. As regards the Regiments being there, they create security, plus a great many people could get onto a Hercules in an emergency. Biddy enlightened me that the neighbouring Africans would murder us if things went wrong, our own staff Neongeza and Nassar would probably kill whites in another settler homestead. There were occasions when Robin and Biddy went to Nairobi for a few days, that I was on my own with the Africans, the nearest other white person five miles away, and no method of getting hold of my lads. It would have been pointless to have felt uneasy.

The British Army were made extremely welcome, their presence much appreciated, none more so than the S.A.S. Due to this and being lucky enough to be included in most events to which Boss and Deputy Boss were invited, during a short break from working, I joined them staying in The Ark safari lodge with a salt lick, woken during the night by an intercom buzzer when particular animals had arrived, either at the lick or for food put out on the veranda. Three rhinos came together, quite close to us, bush buck, buffalo, hyena, cape hares, white-tailed mongoose, elephant, and the noise of the frogs croaking nearby was amazing. Part of the lodge was not glazed, so we could hear the elephants nosing (can an elephant 'nose'?) through the earth, digging it loose with their tusks. What wonderful animals, I had never seen wild elephant so close! Because of being with my lads, we seemed to be guests, free, treated like V.I.P's., and if they signed visitors' books, I was expected to do the same as one of the Regiment. Next morning, Boss was collected from the Safari Lodge in the Gazelle much to the interest of onlookers, and the news was circulating that Maggie Thatcher had just won the general election again which seemed to delight everybody, more British than the British!

Back at work I was doing well getting the material I needed for the painting. Somewhere I'd picked up a tummy bug, felt faint out in the bush while photographing, said nothing, slid into the shade of a tree close by, and Boss presuming I was finding the hundred degrees of heat a bit much, took my back pack for me, asking me to join them for a brew when I'd finished, and I recovered. But a couple of days later I still had the bug, Biddy gave me something for it which she gave to the dogs and worked for her! It had no effect. I had been told by the S.A.S. medic to go to him if needed, but my stupid pride got in the way, and I had felt slightly shy and embarrassed at having to admit I was feeling wretched. At that point I had a couple of days free, Robin and Biddy were away, so I collapsed on my bed to try to sleep it off, Neongeza bringing me drinks at intervals and telling me I was extremely ill! Still feeling lousy, I got desperate and went to see the S.A.S. medic and found many of my lads had also suffered, and the tablets he gave me cleared it up immediately. Served me right for not going to him in the first place!

One Sunday Biddy and Robin wanted to take me to a game reserve, so we left at dawn to spend much of the day there. As I was working that afternoon, a suitable map reference was chosen where we, in the Landrover, could meet up with the helicopter. Once in the game reserve, our real treat was watching a leopard for a couple of hours; she had killed a large white bird and was enjoying her meal up in a tree. We had superb views of her. At that time, seeing game was a peaceful, pleasantly lonely delight, no convoys of tourist vehicles. We came across a herd of elephant including some very young being carefully shepherded along by the adults, these small calves looked so vulnerable, yet even in a throng of massive full grown animals, would not get mislaid or trodden on. We enjoyed our picnic in the shade, cheeky baboons hoping to disturb us no doubt to steal any leftovers. At the appointed time I slipped into my camouflage gear, miraculously the chopper appeared over the trees as expected and I joined my lads, though meeting up in the middle of a game reserve, not a signpost in sight, seemed incredulous!

Out in the bush, going was tough. We met some Samburu tribesmen complete with necklaces and spears, and my lads had a great time bargaining on what I was worth if they swapped me for spears! Five! Good to know of my value! The African tribesmen were very surprised to see a woman with the Army. Some of my lads could speak Swahili, and told me they had explained I was a strong, brave soldier! Cheers! My four tonner suite awaited me that night for the last time, as I progressed to a Landrover with my feet sticking out of the open door, and finally to dossing down on the ground amongst the men, which I thoroughly approved of!

Back at the farmhouse the dogs had found the rotting carcass of one of the cattle, had both eaten and rolled in it, then come into the house, the stench was absolutly sickmaking and quite ghastly. Biddy turned the dogs into the garden but it had little effect on the smell indoors. Thankfully I was out in the field before six next morning ready for the chopper. With my lads, again going was ardous. Everywhere seemed to be thorns that grabbed us affectionately as we passed through them, and stabbed us if on a steep slope we were foolish enough to put a hand down. The two essentials for living out in the bush were clean teeth and clean socks. Nothing else seemed as important! I had helped to make up an ammunition belt, and fired a rifle next day in a cross-legged seated position as they thought the kick might knock me off balance, consequently it wasn't as bad as I expected. I fired it several times.

Back to the farmhouse, I spent next day with Caroline, setting off at dawn, going up Mount Kenya to eleven thousand feet, finding it not unlike Scotland, wide open moorland, rocky crags, and breathtakingly beautiful. Caroline was an extraordinary woman, had undergone many, many operations on her mouth for a cleft palette, knew a great deal about animals, yet made almost no effort with her appearance, contentedly looking both happy and scruffy. She was fascinating company and could tell wonderful stories of her life in Kenya and training animals for films.

My lads held a barbecue one evening for a few settlers. My pony-tail hair and camouflage gear were changed to suit the occasion.

"Didn't recognise you Penny," one of my lads said with a twinkle.

"Just thought I'd prove I was female!"

"We've none of us had any doubt about that!"

Amongst a group of my lads towards the end of the evening, one of them, having consumed a fair amount of alcohol, said he thought it was wrong that I should be out there with them as I cramped their style. The reaction from all the others was immediate, emphatically denying it as 'rubbish.' One man said he'd ceased to notice me, in his opinion proving that I was just one of them. That, I took as a compliment!

I was due to join the Mobility group, as they were part of the painting, and was picked up in a wonderful old fashioned ambulance being the only vehicle available, meeting up with the chopper later. I joined them with the vehicles out in the bush, very surprised to see pink Landrovers - yes, pink! Very pretty, just the opposite of the tough group dealing with them, but as regards camouflage, these vehicles just merged into their surroundings - as they do in the desert - the colour having been well tried and tested. It was astonishing how a group of men could cut their way through the bush, over hills, down ravines, where there were no roads and no vehicles had gone before. This would be a pleasure to paint and I grabbed material as fast as possible.

We moved our area for working to the coast, the R.A.F., who had just arrived from the U.K. joined us with the Hercules for parachuting - another part of the painting - and the R.A.F. were booked into a hotel, a room reserved for me if I wished. I didn't! Not only was I totally content with my lads, but I think I would have got lynched and been treated as a deserter had I taken up the offer! It was an interesting contrast that some of the R.A.F. staying in the hotel were quite young, living in comparative luxury, the reason given that when dealing with aircraft maintenance they had lives in their hands so needed a proper night's sleep, while my lads, some of them mid thirties and I, lived in the rough, taken to and fro to the Hercules in a four tonner along a heavily rutted dirt track, inside which we were flung drunkenly from side to side if not hanging on for grim death! Another contrast was when there was a delay at the DZ; I was with several of my lads on the ground, waiting for the parachuting, and due to a slight delay there was time for a brew, and although we were miles from any civilisation, the R.A.F. set off in their vehicle to try to find a cafe, and my lads merely removed a small piece of turf, lit the stove that they carried, made a brew, and replaced the turf, all in seconds it seemed. Some of the DZ's proved unsuitable for parachuting, the higher the altitude the less oxgyen, and the faster the men fell, dangerously so. However, other places were excellent. Having got material of the parachutists landing, I joined them in the aircraft, from which they would be jumping into water. I was watching very experienced, confident free-fall experts. The Hercules was equipped for the Special Forces, the crew extremely proficient. The tail gate was opened like a huge mouth at about twelve thousand feet, the captain gave the aircraft a slight flip to lock the top in position while we all experienced G force, and in order to see and photograph my lads leaving the aircraft, I was fitted in the side of the tail gate, replacing a tea caddy! We were flying at around twelve thousand feet, and as the tail gate opened and I caught sight of the space and ground below me, my face must have shown my amazement for I discovered my lads were grouped together watching my expression! They weren't disappointed!

We used as our base a small airport away from prying eyes; there was an occasion when we had to hang about for a couple of hours while the Herc had attention. This meant a chance to sunbathe and relax, stretched out round the aircraft, and one or two of the men stripped completely.

"Hey mate, should you do that, Penny's here!" said one of the men.

"Oh Penny doesn't mind!" answered another!

At night we slept together in grass huts on the beach, mozzi nets an absolute essential and thank God one of the hotel based R.A.F. had lent me his, for the insect wildlife wished to eat us alive! At the right time of year when there were no mosquitos or sandflies about, these were luxury back-to-nature huts built of rushes and palms, situated right on the beach, used by the rich and famous including Elizabeth Taylor and Richard Burton. A low rush wall surrounded each, could be stepped over but kept crabs out, the huts had no glass in window openings or doors, a few palm trees in the area, a glorious beach and extremely romantic. It was a chance to swim and relax ... and work. Imagine this wonderful setting, wandering along the beach, nobody about, the most tranquil, peaceful scene, out to sea not a boat in sight, just the lilt and gentle swish of the waves breaking, the rhythm of the water singing one of nature's lullabies, I was totally alone, all was calm as I watched the waves, almost mesmerized ... a slight movement among them, something dark, black, eerie, and ... out of the water crawls a man, black wet suit from head to foot, only his face visible - or rather invisible due to camouflage cream - and ... he is fully armed. What a contrast! At night, if taken unawares by this unexpected experience it could be extremely frightening and very unnerving, but then the chances of anybody actually seeing their stealthy arrival from the ocean would be extremely unlikely. I was expecting them! Even so I found it quite a shock!

Next day canoes were assembled, one needed patching so as a dressmaker I showed them herringbone stitch. 'One girl is more use than twenty boys,' to quote from Peter Pan! We also had Gemini boats. The S.A.S. work exceptionally hard, but situations are often dangerous even in training. One man got into the propeller blade, badly sliced down his left side and buttock, flown to hospital in Nairobi. Next day from the Hercules, we said our farewells to some of the boat troop and free fall lads, and left with the customary low pass at a hundred feet as salute, then the Captain told me smilingly, to hold on tight, then banked the aircraft up and away 'putting G force'. Quite something in a Hercules! We returned to Nairobi, and I joined my lads out in the bush once more.

We had another parachute session inland, time for this fast running out, but conditions were appalling with wind gusting suddenly, and many men got blown off course. No more jumping; I was with the ground crew, and we spent the rest of the day collecting men from different parts of the bush, some as far as a kilometer away, two chutes being a total write-off due to the thorns. Our Landrover punctured twice, and it was all pretty impossible but thankfully nobody was injured. An amusing incident happened on our way home, when with several more punctures we were repairing one of the tyres when a group of Africans came past in a truck.

"Don't worry," they shouted as they passed, "If you need help the S.A.S. are based not far from here!" Lovely! Of the four wheels, we had two punctures in one tyre, four in another, twenty-six in the third, and twenty-eight in the fourth! So much for thorns!

We were now reaching the end of our time. Another chopper flight from the farmhouse, various tasks on route, and we joined the mobility group again. They had made astonishing and rewarding progress. The vehicles had inched forward as a track in front of them was cleared. The men worked incredibly hard trying to reach the top of a ridge. As we had the Gazelle there it was a chance for a recce. It seemed the most impassable terrain had been achieved over the first two thirds of their distance. We had a look at the lake nearby, crocodiles about fifteen or sixteen foot in length, basked below us. That evening heading back for the farmhouse, I had done over five hundred miles in the Gazelle that day.

Shortly afterwards it was time for me to leave with the first group of those going back to the U.K. These included any of my lads who had been injured. We refuelled at Luxor, incredibly hot, and on to Crete, which after my weeks in Kenya seemed clean and tidy, the reverse of my feelings about it on our way down! Here we had a meal out. I was with a group of men who were clearly injured, limping, in plaster or on crutches. These, the S.A.S.? We all saw the funny side. A waitress wished to know why?

"Playing rugger," was the reply! 'Scouse' said if she thought we were mercenaries from Africa, I must be the cook!

Back in the U.K. after being at a reasonable height for several weeks, I felt wonderfully invigorated, energy abounding. Over the period, we had all become more 'lean, mean and dangerous', and looked it, even me! I had left at my lightest weight and lost nearly a stone. I had lived through the most amazing experiences, and had observed and participated in activities that I would never have been involved with in civilian life. It has been very hard to write this part of the narrative, because I am not at liberty to talk about it. Once again, what I saw, learnt and heard, is for myself, alone. However, as part of my visit to Kenya was staying with white settlers, it would have been a pity to produce a totally blank piece of paper!

Once again I had been the only woman amongst a group of men. Again I welcomed that comaradarie, a feeling, an atmosphere, a closeness, a loyalty linking them which is impossible to describe. If I try, I will not do it justice. It is that indefinable intangible something - a quality totally unique and extremely vital and special. I spent longer at any one period, with the S.A.S. than with any other Squadron or Regiment, I was therefore enormously privileged to be a part of it, to share this unique experience and be welcomed to do so with such warmth and acceptance. It is something I shall never forget. I feel certain this mysterious quality would never be found within a group of only women.

I was in the T.A. for six months then given my discharge papers. I was amused that the covering letter told me not to bother to get my signature witnessed on the form, to send it back and they would deal with it! I was not being paid for being in the Army, but presumably the computer didn't know that, so finally I received a document from the Paymaster General saying that I had been paid nought pounds and nought pence! I imagine the computer was satisfied! The completed painting was divided into four, and showed mobility, mountain climbing, parachuting and a Gemini with frogmen.

Although the Eastern Counties Newspapers put an article in the paper under, 'Artist with her head in the clouds,' it referred to a painting of a Spitfire flying amongst some clouds, which the Press commissioned for one of their staff as a retirement present. The truth was, after the tour in Kenya, I had to come down to earth.

After working with 22 S.A.S., I was commissioned by 23 S.A.S, and headed north to meet a group of them to discuss the forthcoming painting. No sooner had we become seated than their Boss handed me a beautiful scarlet rose - it was Valentine's Day!

23 S.A.S. are volunteers. In working life they were in a wide variety of civilian jobs, their Army lifestyle unknown to all they were working with and

kept secret, and they would meet at the S.A.S. HQ in their particular area, change into Army gear, metamorphosing into trained soldiers. They wanted many different small paintings on one canvas. This is always difficult, and does not necessarily work. The Armed Forces tend to feel they are having several subjects depicted while only paying the fees for one canvas. It isn't always the answer, but this time it worked well.

To get the material I travelled all over Great Britain, joining many different groups for various activities. I was apprehensive of working with one group, partly because I guessed they would be the toughest bunch of the lot, and also, as they had a very strong Scottish accent I might have problems understanding them! My anxieties were totally unfounded, as a musical ear is quick to latch on to a dialect, they proved great fun and presented me with a silver quaich inscribed, 'Presented to Penelope Douglas by 'A' Squadron 23 S.A.S.(V) June 1986.' Understandably I am very proud of it.

The painting, on a large four foot by three foot canvas had a central picture of a four man patrol, with twelve small paintings framing it. One of these was of the changing room, important because every single man passed through that, my presence there caused much amusement, and as required, a small Mickey Mouse tattoo on the right cheek of a certain buttock was included! The painting was made into cards for the Regiment, all cards and prints available to both 22 and 23 S.A.S.

Some months after returning from Kenya, I went to the Ministry of Defence to make arrangements for the next Regiment going on detachment to Kenya, to take a video out to Robin and Biddy for me. All parcels that arrived by post in Kenya were opened, contents confiscated, but I knew it would reach them by this method. While I waited, I glanced at the row of seated men also in the room. One in particular made me think ... I had never met him before, but just the way he was sitting, his footwear, just in glancing at him, some sense told me he was one of the S.A.S. As I was leaving the building, the man approached me,

"You're Penelope Douglas. I've seen you at Hereford." We exchanged conversation briefly before I went on my way; after working with the S.A.S. so closely, my sixth sense had been right!

CHAPTER 17

A VISIT TO THE GUNNERS

I gave talks - photographic slide shows - calling them, 'Travel, Art and Aeroplanes.' These were to art groups, Women's Institutes or whoever asked me to speak, and I showed a mixture of photographs of paintings and places I'd visited while getting the details for them. In Barnham Broom, near Norwich, a new village hall had been built and I decided to give a talk there. I had not exhibited at the Assembly House in Norwich since my break from painting, so produced new, small landscapes, and included unsold early paintings, turfing them out of the cupboard, putting a low price on them, having a good clear out! I advertised the evening a couple of times in the Press, and with help once again from Michael Brett, prepared the room, optimistically putting out thirty chairs. Nobody was more surprised than I to find over two hundred people had come, many having to stand after we ran out of chairs! I didn't charge people an entrance fee, but two friends held money boxes at the door as people left, and the donations went to the Friends of the Norfolk and Norwich Hospital, for anything from new curtains round a bed to medical equipment.

Private commissions followed, some of aircraft. I found models a great asset. Ellis and Barbara Holden lived nearby, and Ellis very kindly made the models for me to a high professional standard.

I had read the true story of the only Second World War 'action' to occur on the island of Coll, Scotland, tragic rather than threatening, when some schoolboys saw a misfiring Spitfire heading towards Kilbride. Although they tried to tell people, the response was,

"'Ach, wee laddies at the war games," so it was three days later that the manager of Breacachadh Creamery, out for a walk along the shore, came across the remains of the aircraft and the pilot near Hyne, a deserted ruin. The young pilot, Stevens, had been on a training mission with two other Spitfires which took off from Stirling, and Stevens never returned. I thought the story moving, an episode effected by the training of desperately young pilots during the war. As the article had mentioned remnants of the aeroplane could still be seen, so of interest to early aircraft buffs, I produced a painting of it for the next Guild of Aviation Artists exhibition - a tranquil scene, the remnants of the old Spitfire with sheep grazing peacefully round it. When the paintings were hung, both Michael Turner who was a Founder Full Member and President of the Guild, and also one of the Joseph brothers had shown aircraft with sheep too. It was the Year of the Sheep, we decided!

I received a letter from an Admiral in the United States Navy saying he was so taken with the painting of the Red Arrows flying above the Houses of Parliament, he wanted a print of it to hang in his office at NATO

Headquarters in Brussels. These had not been made but I sent him a photographic enlargement of the painting. It was not unusual to receive correspondence about my work, nor for curious things to crop up. On one of these occasions, I was to meet up with somebody working at the Ministry of Defence, and arriving at the allotted time, as I walked up the steps to enter the building, he came out.

"Penelope Douglas?" I confirmed it. "Can you read music?" It was the last question I was expecting.

"Well, yes, after a fashion."

"Good. Come with me!" He led the way to the Guards' Chapel, explaining as we hurried across Horseguards Parade that he was due to take an organ examination that afternoon - the highest possible - and wished to run through his music once more, needing somebody to turn the pages for him. It was an unexpected lunch hour to say the least! For the organ there are three lines of music to read, the lowest being for the feet. I had learnt the instrument for a year at Sherborne, (and with a rectorial father had the organ available at any time,) and although following such a complicated score was a challenge, I revelled in such beautiful music as it echoed around me. It was immensely stimulating and satisfying.

When I am commissioned for animal portraits, I go to see the animal as soon as possible, even if there is a delay while completing other work, before I can start on the picture. On one occasion I was asked for a cat portrait, and was told that it had kidney problems but there was no hurry. I went to see her the following day, it was sunny, and I took the photographs I needed, thankful later that I had acted straight away, for the cat had deteriorated suddenly, put down the day after my visit.

Having completed various orders, I was asked to do a large three by four foot canvas for the 26th Field Regiment Royal Artillery, and drove down to the south coast to Thorney Island, to meet Lieutenant Colonel Hugh Welby-Everard. It was to show guns and crews, with the estuary in the background. Estimates for the work proved acceptable, and I started collecting information. On Thorney Island, watching the vehicles and guns being manned was fascinating. I met up with them at Larkhill on Ministry of Defence property. It was during this, sheltering with others, the guns some distance behind us, the target ahead, I could hear the whistle of the ammunition as it passed above me! Every part of the painting had to be extremely accurate, and I impressed on Hugh that I would not have the knowledge to realize if some technical piece of equipment was incorrect, and he was excellent at making sure things were as they should be.

"Don't put the kettle in the picture, will you Penelope!" said one man cheerfully looking at his glintingly bright kettle sitting beside one of the guns!

While getting details for pictures I probably appeared rather silent. This was simply because things often happened quite quickly, time was possibly limited, and mainly because my brain was going like the clappers on endless decisions as to HOW I was going to show the subject. By the time I'd got all the information assembled and worked things out, I couldn't wait to get at my brushes!

This painting went well; when visiting I enjoyed staying with Hugh and his family enormously, and the picture included plenty of action and several guns and vehicles, and had prints made from it. As usual I quoted the costs of all the prints and delivered them, leaving the Royal Artillery to set their own selling price and deal with the marketing.

The formal Guild dinners had come to an end, but I continued helping by being on the committee. Sometimes I was on the Selection panel for the annual exhibition, perhaps with a different approach from many people, for I certainly didn't know every nut and bolt of each aircraft, but instead, judged a picture more on the general appearance, appeal, tone, and painting technique. For many years I worked with the Selection panel, making notes on each painting entered for Submission, the vote on whether it was accepted, rejected, or doubtful and to be seen again, and keeping a running total of those accepted, so we had approximately the correct number to hang for each particular gallery. I enjoyed these times. Almost without fail, after several hours of intense concentration, all the paintings had been seen and the selection panel was about to relax, Yvonne arrived like a Force 10 gale among paper boats, insisting that some person's paintings which had all been rejected, be seen again and one, at least, accepted. She always had reasons for giving the artist a second chance, but those of us who knew of this after-selection-ritual would groan inwardly and wish we were in the Bahamas!

CHAPTER 18

OH GOD!

On 21st May, 1987, I received a letter from Raymond Hubble, the padre with whom I had worked in Germany. He had left the R.A.F., becoming vicar of All Saints Odiham, Hampshire, where he inherited a gulf between R.A.F. Odiham and the parish church, mainly due to the previous incumbent being more ready to ban the bomb than acknowledge the Armed Forces. The Station Commander Group Captain Tim Garden MA MPhil RAF wished to make tangible the link between town and Station, Ray had suggested installing some glass in the church, and his letter invited me down to discuss the possibility of my producing a design.

The visit was a fruitful one. Over the vestry door was a large window shaped to a central point at the top, measurements roughly six foot eight inches across, eight foot six inches in height. It had plain clear glass with the Lord's Prayer inscribed on the lowest section. I was to design a replacement. It was to be an R.A.F. window.

R.A.F. Odiham is the home of the Tactical Helicopter Force, several Squadrons stationed there in the past, others currectly based there with Pumas and Chinooks. During the discussion my immediate thoughts were to represent each Squadron by using their individual badges, leaving out the surrounding crown and laurel leaves common to them all. The badge of R.A.F. Odiham could be worked in as well. My Squadron designs were 18 Squadron - Pegasus, 7 Squadron - The Great Bear, 33 Squadron - a hart, 72 Squadron - a swift, 230 Squadron - a tiger, and 240 Squadron - a humming bird. They were a perfect way to represent each. The R.A.F. also wanted two helicopters operated by the Squadrons incorporated in the design, the Puma and Chinook.

Again I got in touch with Dennis and Michael King in Norwich, who were delighted to take on the work of making the window, and I had several meetings with them, mostly to discuss whether my design would be possible, what shapes could be cut in glass without it shattering, and where best to put the leads. Once more, I had almost no knowledge behind me, working with top professionals, and I spent an enormous amount of time thinking about it all and trying out different ideas at home. I was not helped by the existing horizontal support bars which apparently would be staying there, one of which was very thick.

I decided to have the R.A.F. Odiham badge - a castle - in the centre. From this I had radiating spokes such as a child might draw the rays of the sun, gold in colour, representative of the sky and the sun giving light and life. They also symbolised part of a jet engine in the form of division into segments. The outside of the spokes joined a gold circle, a reminder that the tips of a Spitfire's propellors are usually gold, and when taxiing the gold circle is quite obvious. Worked into the segments, and close to the gold circle would be four of the Squadron badges at the points of north, south, east and west, a further two below the gold circle, with the two helicopters at the bottom. Both badges and choppers would be surrounded by coloured glass. As the window was internal and over the vestry door, it needed to have as much light in it as possible, so round the outside of each chosen symbol would be a band of colour, then clear glass, that within the gold circle divided up with circular leads, those outside it with vertical and horizontal leads. At the very top of the window I had three half moon symbolic shapes of cloud, below them the gold R.A.F. Eagle. The glass would be beautiful hand made glass, full of movement, ripples and tiny bubbles.

The next stage for the R.A.F. and the town, was to raise the funds to cover all the cost of production, starting with the approval of the Parochial Church Council in Odiham, and for me, visits to R.A.F. Odiham to work with the Squadrons, see the helicopters, and sort out how best to represent each one. I had an exciting flight in a Chinook when they took me over some woods, then descended vertically into a clearing to land, showing me the versatility of the aircraft. I also saw them flying with a lorry slung underneath, deciding this should go in to the window design. The Puma would be shown on the ground, having just landed two soldiers.

Having completed the draft, it had to go before a delegation of the Diocesan Advisory Committee, who wrote to Ray Hubble to say they were not entirely happy with the proposed design. It was felt the metal frame of the existing clear glass screen in the tower arch had 'somewhat compromised the artist's proposed plan. The broad bar across the aperture is far too obtrusive and should be entirely removed, together with the other thinner bar and the upright staunchions ... ' Thank goodness! We were all delighted! It meant the whole scheme had to be drawn out and painted again, submitted again, a meeting of the D.A.C. again. It seemed a lengthy process, but interesting to learn all about the channels through which a church window design had to pass. Without the existing leads, the blueprint looked greatly improved.

Michael King was enthusiastic, and they agreed to make the window providing I did the actual painting on the glass of each of the badges and choppers. This meant I would be using a totally different type of paint and range of colours, none of which was familiar. How would firing affect them? That in itself was a major headache to me. I knew my oils intimately and what colour would appear. New paints were a whole new ball game. Painting on glass was the same. Added to that I had another problem looming large on the horizon, that King would make the window and deliver the glass, but not put it into the church. More complications! The R.A.F. wanted the window installed by the Battle of Britain memorial time of September 1989, and in August 1987, King felt they could reach that deadline. Although they would have preferred November, they thought two years would give them sufficient time. The D.A.C. wrote to Ray saying they were happy with the altered design, and could now recommend a faculty for the work. Another official procedure! In September, I received the official quotation from King.

During the following year funds were raised, and I got on with other work. Eighteen months later in February 1989 Ray wrote to say he had asked J.H.Glazing of Croydon to install the window, and would arrange the necessary faculty authorisation for the proper ecclesiastic procedures. Once we had that, I could do the cartoon - the life size pattern. All seemed to be in place ... or was it? In March 1989 Group Captain John R.Day OBE BSc RAF took over as Station Commander at Odiham, and requested the addition of the Wessex helicopter in the design.

At that point, the Guild was honoured in having His Royal Highness Prince Edward to open the annual exhibition. I had planned to exhibit the window design, but having been asked to include a third helicopter, there was no time to re-do it in time for 'selection', and it was disappointing that for once I had no paintings hung, for I would not have been happy showing a design that was inaccurate. Nevertheless, as only Full Members were present when Prince Edward viewed the paintings, I enjoyed being there.

Group Captain John Day gave me all the details I needed for visiting R.A.F. Chivenor, Devon, where the chopper was based, who to get in touch with, see it in action and work out the best way to depict it, then add it to the project. He also informed me that the Service of Dedication was arranged for Sunday 3rd September, he had secured the services of a Regimental band with a fanfare of trumpets, and compiled a distinguished guest list. He was obviously very excited about the forthcoming event.

I wrote to Michael King immediately, giving him the latest information, and yet again, re-did the design to include the third helicopter.

That year I had moved to Devon into a farming partnership with several others, optimistically hoping to combine my art work with my love of animals and the countryside. Having visited Chivenor and added the Wessex to the scheme, and drawing and painting the helicopter panels the actual size that they would be when the window was installed, I thought it was important for the Station Commander to see and approve them before they were reproduced in glass. It would mean going to Odiham, so I rang him for an appointment.

"Why don't I come to you Penelope? I could come by air."

"Well, that would be marvellous. Would you come to Chivenor, or alternatively, what about landing here?" I had no idea how this suggestion would be received. It sounded outrageous but worth a try!

"How big a garden have you got?"

"How does a hundred and ninety-six acres suit you?"

"I think even I could land in that!" John replied.

Map references were sent to him, a plan of the farm to show which field would be suitable, day and time fixed. Silage had been cut, they could land near the house. Again I notified the local Police. We were baling and carting hay in to the barn that day with help from the neighbouring farmers, the Marshalls and Skinners, so there was great excitement when the chopper landed, Fred Marshall particularly interested in being shown the inside of the aircraft. Ray Hubble was grinning happily at being included in the flight, we provided lunch, the three paintings were seen and approved. I was given a couple of circuits in the chopper, able to look at the farm and village from the air, looking down on our three hundred ewes, and the forty cattle or so all individually named, the three Guernsey house cows Lily-Ann, Merry and Sylvan, and then it was all over, John landed in the field while I slid out and got clear of the rotors, then he lifted the chopper off the ground, and they were gone.

So finally, for the stained glass window, everything seemed ready and all arrangements made, 'no stone had been left unturned', the problems seemed sorted and solved at last. It was all systems GO. I had received no word from Michael King but presumed they were working on the window. It was therefore one hell of a shock when Dennis King telephoned me at the beginning of April to say that son Michael had an ulcer, had been in hospital briefly, they were so sorry but were unable to take on the R.A.F. window after all! Oh God! That was all I needed. Was this really happening at this stage of the proceedings? I was shaken to the core, furious and frustrated too, not over Michael's illness but they appeared to be so casual about the situation and surely could have let me know sooner. The window was being dedicated within FIVE MONTHS! I was in a total nightmare! The R.A.F. had made all the arrangements for the dedication service, I'd practically been told where to park my car for the event, now I was in one heck of a muddle, worried sick about the likelihood of letting everybody down, and the whole thing rested on my shoulders alone. HELL!

I gave up swearing and started praying, literally! In my usual one to one conversation I had words with the Almighty! I reminded Him that this entire thing was for His benefit and I needed help! FAST! I didn't mince my words! I was desperate!

King returned all my work by post, and in reply to my query of whether they knew of any other glass maker, suggested Caroline Benyon might be worth contacting. I confess there was a bit of me which thought that perhaps a woman might be more reliable! I telephoned her immediately, putting her directly in the picture, trying to sound as calm as possible. Even listening to her I sensed I had the right person, for like me she seemed practical, down to earth and organised. Another query was, would she be happy with the same fee as King? As costs had been agreed, nobody would wish to start further fund raising. I got all the drawings and information to her promptly and heard from her on 13th April that she would indeed be able to do the work for me and for the same fee. I was to go ahead with the cartoon. THANK YOU GOD!

Caroline was based in Fulham. Sylvia my aunt was in Barnes and with her artistic background and interests, generously welcomed me to take over her sitting-room. With furniture pushed against the wall I just had space to fit the whole window design onto the floor if I put the point of the window under the grand piano! I was within reach of Caroline so we could work easily together. My scribbled notes give some idea of how complex it all was:-

1 Check if red roundels OK
2 Who is doing armature? Metal or wood? Beads made?
3 Use 3/8, 5/16, or 1/4 leads.
4 Ask R.A.F. to give Caroline part of her payment ahead, part in the middle, the rest at the end.
5 Ask John (installation) if he can shape bars across centre round Odiham badge.
6 Do eagle boldly - long way from floor.
7 Draw up badges for inside measurements, do in shades.
8 Choppers not more than 12"
9 Check exact colour of hind.
10 Horizontal bars in panels 1/2
11 5/16 around roundels. Divide in 1/4
12 Ask John to do templates and give to C. by 14th May.
13 Do drawings & details of paintings of choppers.

I got going, a huge roll of cartridge paper, ruler, set-square, black ink, nibs, brushes, paints. I felt nervous. It had to be incredibly accurate which took a great deal of time and labour, not least because it involved meticulous measurements and I was hopeless at maths, having to check again and again. Sylvia was a wonderful support, put up a trestle table for me, produced meals, shut the door on me and left me to it. For once I didn't have my music. I had to stop after supper and tidy things away so that she could use the room in the evenings, and the number of hours I put in, the crouched position on the floor, wielding enormous sheets of paper without tearing or creasing it gradually produced the finished cartoon. It was during this that I met Oriel Sutherland - she had retired from the concert platform in 1978, and among her many performances had been chosen by Sir John Barbirolli as the mezzo-soprano soloist for the Henry Wood Centenary performance of Verdi's Requiem at the Royal Albert Hall in the presence of The Queen - she was blessed with what she herself describes as a 'rich dark chocolatey' voice; those words could also describe our friendship, and the music and laughter we have shared.

Caroline's studio was a fascinating old place with all the character of that profession, full of racks shaped specially to hold different colours of exquisite hand made glass, glass that when held up to the specially designed vast, tall windows, would glow and come alive with sparkle. Wood is kind to glass, handles it softly, and every surface seemed to be wood, the colour enriched by age to treacle-dark, smoothed to silk from being handled for many decades, a real pleasure to be in such a studio, and a joy to watch a master craftsman at work. Embraced by such surroundings I began to unwind. Caroline was enormously talented, could produce both classic and modern designs, for church, industry or private home. As she tackled my Squadron badges and aircraft, husband Tony helping, my feelings of total relief as I watched sections completed, fitting in with others, the whole design taking shape, were colossal. Caroline's father, Carl Edwards, had been in the same profession, had designed the east windows in St. Clement Danes, and had encouraged her to 'draw large' when she was only eleven. With this family history of glass making, she must have felt enormous sadness when forced to move out of the studio, severing these links a couple of years later.

The panels were finished, and I was relieved to see the three helicopters correct as regards colour. I was not involved with either the transport of the panels to Odiham, or the installation.

Service details were printed, and on the front cover was the introduction,

'A SERVICE FOR THE DEDICATION OF THE ROYAL AIR FORCE ODIHAM AND SUPPORT HELICOPTER FORCE STAINED GLASS WINDOW, AND COMMEMORATION AND THANKSGIVING FOR VICTORY IN THE BATTLE OF BRITAIN, 1940 WITH THE LAYING UP OF THE STANDARD OF NO.18 SQUADRON ROYAL AIR FORCE. SUNDAY, 3rd SEPTEMBER, 1989 10.00a.m.'

The previous evening I travelled to Odiham church for a rehearsal by the R.A.F., seeing the window in place over the vestry door for the first time. I marvelled at it, mostly in wonderment that after all the problems it had actually materialized! I couldn't take my eyes off it! Caroline had assembled glorious glass, it seemed to breathe life from the natural ripples and bubbles, and now installed in place to a high professional standard, although I knew every inch of the design, studying the completed product was overwhelming. Was I really a part of it? Had it all come to fruition, finally? My eyes were swimming with a kaleidoscope of emotions.

I had sewn a dress to wear for the service to go with a hat that was very fashionable at the time, a small affair perched on top of my head with feathers at the back. Tony and Caroline said they quivered throughout the service - was it nervousness or excitement? The church was packed, the R.A.F. in number one uniforms looking extremely smart formed a guard of honour up the church path. Inside, music was played by the Band of the Royal Army Ordnance Corps. A fanfare of trumpets, then Standards of No.7, No.33, No.72 and No.230 Squadrons were paraded into church. Prayers, then 'Praise my Soul the King of Heaven,' the church echoing to the volumn of the music and voices, more prayers, then Psalm 150. A fanfare of trumpets heralded the Standard Party moving towards the altar, handing the Standard of No.18 Squadron over to the vicar, Ray Hubble, 'for safe keeping in this House of God.' The National Anthem, both verses, then the clergy moved down to the west end of the church, the congregation turning in their pews to face the new window for the dedication by The Right Reverend Francis W. Cocks, CB, MA, RAF (Retd.), recently Bishop of Shrewsbury and at one time Chaplain in Chief of the R.A.F. Once again I felt that confusing mixture of pride and embarrassment! All being well, the window would be there for several centuries long after I was dead, a little bit of me would remain. I felt emotional and enormously grateful, for life, for everything. The hymn, 'O Worship the King,' lessons and anthem, a sermon from the Bishop mentioning the window and bringing in the work done by both Caroline and I - only once before had I ever been mentioned by name in a sermon, when my brother and I were children, misbehaving in the choir stalls and my father had felt compelled to repremand us - the service at Odiham continued with Battle of Britain prayers, ending, 'Never in the field of human conflict was so much owed by so many to so few.' After the service we gathered in the churchyard for a flypast by helicopters from R.A.F. Odiham. For once in my life, my father looking down from above on the window might have approved of his daughter's efforts!

Amongst all the official V.I.P's present at the service, several of my friends and relatives came to support me including Sylvia, Peter and Katharine Makower. Sadly my mother was too disabled to tackle the journey from Norfolk. However, when she moved back to the West Country to join me at the farm for the last two years of her life, I drove the car right up to the door of Odiham church, helped her out, and finally she saw the window in place. A very happy moment for both of us.

All Saints church Odiham was mentioned in the Domesday Book of the great land survey carried out by William the Conqueror in 1086. It has two contemporay windows over the high altar and in the Lady Chapel executed by Patrick Reyntiens, the colours of which are vibrant and stunning, but because of their modern designs many people told me with obvious pleasure that they could understand my window, unlike the others! It's true there was no doubt, my design, colouring, the whole, was immediately loved by all who saw it. However, without the dedication and hard work by Caroline, it might never have existed! Without doubt, she had come to my rescue!

After the service I went on to the Officers Mess for the official luncheon which rounded off the event in great style.

Publicity flowed, articles on the window appeared in several newspapers, and the R.A.F. had cards made with a photograph of the window flanked on either side by the Standards, the symbols of each echoed in the glass, and an airman beside, head bowed. The R.A.F. also sent me a framed photograph of the window. Odiham, being only a couple of miles or so from the M3, has meant I have returned there several times, to sit quietly and thankfully in the church.

The Chief of the Air Staff, Air Marshal Sir Peter Harding, who had been unable to attend the service due to a prior work engagement, visited R.A.F. Odiham later, and went to All Saints Church to see the new support helicopter window. Back home in the studio I did a painting of the window, and the three helicopter panels separately including the red border surrounding each, all framed, and submitted them for the next Guild exhibition. I included a photograph of the airman standing beside the finished window. I was disappointed in the Guild, for to have aircraft in a stained glass window, and for posterity, could have been a notable first in the country, but the three helicopter panels were rejected, only half of what had been submitted was shown, and there was really no interest from the Guild.

CHAPTER 19

A PROBLEM PERSPECTIVE IN PANGBOURNE

From Squadron badges in stained glass to little metal button ones! In her youth my mother had been an excellent horse-rider. My brother and I both had a pony, making many friends through mutual interest. As children, John Labouchere and I had read the story of A.F.Tschiffely who rode from Buenos Aires to Washington DC in 1930, an amazing feat, mostly without maps, roads or financial assistance. In 1990 John set out to do the same route, also with Argentinian horses. Wishing to ride with a souvenir to give away on this mammoth journey, essentially small and weighing almost nothing, he settled for badges, asking me to design them. They showed him mounted, two other horses as pack animals, a background of mountain peaks, with 'Latin America on Horseback 1990 - 1992' and 'John Labouchere,' below. Time was tight. I tracked down a manufacturer who ignored my design and assembled a badge that was irrelevant and unsuitable, but at the insistence of both John and me they re-made them to the design we wanted, and with John already departing, the badges were rushed to him at Norwich railway station! They travelled in his saddle bag during his five thousand mile year long expedition, were well received especially in remote villages high in the Andes.

Down in Devon, the farm was on the market. Whilst working with the livestock had been enormously rewarding and enjoyable, especially the lambing - I had been well taught by John and Lynn Odell in Norfolk - I was an experienced ewe obstetrician and gynaecologist, and as I laughingly called it a ewe paramedic when Fred and Sylvia's sheep had a birth problem on the neighbouring farm, the work load was very time consuming. Painting became more and more difficult to fit in, and so was the mental adjustment of searching for that inner stillness and peace which goes (hopefully!) with the deep concentration needed. Although I had a year between our stock sale and leaving the farm, I enjoyed checking the cattle and sheep belonging to Nigel and Maureen Brock who rented our grazing, and it wasn't until I'd found a new home, staying in the West Country where I'd been born, I was able to give my work undivided attention once more.

Commissions increased, so did my fees, many were for animal portraits, others aircraft. Richard Crosskill - he and his wife Merry great friends of mine - had been newly elected chairman of Norwich magistrates, and commissioned a Spitfire painting to be presented to Pat Hood, an ex-pilot and his outgoing predecessor. Other commissions included notelets with pen and ink drawings of otters sold in aid of Tarka Radio, Barnstaple hospital radio; a portrait of a retiring headmaster to be hung in his school; model radio controlled yachts racing on the Broads; British White cattle; somebody's pretty cottage; the list was wonderfully varied. Often asked what

I prefer painting most, I usually answer, a change of subject matter from the previous commission!

Over the years my animal portraits on velvet had improved with the use of a more exacting template and thicker paint on the velvet, and I still needed two clear days to do each dog, and an extra day for a horse. Smooth coated animals always took longer. Perhaps my technique with the paintings on canvas advanced too. It was hard to tell. I certainly used my brushes to greater effect, with a large sky working them in a circular movement or from different directions, never just from left to right. But as the subjects became more complicated I spent a greater time on planning the arrangement of the overall picture before I ever picked up a brush. The Golden Mean is a method of calculating what is supposed to be the ideal proportion between two objects, used in both architecture and art. Many artists use it as a guide, such as for placing an aeroplane in a picture. No doubt it is an important feature learnt at art school. I never consciously used it, and arranged objects on a canvas by eye, until it looked right. When executing my pictures, I continued using a water colour brush for small details in oils.

When I started painting, going to art school never seemed to manifest itself, either as a personal idea or a suggestion on anybody else's part. I held that very first exhibition, received commissions, and simply ... got painting. I already had a training behind me plus secretarial experience and probably wouldn't have wished to return to student days, though undoubtedly would have enjoyed and been stimulated by the training and experience. My main objective had been to see if I could paint full time. If I had stopped for art school, with whose techniques would I have qualified? Would professional lecturers have left their mark upon my work, and if so, would it have greatly improved my craftsmanship and competence, or was I an original product simply by being myself?

A commission that was a real nightmare of perspective - I feel sure art school would have taught me mathematical calculations for this - was for Pangbourne College, a boarding and day school for about three hundred and twenty pupils. It was founded in 1917 as a Nautical College for boys wishing to join the Merchant and Royal Navy, and as they had no permanent Chapel - the current one was shared with drama and other events - plans were being made to take down an 1896 Grade II Listed Methodist Chapel in Milford Street, Salisbury, which had not been used for ten years, originally built the same year as Pangbourne College and with similar architecture. When the Falklands war ended, two hundred and fifty-seven British families had lost sons or husbands in land action above Stanley or at Goose Green. Many other servicemen were lost in Her Majesty's ships and Fleet Auxiliaries - the guided-missile Destroyers and Frigates which protected the troop ships, bombarded the enemy positions, and took the brunt of the Argentinean air attacks, the Landing Ships and Merchant Ships. More than half the British casualties were Officers and men from the Royal Navy, Merchant Navy and Royal Marines. The Trustees of the Falkland Islands Memorial Chapel Trust had been offered the Chapel in Salisbury, it was to be removed brick by brick, rebuilt at Pangbourne College, and dedicated to all those who lost their lives in the Falkland Islands conflict.

My job was to paint a picture of Pangbourne College with the Chapel already in position behind the parade ground, ahead of it actually being moved and rebuilt there. Showing the two buildings together would be an excellent way of helping the fund raising, for over a million pounds was needed. I went to Salisbury and found the Chapel in a narrow street with buildings opposite it. Standing back to view it and get the material I needed was totally impossible. Cross roads near by showed the side, but not the angle I needed, and certainly not the front of the building which was the essential part of the commission. Fortunately there was a hotel opposite and the owners were a great help, allowing me access to a room overlooking the Chapel, and from every floor, and this was my only means of seeing the front from various heights. I took careful measurements too, for I knew where the Chapel would be placed at Pangbourne, but I also needed to get the scale correct. Another mathematical headache! The main building at the school was also difficult to paint, fiddley with all the white windows in red brickwork, but it stood magnificently with mown, tiered lawns and banks, each set higher, drawing the eye like a magnet to the superb architecture set above them. During one of my visits, my timing was bad for I needed to include some pupils and by chance had chosen half term, however I had my teenage Godson Mark Jacob with me, and with a series of signals between us that would have done the Navy proud, Mark walked along a path below the building while I signalled from an upstairs dormitory window in another building when I wanted him to pause. With figures half an inch tall, who would know that every single one was Mark! He was excellent, giving me both the scale and movement.

The painting was completed and framed, hung in the headmaster, Anthony Hudson's room, was studied by The Princess Royal when she visited, and used on various cards and brochures. I went to one or two functions at the school, and met Admiral Sandy Woodward who was very much involved with the Chapel project.

Copyright is a difficult subject. Basically, the artist owns the copyright even when a painting changes hands. Reproduction may only be made with permission of the artist. In some cases the artist can sell the copyright. I knew that the Pangbourne painting would be used for fund-raising, and had stipulated as usual, that they could do so on condition that they included below the reproduction, 'From an original painting by Penelope Douglas G.Av.A.' and had put it in writing. Sadly it was omitted on more than one occasion. I wrote again. Next a particularly large brochure was beautifully produced, but my painting inside the front cover had no mention of my name, not only that, but with plenty of room to spare they had only printed on part of the page, reproducing half of my original painting which I took exception to. It certainly didn't follow the law of copyright! These brochures were sent all over the country and overseas. I had made the rules clear from the start, so it was extremely aggravating and disappointing, especially as many artists receive orders for work because other people have seen their originals or reproductions. It was one of my main sources of commissions and therefore my income, and vital that my work was attributed to me. Indeed, this Pangbourne commission had come through Edward and Pippa Tildesley, who knew my paintings. Printing half the painting only, was not representative of my work. On a previous occasion, the Public Relations Officer from R.A.F. Catterick wrote requesting permission to copy a painting and enlarge it for use in the Royal Tournament, and I cannot recall refusing permission for a canvas to be reproduced when specifically asked.

The Guild of Aviation Artists had grown in numbers and I continued having paintings hung, with a picture in the Gulf Conflict exhibition, 'Behind Enemy Lines' showing Commandos being dropped from a Sea-King. The Guild had started several local gatherings for talks and critiques, one of these being based in South West England, started by Ron Beecham. Roger Steel, Miles O'Reilly, and I were the three Full Members in that region, and we helped with the criticism of any work that was brought for that reason. It was always interesting to see other people's work, and although I gave criticism, I hoped I did so in a manner that as no offence was meant, none was taken, and I added humour when possible. As I do with my own pictures, it was enlightening to see an unbalanced painting if put on the easel upside down! Constantly I looked at my work that way, and in a mirror. Both gave me a fresh and original view and faults became more obvious.

At the Guild's annual exhibitions I often attempted something different, seldom interested in submitting a picture of an aircraft batting across a blue sky, fluffy white clouds included or not. As a result they were often mentioned in the Chairman's Report which was rewarding and meant a great deal to me. One such painting was of a group of five children gathered round the kitchen table in the evening making model aircraft. The children were very patient being artist's models, for I set the scene deliberately, with Mark Jacob, younger brother Peter and three friends. I showed them illuminated by a table lamp, all engrossed, a half-eaten piece of Christmas cake beside them and called it, 'More cake for anyone?'

For Guild exhibitions I was able to use material I had obtained from commissions for the Armed Forces. Although I have shown the Spitfire and Hurricane often, I have never painted a wartime dog-fight. I don't think this was anything to do with childhood experiences, more that I hadn't seen it as an adult other than in films, so might not have portrayed it accurately. My memories were those of a small child, and to us children war was exciting! I didn't understand the death, destruction and horror of it all. We lived in Rochester, my father was Chaplain to St. Bartholomew's Hospital. His parish was ten thousand people, and he visited Chatham and the dockyard regularly. I remember he used to sleep in his clothes, just with his shoes and jacket off, so that when the casualties arrived at the hospital, he could get there immediately. We had a shelter built in the garden, and even now the smell of wet concrete never fails to bring back memories of its construction.

When the air raids were constant we slept in the shelter all night, or were summoned by the siren to troop out to it in sleepy state. Annie, a residential cook my parents employed, came too. She was amazing to us children because she could take her teeth out! Trying to see this happen was one of the strongest reasons for another night in the shelter! It was thrilling and great fun to sleep in narrow bunks, AND with our parents! The sound of the 'doodlebugs', like the smell of the concrete, became implanted on my brain for ever. The raids from these flying bombs carrying more than a ton of explosive, began in July 1944, and within a fortnight there were over six thousand casualties. Rochester was on their flight path for London. As long as the engine kept going and you could hear it, you were safe. It was when the sound stopped that it was dangerous. If home was not within reach when the sirens went, we children were told to take shelter in the nearest house. I recall my father hurrying across his study in the silence after a 'doodlebug' engine stopped, perhaps wondering which of his parishioners was about to be killed, and the French windows blew out as he reached them so he just went on walking out through the gap! We stood there open mouthed with surprise, grabbed by my mother from rushing out to join him, for there was shattered glass everywhere. Our real treat was when the ice-cream man came up the road. He had a huge container attached to his tricycle and even now I can see the sort of steam that escaped from the ice cold compartment as he opened it, and the wonderful smell of both the ice and the luxury, quite unlike today's ice-cream. For a short time my mother took us children and stayed with her sister and husband in Headington, Oxford. (Years later she told me that separated from my father, they set a time of day when both would pray together.) I was chirpy, active and seldom stopped talking, but my Uncle Harry could reduce me to trembling silence in seconds. He had been injured in the First World War with poor eye-sight as a result … and found me hard to tolerate. He listened to the wireless bulletins of the Second World War avidly, everybody wishing to do the same, he appeared to dislike me, and only spoke to me when absolutly forced to, his main words were only three,

"Keep quiet child!" I was terrified of him.

At one time my parents must have been desperate in Rochester, and sent us both away from the bombing, my brother to Uncle Mellis and Aunt Constance at Pakenham, Suffolk. I became a refugee. I was packed off like a parcel, a label attached to my coat buttenhole, to Aberdovy, Wales, with and to, total strangers. I suppose I took it all as a matter of course, though I couldn't understand why suddenly I had been sent away from the three people I loved best in the world, with nobody familiar to me, everything strange, and with a rail journey that had gone on for ever. Children there were mostly boys who bullied little girls, tied us to a post and made us watch while they sliced a live grass snake into pieces on a rock. Pure torture to a small girl. And a lover of animals. A vivid, horrifying memory. Personal possessions were clung to, they were so few and the only link with familiarity and home, and I still remember how desperately upset and

evacuee

miserable I was when one of the adults took away my dressing-gown cord in order to tie our bedroom door shut from outside the room, as one of the two Spanish sisters with whom I was sharing my bedroom, had taken to sleep walking. The grown ups wanted to make sure she couldn't get out of the room and fall down the stairs. I remember suffering agonies without my precious cord, worrying that it might never be returned to me. My special love was Little Teddy, a small bear about ten inches high who had left Rochester with me and was my closest companion during my evacuation. (Big Teddy sits on my chest of drawers as I write!) In Wales, Little Teddy disappeared! Presumably he was stolen. Deepest heartache.

How long I was kept in Wales I don't know, but eventually I was moved to Suffolk for a month or so, at long last united with my brother. Uncle Mellis, my father's brother was also ordained, and I remember he held family prayers after breakfast every morning in the drawing-room which was the only time the staff would have joined us there. We had to find a chair at which to kneel, but to us children this was not so much a collective plea for peace and the safety of those we loved, but once again the fairly innocent delighted happiness and giggles of two children together at last, and peeping through our fingers at each other we were incapable of bowing our heads devoutly! Neither of us were models of good behaviour!

My other vivid memory of the Rectory, Pakenham, was the occupant of a window overlooking the drive. Long ago the window had been bricked up, this brickwork set back in the recess where frame and glass had been. Painted on this was a false window, white bars matching other windows in the house, and seated inside was an elderly gentleman with grey wig, his attention drawn away from his candle and pile of books, to the driveway outside. It didn't matter where I stood, his eyes followed me, and I looked on him as a benevolent, personal friend and member of the household. He was painted by Rex Whistler who used to visit my Uncle and Aunt regularly, and with his sense of fun and imagination had decorated the window with a character from the past. I believe it now has a preservation order on it. From Pakenham, we returned to Rochester with the noise of the 'doodlebugs'. Outwardly I was unaffected by the war, but my mother told me I often talked in my sleep about trying to rescue my guinea-pigs and carry them to safety away from the bangs and bombs.

CHAPTER 20

'ESCORT FOR A V.I.P.'

The R.A.F. Museum put on an exhibition, VISIONS OF WOMEN, VISIONS BY WOMEN and as they had several of my paintings, I was asked to exhibit, putting in a canvas of an R.A.F. helicopter airlifting a casualty. A canvas by Dame Laura Knight was shown, so I was in rather exalted company! I accepted the invitation to the official cocktail party, and pleased to be mentioned with five other artists in the publicity spread.

During the first years of the Guild's existence, Yvonne Bonham had played a major part in the organisation. She was often late for things, and by way of explanation to members, I wrote a short article for the Guild newsletter explaining that she ran on Bonham Time instead of Greenwich Mean Time! She was usually doing half a dozen necessary jobs on route, hence we were often kept waiting for her, invariably on cold windy corners! When she retired from the main bulk of responsibilities, several of us were asked to produce something to mark the occasion, all to be mounted in a volumn to be presented to her. Having worked with her in the days of the Guild dinners, I wrote the following:-

Guild dinners were arranged with care,
Each one a lavish, grand affair
We worked upon the seating plan,
Laughing, as two women can -
"There's Mr and Mrs So-and-so ... "
"She's not his wife!" "I didn't know!"
"Not those two Johns on table five,
They'll fight 'till only one's alive!"
The restaurant manager's irate,
"Which menu? When? You're much too late!"
And we 'old timers' quote the line,
"Yvonne just runs on Bonham time!"

Cuneo's mouse - we made it zoom
By parachute across the room,
And Dudley, quaking in his shoes
Practised his speech inside the loos!
The time we faced the manager's wrath
For sketching on the table cloth!
Our thanks to you? A bunch of flowers,
For verbal thanks need several hours.
And you, without the least remorse

Arrived before the second course!
And we 'old timers' quote the line,
"Yvonne just runs on Bonham time!"

Exhibitions come and go,
You organise each minor show.
A group of helpers wait to hang!
You've volunteered this merry gang.
Things can't get going 'till you arrive,
It's due to you the Guild survives.
You've not been idle, stayed in bed,
But done the donkey-work instead.
A newish member dares to say,
"So where's Yvonne? Not here to-day?"
And we 'old timers' quote the line,
"Yvonne just runs on Bonham time!"

Our Annual show's the major thing,
To it your special talents bring
Selection panel organised,
Each sub-committee supervised.
At ten o'clock we are to meet,
And clutch our paintings in the street.
We stand outside for half an hour;
"My painting's soggy in this shower!"
"At last! Yvonne! You've got the key!"
"Been waiting long?" she asks with glee,
And we 'old timers' quote the line,
"Yvonne just runs on Bonham time."

You've helped the Guild from strength to strength,
Encouraged all our plans at length,
But then of course, you ARE the Guild,
Your place, with ten, could not be filled.
You are, in fact, the Guild's right arm,
With warmth and humour, tact and charm.
And we 'old timers' understand
When things take longer than you'd planned.
Guild members mutter in refrain,
"Oh where's Yvonne - not late again!"
And we 'old timers' quote the line,
"Yvonne just runs on Bonham time!" *

Members of the Guild were invited by the American Society of Aviation Artists to put on a joint exhibition at Dayton, Ohio. The Guild sent thirty paintings to the United States, one of which was mine of the Red Arrows

* Years later, at Yvonne's funeral, this poem was put for all to read, I gathered!

over the Houses of Parliament. This time my picture wasn't stolen! At the same time the Guild had its twenty-fifth birthday, celebrating with a Jubilee Luncheon.

'The R.A.F. To-day,' was another exhibition put on at the Hendon Museum by Guild members, but for the first time paintings did not have to include aircraft. This gave me the chance to do a portrait on velvet of Caspar, an R.A.F. Police dog, these being based at R.A.F. Brize Norton. The dogs were mostly German Shepherds, and I got material of Caspar who had been born in 1988, donated to the R.A.F. four years later from the civilian Police after his handler had died, and in a few months was placed first in the R.A.F. Police U.K. Working Dog Trials, giving him the title of champion for that year. Painting Caspar's portrait avoided showing one paw heavily bandaged! He was a beautiful creature. Within a matter of weeks the girl grooms were going to be phased out, so I recorded them for history in the painting, which showed the day to day work of Police dogs guarding the base, agility and personal attack. All the dogs commanded the greatest respect, I had to keep well clear of one or two with their intimidating snarls and barks showing they certainly meant business, some liked to meet me first, after which I was accepted, others were loving and friendly. Caspar's portrait was put in a glass case at the Museum, they were anxious that the public could not touch or damage it, so it was not shown at its best.

Tim Gauvain had left the R.A.F., and become Executive Director of St. John Ambulance, and on 26th June 1991, with co-pilot David Hughes, entered the Dawn To Dusk Challenge, a prestigious international flying competition. At 4.30a.m. in a little Piper PA28, they took off from Denham airfield in Buckinghamshire, with forty-seven touch and go landings at different airfields in 16 hours 59 minutes, finally making their last touch down at Northolt airfield. With one minute to spare if the flight was to qualify for the Dawn to Dusk Challenge, it was certainly a nail biting finish! For Tim it was a dream come true, a remarkable achievement, and all over the country members of St John turned up to greet them and wave them on their way immediately. Tim's wife Sandy, had commissioned a painting as a surprise for Tim, so I met up with he and David when they touched down at Exeter airport, a refueling stop for both aircraft and pilots! A few years later, it was sad news indeed when I learnt that Tim had died of cancer.

Although I had worked in oils for years, I was determined that once I found a home and became settled, I would like to learn about water colours, so in the summer joined Denis and Valerie Pannett in Sussex for the three day water colour course they run annually. Denis was a Full Member of the Guild, he and Valerie had been very good friends of mine for many years, and I had always admired his pictures enormously. In the past we had painted on the North Norfolk coast together. Juliet Pannet M.B.E.,F.R.S.A., Denis's mother, who had been a professional painter all her life with twenty-two portraits in The National Portrait Gallery, gave tuition too, and I had the time of my life! The Pannett family were enormously generous to me, I moved in with them for the duration of the course, spent a glorious night sleeping in the garden on their swing-seat accompanied by Rosie, my very loving retired sheep-dog (I had trained her as a working dog while farming,) and when the weather worsened, we moved indoors. Denis and Valerie had Chloe, also a Border Collie, and she and Rosie accompanied us during the course and were inseperable. Both had such beautiful manners that they were a pleasure to have with us. In spite of my having been a professional oil painter for many years, a whole new world of art opened up to me which I found immensely refreshing and stimulating! After working with sticky, relatively stiff paint, I really had to think WATER to force myself to extend my knowledge and achieve the subtlety of water colour and use it to its full potential. One of the major differences was that when dry, colour would be lighter. The use of tone was still vitally important, but it all seemed much more fragile!

Full of the enthusiasm gained from the novelty of working with a totally different medium, I put two water colours into the next Guild exhibition and sold both during the official opening. Admittedly one went to Michael and Clare Brett and family, for following up the past idea of the picture of children making model aircraft round the kitchen table, I wanted to extend my imagination with the use of models again, painting the Bretts on the beach in Devon, Clare with daughter Helen playing with some models of the Red Arrows, Michael with spade making an aircraft carrier type of ramp take-off for an Andover - quite unheard of - and Helen's brother Tom lovingly holding a Spitfire model. The picture was called, 'Sun, Sea, Sand and Imagination.' The other painting showed flowers with a hot air balloon above them, and this got a favourable mention from the Guild's President, Michael Turner, in his report. Thanks Mike!

Following up thoughts after visiting the Police dogs, in 1997 I produced a water colour Christmas card of Father Christmas being escorted by a Police Dog Handler with Alsatian, 'Escort for a V.I.P.' I offered the idea for Christmas cards of this, to the Provost and Security Training Squadron of the R.A.F., they took me up on it, bought two thousand cards, and commissioned a painting!

Flight Sergeant Pam Gordon was extremely efficient in organising when and where I could get details for this picture, as again, it was to be five scenes on one 20 × 30 inch canvas. In the centre, the Basic Police Course Pass-Out with the Provost Marshal awarding the individual prize of the Baton. The corners were to represent the Control of Entry Duties with the Police manning the entrance to an R.A.F. Station, Dog Handling Duties with a dog patrol duty on the airfield, Air Transport Security Duties in the departure area where hand baggage was checked, and Investigative Duties showing an interview of a possible offender by R.A.F. Police. I returned to R.A.F. Brize Norton for a third of the material, and obtained the other two thirds at R.A.F. Halton, watching a Passing Out Parade. The Provost and Security Training Squadron gave a drinks party for the unveiling of the painting which was draped in navy coloured cloth not unlike velvet.

"It's actually a tablecloth!" Pam confided in me, "but it's very suitable." It was both! The painting was concealed on an easel and I managed to unveil it without knocking down either! Although five hundred prints had been made, to be sold in the Provost and Security Training Squadron shop, the whole enterprise had been kept a secret and therefore a surprise until the unveiling, yet the day before, an order for a print had come through from Aldergrove, Northern Ireland! I had been asked to sign all the prints - usually I signed between twenty-five and fifty - such a large number took a full day's work. I made a mental note that if asked to repeat this, I would make a charge for a named charity! A second water colour Christmas card was painted, this time of an R.A.F. Policeman at entry gate or picket post, stopping Father Christmas with reindeer and sledge and asking for identification.

The scarlet helicopter, Devon's Air Ambulance - The Messerschmitt Bolkow Blohn BO 105DB - was a subject that I was longing to paint. I discussed the possibilities with them, wishing to show a casualty being picked up from the beach, an unusual venue for an aircraft. They were very keen on the idea, so I went to Exeter airport to get material on the chopper. They were short staffed that morning, so I was asked to provide my own casualty! Great friends of mine, Tim and Clare Hornsey with daughters Emilia and Naomi, lived nearby - Clare an immensely talented artist - and Naomi acted as my casualty, and I took Natasha her school friend, too. Both the pilot Rob Mackie and paramedics Mark Hale and Chris Wyatt wore orange flying suits, and as I had anticipated, it was going to be a colourful painting. Naomi was strapped to the stretcher, air paramedics buzzing round her. She commented later that it was scary because her feet were strapped tightly so that she couldn't move them! She was loaded into the aircraft. Natasha as anxious friend at the scene of the accident, gave me the scale of an upright person beside the stretcher, as the paramedics were bending down dealing with the patient.

Next week, Tim and Clare put in an Oscar winning performance gazing at their lawn pretending to be deeply concerned about their daughter's plight although at the time there was nothing in front of them but grass! They would be standing beside the stretcher for the painting. Next I drove to the beach to get my background, and as I wanted onlookers at the scene, from back view, I asked several strangers if they would stand and look at a chopper that wasn't there, while I got details of them. My cousin Ella, husband John and their three children, Louis, Jack and David who were visiting me at the time, were added as interested onlookers. I put the jig-saw together on canvas, took it up to the Air Ambulance base and they were very pleased indeed, one of the team, Mark, amused me by saying that it was such a sunny picture all he wanted was to go and buy an ice-cream! At my expense I provided them with around a thousand prints which they could sell to raise funds, for the Devon Air Ambulance is a Registered Charity and relies on public funds. They felt my gesture generous but as I knew it cost in the region of eighty-five thousand pounds every month to lease and fuel the chopper complete with the costs of its pilots and maintenance staff, the sale of my prints and the ten thousand they would bring in was a mere drop in the ocean. However it had proved interesting and rewarding, and they had been a great help in setting up the scene for me. Somebody commented they felt certain the casualty made an excellent recovery! In view of my having painted an accident, I appreciated the comments as I had no intention of making the same mistake as I had over the Alexander Keilland oil rig disaster, and it was important that the painting appeared cheerful enough for the prints to sell. The Devon Air Ambulance fund raisers were a first rate example of how copyright should be respected, for they produced the painting on certificates presented to the general public as a thank you, and also on a calendar, always asked permission, and printed my name beneath the reproduction.

Sometimes, because I am an artist, I find myself using paints for unusual ideas, as was the case for Kate's bedroom! At the farm, with my mother disabled, I needed help for her on the few occasions I was away for a couple of days, so advertised in The Lady. It read, 'Stroppy dependent ancient Mum needs watch-dog on Devon farm.' Kate replied, saying she was, 'a stroppy independent Grandmother, and hoped she would do'! She proved invaluable, and we became very close friends. She had moved from the outskirts of Truro to a rented property in the heart of St. Agnes, but her bedroom had one utterly depressing dark brown stone wall, making the room very gloomy. I bought a large piece of loose canvas several feet deep and even wider, and on it painted a sunlit view as if looking out of a window, several headlands, the sea and waves breaking onto the beach. A baton of white painted wood along the top and bottom gave the impression of the window frame, the window catch painted in, and curtains either side covered the raw edge of the canvas and extended the width to cover all the brown stone. Once up, various letters went to and fro to Kate, all enjoying her delightfully wicked sense of humour, such as from estate agents asking if the property with the sea view was for sale!

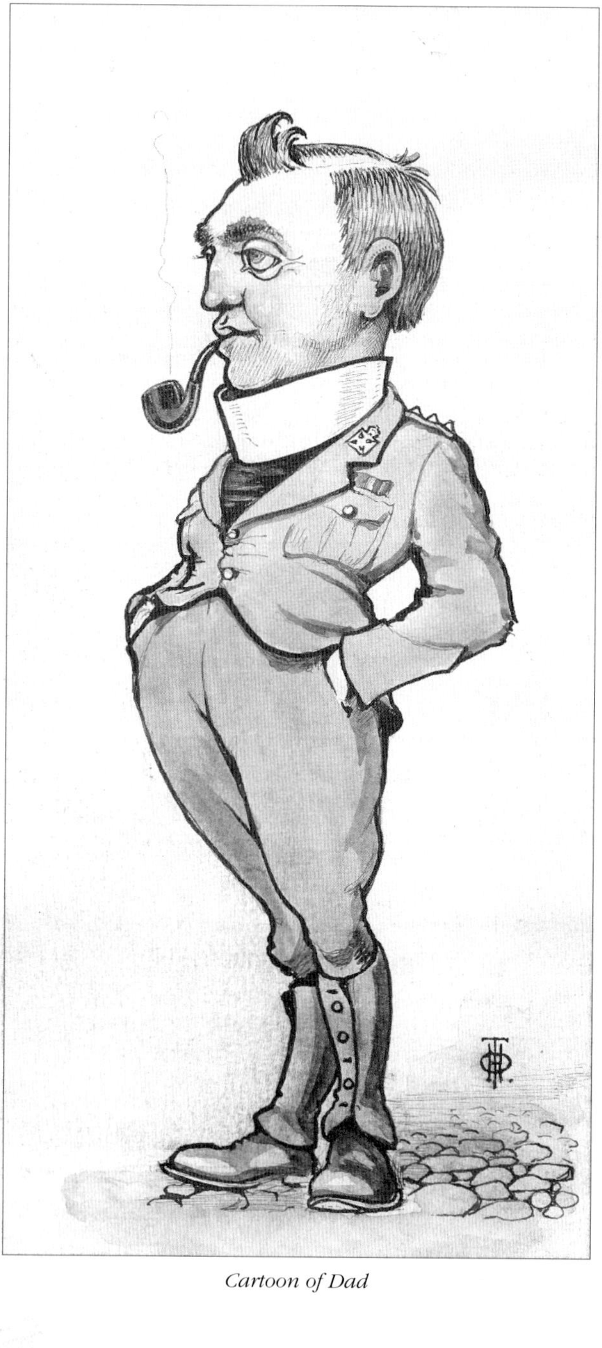

Cartoon of Dad

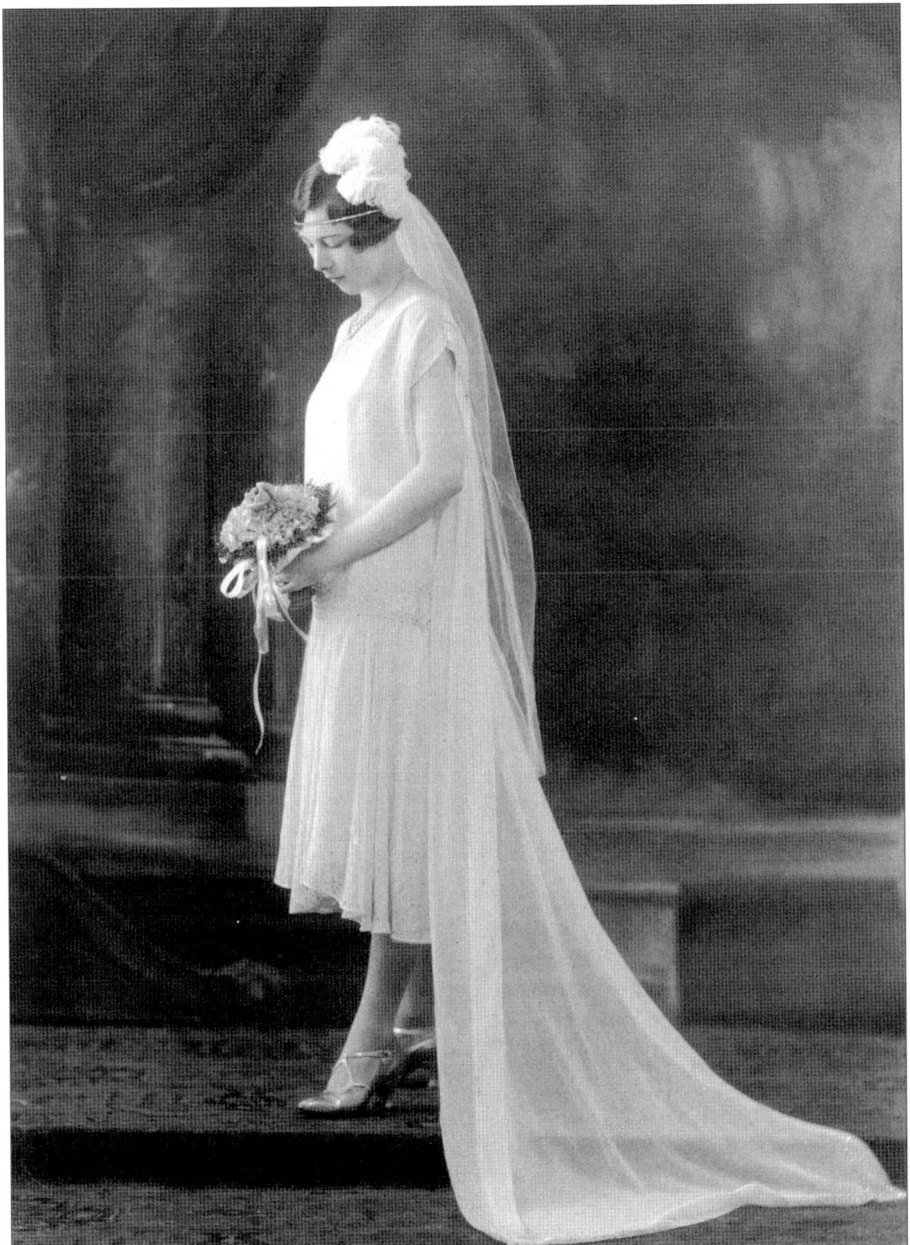

My mother Enid Chetwynd – Presentation at Court

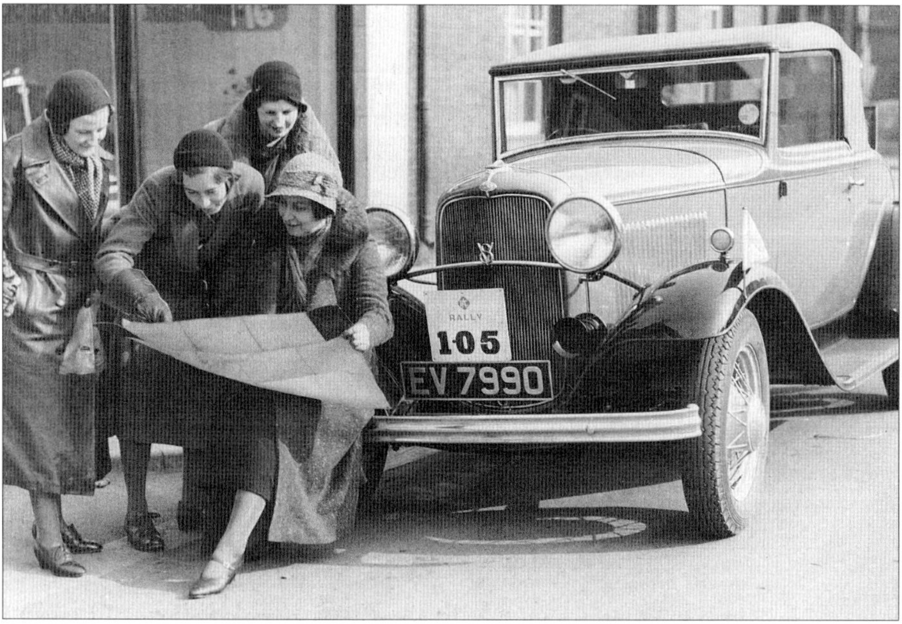

Enid (centre) R.A.C. Rally

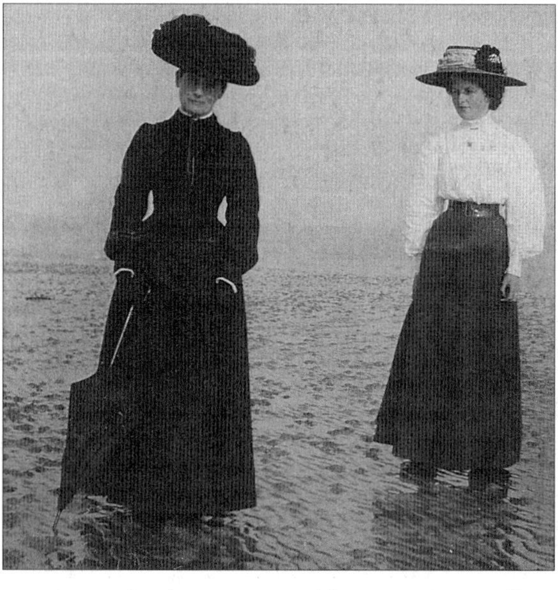

My grandmother Augusta and her niece Gwen Evill

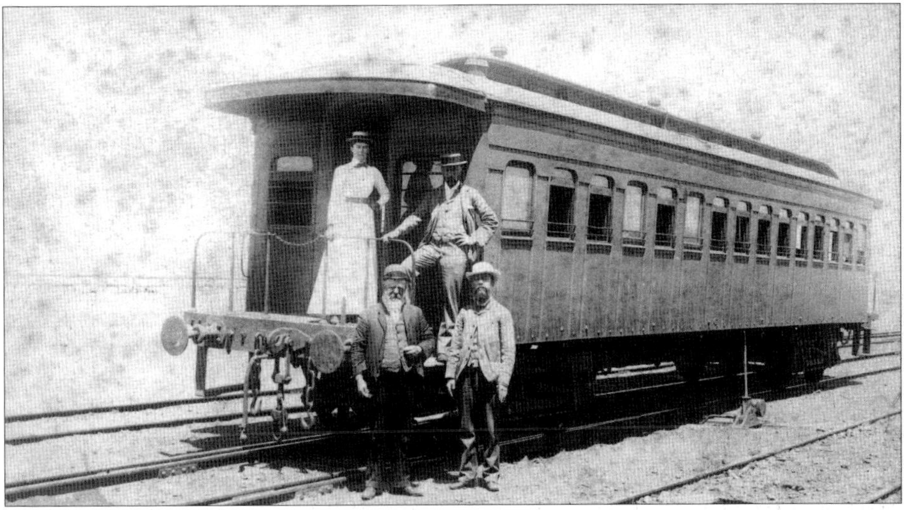

Grandparents' honeymoon

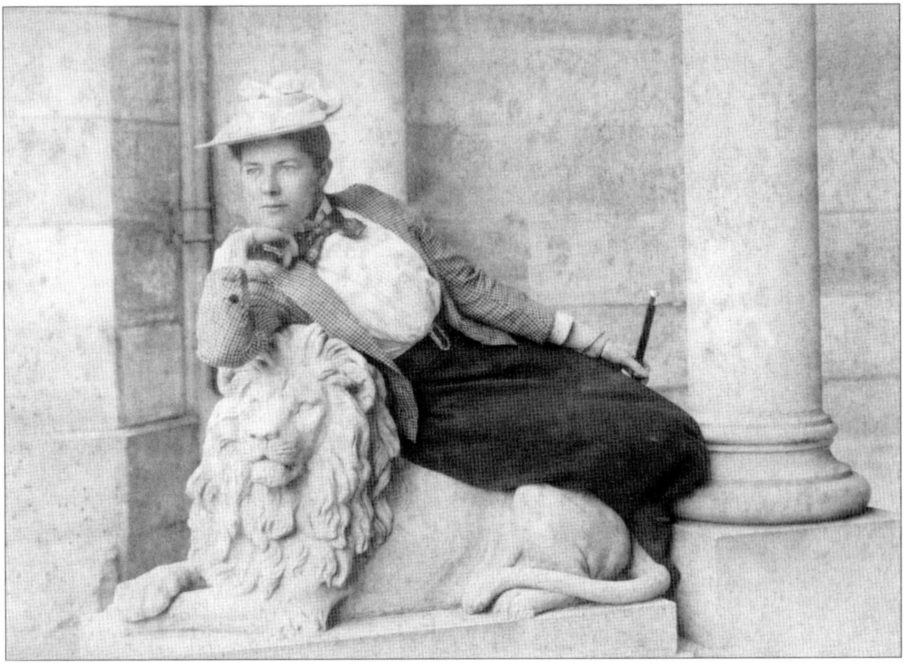

Eva Chetwynd, my grandmother

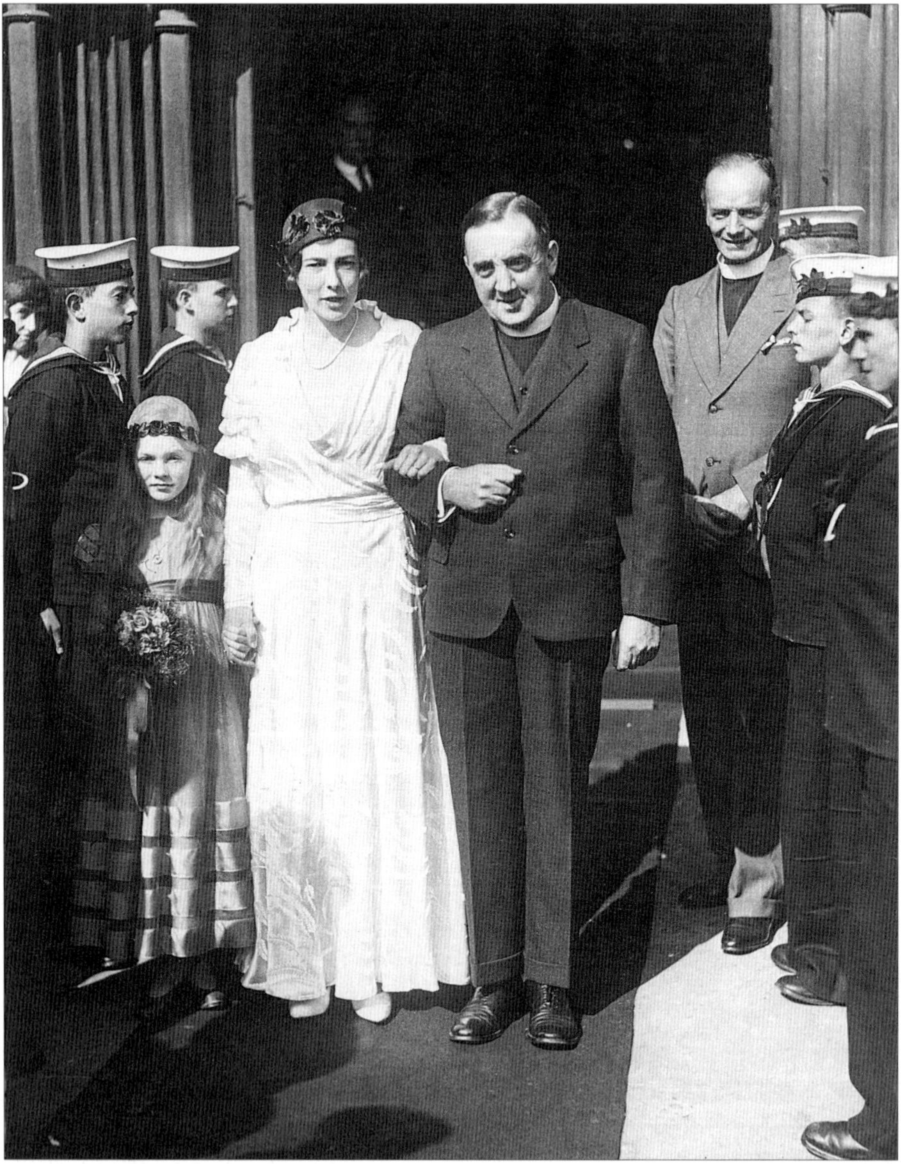

My parents' wedding

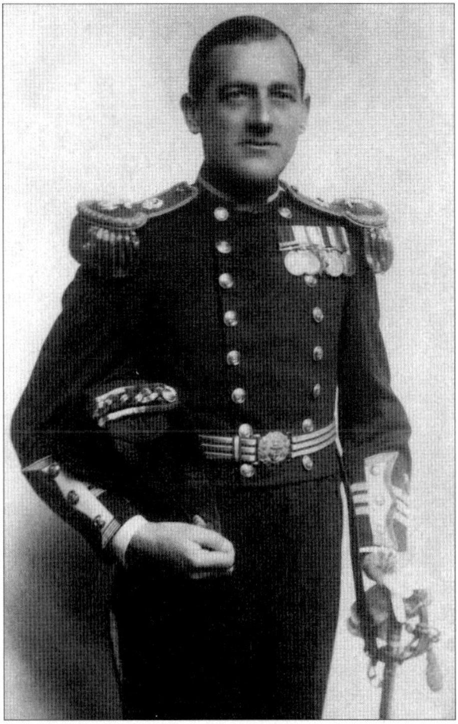

Uncle Stopford

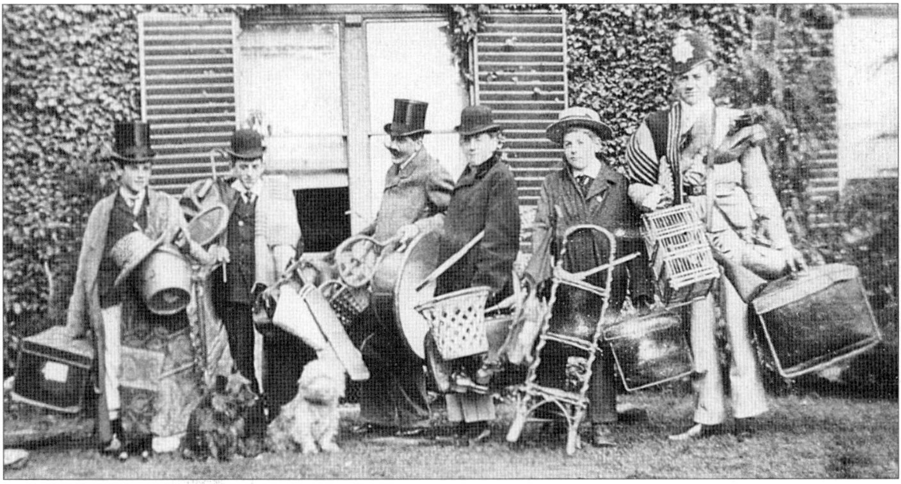

"Off to the seaside"
Make-believe for the camera – my father (second from left) and some of his brothers

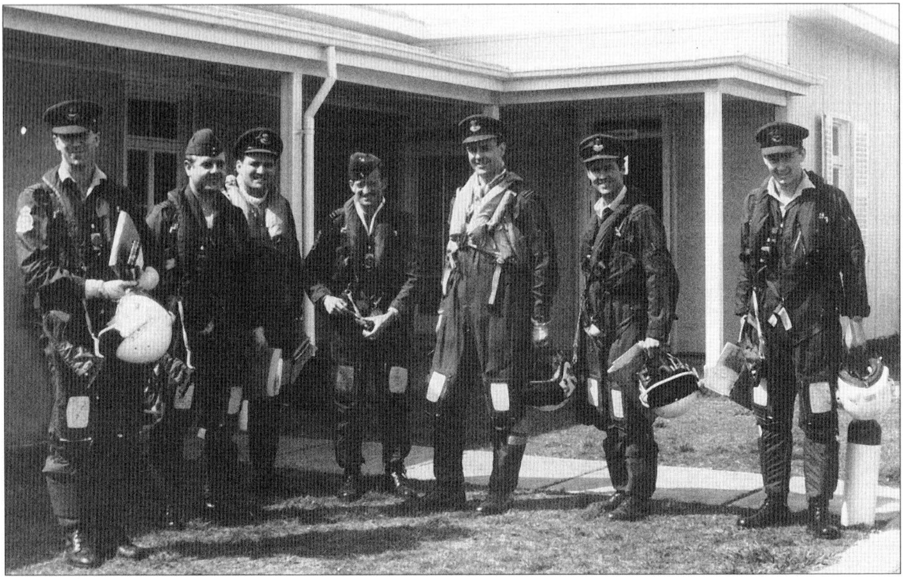

1 Squadron – Akrotiri
Pence, Porky, Bruce, Ken, John, Neal and Roger

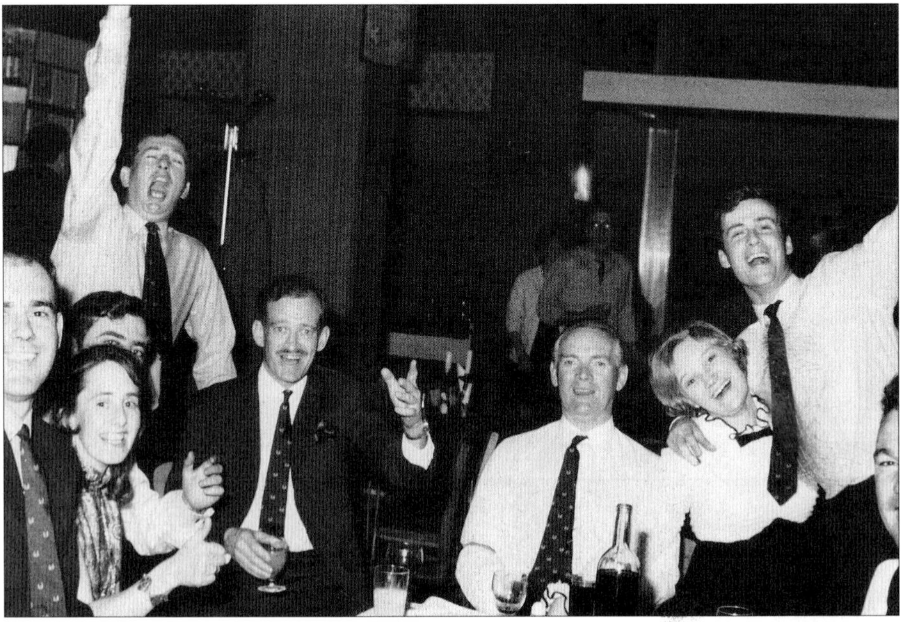

1 Squadron – Akrotiri – a break from flying Harriers
John, self, Mike, Brian, Ken, Harry, Lynn, Neal and Bob

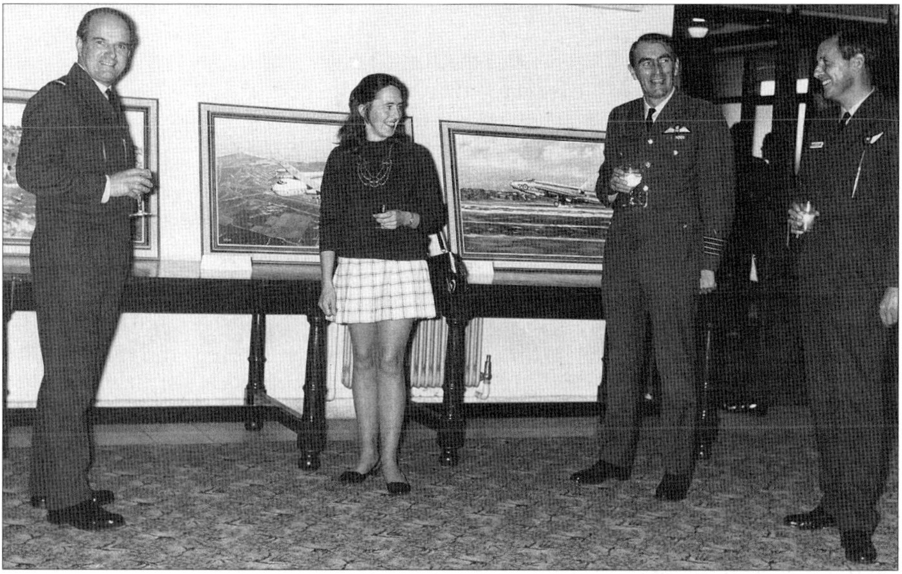

Air Commodore Stacey, self, Group Captain Mike Beavis, Keith Hepburn

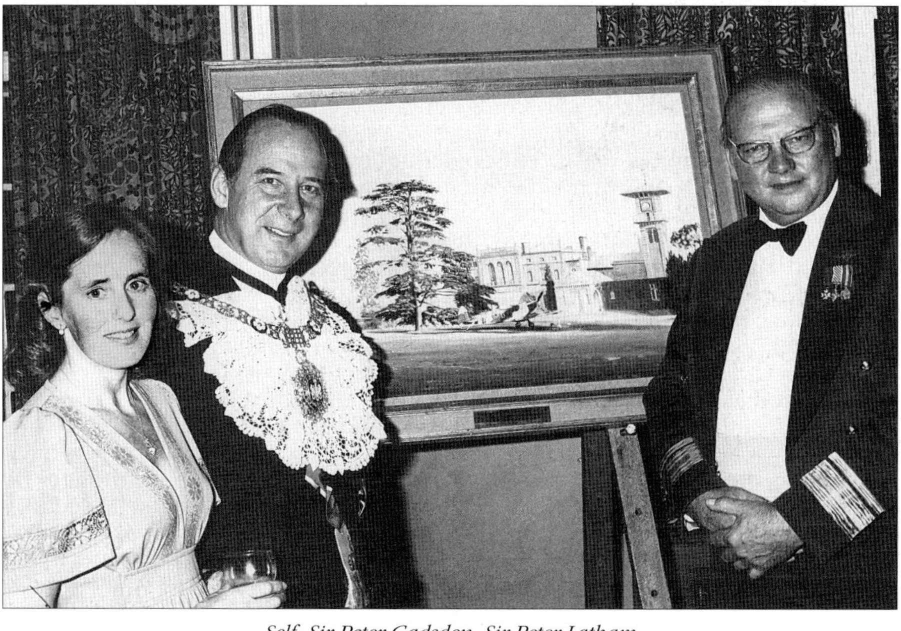

Self, Sir Peter Gadsden, Sir Peter Latham

CHAPTER 21

TO PONDER A LITTLE

Why had my brother and I chosen to follow artistic careers, he as a film writer and producer, I as artist and to a smaller extent, writer? I delved into my past and background to see if any of my ancestors had been artistic, and if this life style I'd chosen was inherited.

On my paternal side, my great grandfather George Mellis Douglas, born in 1809, left England and went to Quebec to join his brother, where he became a doctor. Both men were strong willed and strong tempered Scots, and George, wanting to see something of the world, accepted a job in the Gaspe Peninsular to run the new quarantine station there, recently established to cope with the increasing number of immigrants arriving from Britain, France and Ireland. In 1836 he was offered the post of superintendent of the main quarantine station in Canada, situated on Grosse Ile, in the St. Lawrence seaway off the coast of Quebec. It was here during a party, that he met the three beautiful daughters of Archibald Campbell, and fell in love with Charlotte, they married in 1839. They had two sons, Mellis, and Archibald, and George took over a neglected farm well away from the cholera quarantine area. After a holiday in England, George heard stories of unrest in Ireland, a failed potato crop and famine, and that sick and starving were travelling in their hundreds to the ports, fleeing to what they believed to be a new life across the sea. George was alert and had the hospital on standby. The Canadian authorities failed to believe there could be trouble, so George, who had asked for an extra £3,000 to improve hospital facilities, was turned away with the pittance of £300 … then he returned to the hospital knowing that he was likely to have an epidemic on his hands. Fortunately for everyone's peace of mind, neither he nor any of the doctors in Quebec had any premonition of the holocaust which was about to descend upon them.

In May 1847, shortly after the ice had broken, the "Syria" arrived with her dead and dying; four days later two more ships arrived, one reporting 45 deaths at sea … By the end of May there were forty vessels lying in the St. Lawrence seaway stretching down river for two miles waiting to discharge 13,000 sick and dying passengers. The hospital buildings were full. The authorities ordered the army to move in to erect tents to house the sick. The tents arrived, but the soldiers refused to erect them, terrified that they too would succomb to disease. George himself and his few helpers were left to erect them. Over the days ahead, they had an impossible task … it proved too much, and George too finally succumbed to the disease though he insisted on carrying on until he was so ill that he could not walk. Nursed by Charlotte, he pulled through and returned to work; but he remained weak and dispirited. Meantime the plague continued. The dead and dying crawled about the beaches or lay where they had been landed, too feeble to move. Bodies were winched off the ship and were buried where they lay in shallow graves, often dug up by rats which came off the boats in droves. In desperation bodies were flung into the sea to be washed up time and time again, for now there was neither time nor space for proper burial. Families became separated, never to meet again, for George was still trying to send only the healthy to the mainland though he knew full well that a passenger passed fit one day could be dead the next, spreading typhus in his wake ... George wrote in his report, '100,000 immigrants had passed through Grosse Ile, that he and his men had inspected 442 ships and had treated almost 8,600 patients, 2,300 had died, among them 900 children and babies. Of those who tended the sick, 4 doctors, 6 priests, 34 nurses, had also perished.'

George lived, but was deeply affected by all that had happened, more particularly when some of the frightened citizens of Quebec wanting a scapegoat, and knowing nothing of the desperate conditions under which he had worked, nor of the failure of the authorities to give him the assistance which he had so earnestly asked for ... blamed him for the arrival of plague on the mainland. Ignorant and jealous, they accused him of benefiting from the misfortunes of the sick, because he sometimes received payment for the milk and vegetables he grew on his farm. Furious and angry, George bitterly denied this and some of the priests who had worked with the sick on the island, testified that he had, in fact, often given freely not only of his produce, but had lent them his horses to ride around the island visiting the sick. Family and friends supported him but the hurt remained.

Meanwhile, with Charlotte pregnant, George bought the small island of Ile au Reaux, away from the island dangers. A model farm was created and the hard physical work and planning of the new home gave George fresh energy, and he became more like his old self. In 1849, Justyn (my Grandfather) was born. A year later Agnes arrived, the daughter Charlotte and George had longed for. 'Life seemed set fair for the young family but it was not to be. George's world fell apart in 1852, Charlotte dying in giving birth to their last son, Charles. George was devastated. Charlotte had been his anchor, his inspiration and his great love. He had depended on her for everything, he looked to her to grace his table, to entertain their friends, to care for the children and to give him the moral support which he now so badly needed. Without her he was completely lost and very lonely. The mainspring of life had gone.'

'Time gradually healed ... George's eldest son, Mellis, was enrolled in medical school, Archie, 12, joined the British Navy. Justyn a shy and sensitive little boy remained with his grand-parents, and George free to travel, took Agnes to England to Charlotte's younger sister Marjory, (married to Andrew Noble), who had offered to bring up Agnes with her own young daughter.'

Back in Quebec, George met Susan Cleghorn, they were married in 1858. 'George was fond of Susan and respected her but he did not love her as he had loved Charlotte ... a baby son duly arrived safely in 1860, but Susan died a few days later and, grief-stricken again, George took the baby to Susan's parents in Scotland.' George again returned to Quebec. Four years later with financial difficulties, depressed, nervous and a sick man, he died on June 14th 1864. From the inquest held that day, the verdict read, 'George Mellis Douglas, in a moment of insanity, committed suicide with a table knife and died as a result of his wound.'

George's eldest son, Campbell Mellis Douglas, born in 1840, qualified as an Army surgeon in Edinburgh at the Royal College of Surgeons. He married Eleanor McMaster, a widow with two young children. He served in the Army for many years, then left. Much of his life outside the Army was spent in designing and patenting Canadian canoes. Unable to resist the chance of further adventure, 'in 1885 he rejoined the Army, helping to quell the North West Rebellion of Louis Riel and his band of half-breed Indian followers ... given the rank of Major he astounded his superior officers when he rescued and evacuated seriously wounded troops down river in his canoe, braving the enemy. His exploits were recognised later as, The Surgeon Major C.M.Douglas VC Armoury.' Back in England he lived in Berwick on Tweed, working on his medical duties and testing his canoes. He quit the Army in 1902, buying an old mill in Dunmow, Essex, and later went to live with his daughter Muriel, in Wells, Somerset, dying there in 1909.

Archie, George's second son, like his brother loved the sea. He could sail his father's thirty-five foot sailing boat single handed before he was twelve, and had set his heart on joining the Navy. He served in many ships, and when on leave, joined his sister Agnes in Scotland, spending time with his mother's sister and husband. There he met Constance Hawke, the daughter of a Devon parson, and married her in 1871. His Uncle Andrew had become an influential director of an armaments firm and urged Archie to specialize in gunnery, and Archie took a three year course on this at Devenport, and became Senior Staff Officer. His next appointment was important, for he was chosen to go to Japan to help them update and modernize their almost non-existent Navy. Following this Archie was in command of a warship 'Egaria,' carrying out various assignments for the Admiralty, often of a secret nature. 'Senior Officers at home recognised that in this young commander they had a man who could command respect in any situation, for he had used a diplomatic approach rather than the use of arms, often successfully diffusing possible trouble.' He served in many ships, with spells of shore duty, and with promotion to Rear Admiral, was in command of the East India Station. Eighteen months later he was appointed Second Sea Lord at the Admiralty, which meant a return to London and office work again, but not for long. In 1902 he received a Knighthood, KCB, and was offered Commander in Chief of the West Indies and North American station. In 1907 Archie hauled down his flag at Portsmouth for the last time and retired. He and Constance settled in a rectory in Hampshire, and sadly, she died a year later. Desolate, bravely he carried on, taking on various directorships including Palmers Ship Building Company where he helped to secure the contract for the building of the Queen Mary. Unfortunately his health deteriorated and he developed cancer of the jaw, with a major operation when his left eye and almost the whole of the left side of his face was removed. He died peacefully at home with his family in 1913. His Majesty the King was represented at his funeral. Admiral Sir Archibald Lucius Douglas's honours were as follows:- GVCO, GCB, Jubilee Medal, Fenian Raid Medal, Egypt Campaign Medal, Order of Naval Merit to Spain, Order of the Rising Sun, and Legion of Honour, Egypt.

Archie and Constance had six children and lived in Devon, Constance was an expert horsewoman, and with Archie often away, she and the children enjoyed country life and their Dartmoor ponies. With the cottage proving too small for a growing family, they moved to Vineyard near Totnes which they rented from their friends the Champernownes. When Archie was based ashore, Constance and the children moved to London where Archie's prestigious appointments involved the family in a great deal of entertaining.

(I shall concentrate particularly on their daughter Isobel, (nee Douglas) born 1874, my father's first cousin.) Isobel escaped the society life in London, renting a cottage in Avonwick, where she could ride and flirt with all the local lads, among them Tommy (Arthur) Champernowne, whose family owned Vineyard, the house they used to rent. Tommy fell completely in love with her, and years later, married her when she had long been a war widow. Dartington Hall and the estate had been purchased by the Champernowne's in 1559, and remained in the family for well over three hundred years. (Sometimes spelt Champernown.) At the beginning of the twentieth century, when family wealth had dwindled, Tommy and Isobel were forced to sell much of their land, and in 1925 the remaining 800 acre estate was sold by the Champernownes to Leonard and Dorothy Elmhurst, who restored the near derelict buildings and renovated the estate. Amongst other projects they created studios and workshops for the practice and performance of the arts; the traditions have hardly changed with the rich choice of adult education available. The Summer School has grown and flourished since 1953

I, like my great grandfather's family, fell in love with the beautiful countryside around Totnes and decided to buy a cottage in the area. It was not until after I had done so that my cousin Bettina Thomson (nee Douglas) from Scotland, wrote the history of the Douglas family and I learnt of the strong family ties surrounding me. Bettina is the daughter of David, the youngest son of Archie and Constance. To her I am greatly indebted, not only for telling me of my family links, but also for allowing me to quote from her recent Douglas history.

So, medicine and the Armed Forces seem to feature strongly in my past, but so far no mention of the arts except for the designing of canoes. I will move on to Justyn, my Grandfather, the fifth son of George and Charlotte. He was born on 14th August 1849. At the age of three, when his mother died, he and his young brother went to live with the Campbell grandparents. 'They were all well read, musical, artistic and deeply religious,' able to provide a secure and happy home. Later he was deeply affected by his father's brutal death, he and his brother the only children at the funeral. On leaving school Justyn went to medical school in Edinburgh, and avoiding the many sad memories of Canada, decided to stay in Great Britain, and was offered a post as House Surgeon at the Cottage Hospital in Bournemouth, setting up practise on his own within two years. There he met and fell in love with Augusta Ram, they married in 1877 and set up house in 'Tantallon', named by Justyn from the hereditary Scottish stronghold, proud of his Douglas forebears. 'Petite and serenely indomitable, Augusta bore him eight sons and a daughter. The support of a good wife and a happy home filled with children was an enormous joy to Justyn, in such contrast to his own stormy upbringing. He loved his medical work and was happiest working among children. He became an authority on tuberculosis and specialized in diseases of the lungs. Sadly, he himself contacted the disease from working with his patients.' The disease took a firm hold, and he died in 1893 at 'Tantallon,' surrounded by his devoted wife and family.' He was only forty-one years old, leaving his widow with nine children to bring up aged between three and sixteen

My father was the sixth child, Eric Campbell, born in 1885. 'They were a self sufficient family ... could almost field a cricket side and half a rugger team! They enjoyed acting, were always playing practical jokes not only on each other but on any long suffering visitor who came to the house, and spent many happy hours on the river with a collapsible canoe, Uncle Mellis's present to them. One of their jokes when meeting a visitor was to enter the room one by one, introduce themselves by name, shake hands, leave, join the queue of brothers outside, then return giving another name, leaving the visitor totally bewildered as to how many children there were! All were extremely musical and had lovely singing voices. When Justyn died, Augusta moved to Sherborne to a new 'Tantallon' with the children, all of whom were educated there. On leaving school, seven of the eight boys got university degrees, Stopford enrolling at Dartmouth Naval College before going to sea.' My father Eric, while at Cambridge, was cox for the Queen's boat. He told me he had a trial for the Cambridge University boat, but sank it! He was keen on both cricket and rugger, and loved anything to do with music and books. He joined the Army and at the outbreak of the war in 1914, joined the British Expeditionary Force and became Chaplain to the Forces until 1926, twice mentioned in dispatches.

Five of Justyn's boys married, ... but only Eric produced a family. He married Enid Chetwynd, the youngest daughter of an old English family whose ancestral home adjoined the parish church ... where Eric had taken a temporary curate's job in order to see more of Miss Chetwynd! Enid fell madly in love with Eric even though he was twenty-two years older, and made it abundantly clear she wanted a family, something the other Douglas men seemed unable to achieve.' (My mother always added with a twinkle, "I don't think they knew how!") After their marriage, they moved to a living at Bradford Abbas, Dorset, where I was born, and then to Rochester, Kent.

My father was a story teller - most parsons write their own sermons - his thoughts told to a captive audience or congregation. He revelled in words.

His sermons were seven to ten minutes in length ('if you can't find oil in the first few minutes, stop boring,' he told a clerical nephew), and he was as likely to quote from The Wind in the Willows, Alice in Wonderland, Winnie the Pooh, Keats or Shakespeare, as the Bible. His strong singing voice echoed through the church - if the organist played too slowly he would turn to her and sing slightly ahead until she caught up - and the organ was at full volumn, encouraging the congregation to join in with alacrity! It was not surprising that his services were extremely well supported, the number of parked cars outside the church every Sunday indicative of the distance from which people travelled to take part in his services and hear him preach.

So on the paternal side, it seems my grandfather was brought up in an artistic household, but there is no mention or record of his having any interest in this. My father did not draw or paint, nor did any of his brothers, many of whom went into the church. Music featured strongly from childhood onwards.

I will move on to my maternal ancestors. My great-great grandfather, Augustus Berney, was the youngest of twelve children, and seeing no hope of ever inheriting either of the family estates of Morton Hall and Bracon Hall in Norfolk, set off for Australia in a sailing ship in 1848, aged seventeen. There he got a job in the Custom's Office in Sydney, and married Matilda Gibbs. (My aunt Sylvia in her family history, says Colonel Gibbs, Matilda's father or grandfather, had relieved Frederick Duke of York, of an embarrassingly pregnant mistress in return for the govenorship of the convict prison in Sydney, and took her to Sydney as his wife.) Augustus and Matilda had three children, two girls and a boy, the eldest of which, Eva, was my grandmother. They all grew up in Sydney, a happy childhood with boating trips in the harbour and adventures out in the bush. They were lively children, amongst their exploits was to lean over their high garden wall and drop thistle heads into the long hair of any girl passing below! When my grandmother grew up, the great event of the year was the arrival of the British Fleet in Sydney harbour.

In 1893, my grandmother married Henry Goulbourn Willoughby Chetwynd, (the eldest son of Henry Weyland Chetwynd,) a Captain in the Royal Navy. In the past, like the Berney family, the Chetwynd's had been great landowners, the last land they held was at Ingestre, in Staffordshire. Here's a fascinating story! In 1717, Walter Chetwynd of Ingestre had been given a peerage and became the First Viscount Chetwynd, and about fifty years later his grandson William inherited the title and land, and was very keen on gambling. He met John Talbot, son of Lord Chancellor Talbot, and William gambled away everything he owned, Ingestre included, and in desperation, added his unmarried sister Catharine, to the stakes. He lost! She married John Talbot, and Ingestre became the seat of the Earl of Shrewsbury. The Talbots added Chetwynd to their surname. From William, the title of Viscount was handed down through the generations to my grandfather Henry, who as the eldest son, was the heir.

Henry had three brothers, Godfrey, Wentworth and Walter, and three sisters, Ida, Katie and Margaret. They were not well off on a Captain's income, but because of their aristocratic descent, kept a foothold in society. It is believed that when the girls 'came out', they could only go singly to invitations, as there was only one hat between them! All three sisters were interviewed at the Palace for positions as Ladies-in-Waiting to Queen Victoria, but were not accepted as they could not sing, and the Queen wished to be sung to in spare moments.

My grandfather Henry, aged nineteen, also set out for Australia, where he trained and qualified as a civil engineer. He became a draughtsman in the main office of the railway in Sydney, met and married Eva, and their honeymoon trip was taken on the railway he had helped to build! They were supplied with a railway carriage as their honeymoon suite! Henry and Eva's first daughter of three, Dorothy, was born at Murrurundi. (A curious incident came to light much later, told by Katie, that Eva's mother, Mrs Berney, was a daughter of one of George II's sons who had gone out to Australia, so that, in her brother's three daughters, two branches of George II's descendants met. Their eldest daughter, Dorothy, owned a ring given by George II to his son. (It is in the form of a snake, the hair within this supposed to be that of the 'Grand Old Duke of York,' and I gather, it is still in the family.) But in 1897, Henry received a letter from Katie saying that if he wanted to see his mother alive, he must return to England at once. Back home he worked on the railway line from Epsom to Tattenham Corner, and during this period, my aunt Sylvia was born. When the line was completed, no other job seemed available, and he decided to try farming which he had always longed to do. They rented Eyehurst, a two hundred year old farmhouse and land near Chipstead, Surrey, around 1904, and my mother, Enid, was born there three years later.

When my mother was two her father died, and the title passed to his younger brother Godfrey, who became the Eighth Viscount Chetwynd in 1911. (Family roots can be traced back to the tiny village of Chetwynd in Shropshire, where the first mention of them is recorded under Adam of Chetwynd in 1190.)

So, I'll move on to Godfrey, Lord Chetwynd. During the first war, in May 1915, the Times printed the information that there was a desperate need for shells, the British attack had been checked, the limited supply of shells being the cause. The Daily Mail ran the headline, 'The shells scandal. Lord Kitchener's tragic blunder.' Godfrey was a qualified engineer, and in America added bridge-building and 'riding sheep trains to Chicago' to his experiences. Before the Great War, he was a Director of Vickers Ltd, the machine-gun manufacturer and ship builder. Lloyd George wrote of him,

'To help us with the problem of shell filling I had the good fortune to secure the services of Lord Chetwynd ... he had a tremendous store of resource and ingenuity. I was, however, warned that he was very sensitive to any attempt to control him by a bridle of red tape.'

Lord Chetwynd had no experience of explosives but knew the need for shells was urgent, and 'set to work with the will and energy of a whirlwind.' He went first to Brunner Mond & Company's works, to study Ammonium

Nitrate. With no time to design special machinery, the obvious alternative was to think of a substance with a similar nature - moist sugar at Tate's factory. He chose the site of Chilwell, near Nottingham, as it had all the components he wanted, near a railway, away from the population because of the dangers associated with high explosive, and a wooded hill where he could store loaded shells on the assumption that if an explosion occurred it would pass over the top of the main factory, and trees would break its force. Once the site was bought, the pace he set himself was staggering. He planned the factory on half a sheet of newspaper, and when the Treasury wired, 'Must see plans as soon as completed,' he wired back, 'Factory half built, will send plans as soon as completed.' Eventually it was to have a continuously running conveyor belt from the AN mill to the Mixing House, with both sugar refining and flour milling equipment in both AN and TNT mills.

The Times report of 14th May 1915 mentioned the battle for Aubers Ridge, where nearly 20,000 men had been killed because the field guns were short of high explosive shells. No wonder Lord Chetwynd was so motivated. By 8th January 1916, the first shell was filled at Chilwell, and the first batch fired at Shoebury-ness, giving results superior to previous methods. On lst July 1916, the assault at the Somme was launched; by the end of that day, 60,000 men were dead or wounded. Losses on both sides were horrific. The British alone suffered 400,000 casualties. The National Shell Filling Factory at Chilwell had filled its millionth shell, supplying almost all those fired at the Somme.

By October 1916 there were 6,000 people employed at Chilwell, 2,000 of them women. Godfrey's youngest brother, Walter, had been ordained, and was Rector of Clifton. He took over the supervision of the factory canteen. Both brothers appreciated proper meals for the staff were essential, plus facilities for sport and entertainment. King George V visited the factory, photographed with Lord Chetwynd for the London Illustrated Journal, standing amongst thousands of shells in the Shell Filled Store, a cluster of them suspended over his head! In August, Lord Chetwynd was made a Companion of Honour for his work at the factory.

By 1918, 10,000 were employed, 4,000 being women, with 30,000 full meals served each day, with a new daily record of 46,725 shells filled in one twenty-four hour period. By early 1918, there had been seventeen minor explosions, with nobody killed or seriously injured. However, on 1st July 1918 - weather so hot that ice had been brought into the factory to keep the TNT cool - suddenly there was a massive explosion. Within a few seconds the Mixing House and extension, TNT mill and TNT stores were completely destroyed, many other buildings damaged. Nearly eight tons of explosive had lifted itself skywards in a horrific blast that brought death and destruction to the factory at the heart of the British war effort. In all 134 were killed, 25 of them women, and 250 were injured. Telegrams of sorrow, sympathy and shock poured in, amoung them one from Winston Churchill, who had succeeded Lloyd George as Minister of Munitions, and one from the King. Lord Chetwynd replied, 'Please convey to His Majesty the King the heartfelt thanks of all at Chilwell for his gracious telegram. Kindly present my humble duty with the assurance that the one thought of all here is to maintain the supply of ammunition of the Army. Chetwynd.'

On 9th July, the factory was given the VC. The honour was suggested for Heroism at Explosion. Chilwell VC was born, taken to the hearts and minds of all. A full investigation into the cause reported there was no fire, no warning. The Reverend Walter Chetwynd was given the O.B.E. for his heroism in the great explosion. Married, but with no children, he died in 1920 aged fifty-five. By 1918, September, the highest ever weekly figure for shell filling, in thirteen shifts, gave a total of 275,327 shells.

After the war ended, Chilwell was allowed to slumber peacefully, but played a vital role in the Second World War. It was closed in March 1982 as a consequence of the 1975 Defence Review. After the war, Lord Chetwynd joined Imperial Airways becoming Vice-Chairman. In later life he returned to North America to renew old memories and meet old friends. The 8th Viscount Chetwynd - Chetwynd of Chilwell - died in 1936. He married twice, with a family by his second wife.

The only information on Wentworth, the other brother, was written by Katie. '1914, Wenty died. He was an expert on the compass, and in the early days of flying, much time was spent finding some way of fooling the compass so that the metal in the aeroplane did not divert the needle. He'd had a fine career in the Navy and fully fifteen years at the Admiralty … we are all so proud of his improving the Naval compass so that one hears the name of Chetwynd. He was a terrible loss.'

The three girls, Ida, Katie and Margaret, all married successfully into wealthy industrial families. Ida married Archie Merrie, whose wealth came from steel and coal in central Scotland. Katie married Douglas Vickers, and Margaret married Sir Thomas Stanley Birkin, a successful Nottingham lace manufacturer.

When my grandfather died, my grandmother's total assets were £180, so she and the three daughters went to live at her parents home of Bracon Hall, in Norfolk, and as the children grew up, much of their time was spent in visiting one or other of their aunts, hence the motor racing and rally interest shared with Margaret's son, Henry (Tim) Birkin, my mother Enid Chetwynd, and Joan Chetwynd.

Much of the history of my mother's family has come from talking to my aunt, Sylvia. My grandmother must have enjoyed painting, because although there is no mention of this, I have a small oil painting of a basket of pansies signed by her, and I'm told she used to copy paintings of old masters. Of her three daughters, Sylvia studied illustration at Chelsea Polytechnic, but there is no record of either Dorothy or Enid being artistic. Dorothy's daughter Hilary Balfour (my parents' bridesmaid) was an excellent draughtswoman in her early twenties - she used to draw wonderful pictures for me to colour when I was little, mostly horses in motion - and was offered a place at the Slade, but didn't take this up because she wanted to work as a land girl during the war. (Hilary is the sister of Tony Balfour, mentioned earlier.)

So, having delved into my ancestry, the only other information I have found is the link with the artists John Berney Ladbrooke and John Berney Crome, both of the Norwich School of Painters. (The current John Berney is my mother's first cousin.) However, this link is sufficiently tenuous to be completely ignored.

The life-style of wealthy families or aristocracy - those who did not have to earn a living - included the study of many of the arts; learning drawing, painting, and music was commonplace, so it can be assumed that on my mother's side, though art could have been important, this does not appear to have been the case.

So what made me take to it? Answers, like fluttering butterflies and falling leaves in the autumn, are illusive to grasp. I am left with the conclusion that upbringing played a large part. From my father I certainly inherited an essential in life, his sense of humour, but it is my brother who has his wit - he laughs ten minutes ahead of the punch line, I laugh ten minutes later! - and rather, I have my mother's joy of seeing the funny side of little incidents in every day life. Perhaps from my father I learnt that I did not come up to (his) expectations, therefore I must battle to do better, second best will not do; I have not been bogged down with this 'battle', although I am very critical of my work, yet have got enormous pleasure and satisfaction from a life in painting.

And my mother's influence? Perhaps hers was the stronger, but quite different. She instilled in me the great importance of simply, trying something. It didn't matter if I was gaining more experience at a thing I'd done before, or whether it was quite new, but this 'trying' had to be undertaken, AND in spite of all the odds against it. I think the latter was very important. One childhood example comes to mind involving my pony. Often we took part in gymkhanas, hacking for six miles or more to reach them for we had no horsebox. I was twelve years old when I was given my pony, Gypsy, I was rather unconfident, and by the time I gained sufficient experience to enter the jumping competitions, I was in the over fifteen age group having to compete on a 13.2 hands high pony against horses that included the legendary Sunsalve. My pony was not what is termed a 'first child's pony,' I'd had many falls from him when he shied high spiritedly, and although he carried me safely over huge Norfolk ditches out hunting, he was adamant that to leap over the red and white poles of a Road Diversion sign in a show ring was ridiculous! He would carry me over half the course, and then refuse, causing me to be illiminated. Of the jumps he did take, he would have a good look, then rocket over them almost from a standstill. To sit tight during this needed determination and confidence. I had neither! I worried about entering, sat miserably in my saddle waiting for my turn while my mother stood beside me saying,

"Of course you can do it!" Entry fee paid by her, it was always too late to back out. If I came off in the ring, Gipsy would do justice to a rodeo, other mothers gasping that this small girl should ride such an animal, but when caught, he would follow my mother meekly, good as gold! Mostly I stayed on and rode out of the ring grinning my head off at having achieved the jumps I had, and given great encouragement and praise from my mother.

She made me feel I'd achieved something, even though I failed to finish the course. The essence of this has played a large part in my life.

I've had wonderful support from close, special friends which has meant a great deal more than many of them may realize. Some are already mentioned in this narrative; to name but a few, Michael and Clare Brett, Richard and Merry Crosskill (and for Richard's valuable help with proof reading this manuscript and writing the back cover), Tony and Mary Sword, Anne Leake, the Jacob family, Joanna and Nick Hinde, Andrew, Oriel Sutherland, Jane Birkett, Rosemonde, Kate, Denis and Valerie Pannett, Clare and Tim Hornsey, and many others, as well as my family. To them all, I owe a great debt of gratitude for their continuous help and interest.

Of the wide variety of commissions I have completed, especially those for the Armed Forces, the people involved in assisting me in getting the material have been truly superb, and without their help I would not have had the opportunity of creating all the pictures I have worked on. They gave me the chance, and for that I shall always be enormously grateful.

I've been incredibly fortunate. Luck doesn't float by on a wing and a prayer. I am a staunch believer in searching for luck and helping it head in my direction, quite prepared to put in a great deal of effort, time and dedication to a career for which I have the most colossal enthusiasm - as I have with anything creative I want to do. I feel I've loved life to the full, even though there have been many downs among the ups - maybe the memories of the former fade as perhaps they should. And if I sound a patronising so-and-so it is not intentional, but failing doesn't matter, it is the 'having a go' that is important! Only by taking that attitude have I found such a tremendous satisfaction and pleasure in attempting a creative course through life. Although I haven't a single qualification on paper, it honestly hasn't mattered. The answer is, 'go for it!' Face the bridges when you come to them!

The variety of subject matter continues, and I was commissioned for a water colour of a Vulcan bomber over a background of Cyprus, a new challenge to produce it in that medium. I enjoyed working on portraits of Alexandra Michael aged five, and her sister Elizabeth of two; the R.A.F. Catering Support Unit has just commissioned a painting with prints, and as a novelty I am to be studied as an A Level Art subject by Sarah Cruickshank!

After staying with my cousin Anne in Dublin and her husband Christopher Fitz-Simon, (and advice from Tony Cloke), I have some unfinished business with a certain Mrs Wilourby-Pond, but that is another story! Recently, Denis and Valerie came to stay, the stormy weather preventing us painting out of doors, but prompting lively discussion on tonal qualities as we considered the Dartmoor landscape during walks. It was through them, the most extraordinary coincidence happened concerning four Bedouin horsemen and … so sorry, can't write more, another commission's come in and I must go …

INDEX OF PEOPLE